Nationalism and Socialism in twentieth-century Ireland

MAP OF IRELAND
Showing counties, provinces, and political boundaries

Nationalism
and Socialism

in twentieth-century Ireland

E. RUMPF and A. C. HEPBURN

LIVERPOOL UNIVERSITY PRESS

Published by

LIVERPOOL UNIVERSITY PRESS

123 Grove Street, Liverpool L7 7AF

ISBN 0 85323 343 8

First published 1977

Printed and bound in Great Britain by
Hazell Watson & Viney Ltd, Aylesbury, Bucks

Foreword

Although it is now more than fifteen years ago, I still recall my growing excitement as I read Erhard Rumpf's published PhD thesis, *Nationalismus und Sozialismus in Irland*, on which this book is based. At that time, professional historians and political scientists had not got very far with the task of producing objective interpretations of Irish nationalist movements of the first twenty years of this century or of the subsequent years of the civil war and its aftermath. The first was a period still enveloped in clouds of 'glorious struggle' mythology and unquestionable hagiology; to probe the second was still to touch open wounds. Rumpf's analysis of the areal and socio-economic structure of the independence movement and of the civil war factions seemed to me to be the kind of systematic work that badly needed to be done, and his findings were both cogent and suggestive.

Rumpf's starting point was the relationship between nationalism and socialism and, although this did not prove to be a very satisfactory frame of reference for Ireland, he was able to show that, at the time of the war of independence and the civil war, the essential social components of Irish nationalist movements could be clearly discerned and be seen to form a coherent pattern. As important, his work demonstrated what could be done, despite the absence of survey data, using simple techniques with the limited official statistics and other quantitative data available. Above all, it is a rich source of hypotheses calling out to be tested.

Unfortunately, the book had little impact and the possibilities it seemed to open up were not realized to any extent. It is shaming to have to admit our insularity, but the main reason, I believe, was that the work was in German, and, hence, unavailable to most English-speaking scholars working in this field of study. Because books about Ireland did not have much of a market, no translation was published. I found it sufficient myself to produce a very rough translation for my own colleagues and students, and a small but continuous trickle of research workers made use of it over the years. The book did not evoke the interest in Ireland that it deserved and would have got, had it been in English.

Now it is. Dr Hepburn's edition will, I hope, renew interest in the areal, socio-economic, and other structural components of twentieth-century Irish political movements. Rightly, Hepburn, with Erhard Rumpf's co-operation, chose not just to translate Rumpf's original but to up-date it and, in the light of recent scholarship, to add to it and to rewrite some parts. In particular, he has added a chapter on Northern Ireland. The maps have been redrawn and new ones added, and the bibliography has been extended to include the considerable amount of work that has appeared in the last fifteen years. In making these additions and changes, Hepburn has shown a sensitive appreciation of Rumpf's essential arguments.

The war of independence and the civil war cast long shadows—and Rumpf sketched these in his later chapters—but the character and sociology of our politics have by now obviously changed. We badly need to plot those changes in the social structure of our parties and other political movements over the years. Hepburn has shown that Rumpf's techniques are still fruitful and there is a mass of data now available or, with the use of surveys, potentially available. I hope that some in my own profession who read this book will think, as I always did when I looked at Rumpf, that it suggests interesting lines of inquiry worth taking up. I feel sure that students of contemporary Ireland and all interested in the origin and development of the Irish state will be pleased now to have Rumpf's pioneering study available in a con-venient and up-to-date form.

                                                    BASIL CHUBB

Contents

APPENDICES

List of Illustrations

MAPS

TABLES

FIGURES

Introduction

When Dr Rumpf was carrying out research for the original edition of
this book during the mid 1950s, a well-known authority on Irish politics
told him that no foreign student could hope to understand the problem.
His very approach, it was argued, betrayed his ignorance: 'there was
no sociological, sectarian, or class problem or angle in the Sinn Féin
movement, or any part of it, from beginning to end'. Although few
scholars, whatever their national allegiance or academic discipline,
would maintain such an extreme position today, there is still a tendency
to analyse Irish nationalism in the terms of its own rhetoric.

Nationalismus und Sozialismus in Irland, which was submitted by Dr
Rumpf for a doctorate at the University of Heidelberg in 1959, was one
of the first works to attempt a more dispassionate approach. During the
past few years its social-geographical method of analysis has aroused
considerable interest among historians and political scientists, and the
authors hope that the book, revised, considerably expanded, and
brought up to date for English publication, will now reach a broader
readership and encourage further work along similar lines. The present
work is based on a translation prepared a few years ago in Trinity
College, Dublin, under the direction of Professor Basil Chubb, for his
private use. Chapter One, 'The Historical Background', has now been
entirely rewritten, and a new section on the Republic since 1957 has
been added to Chapter Four. The chapter on Northern Ireland has
been written specially for this edition, as has the second Appendix, an an-
notated listing of political groups and parties which have appeared

in Ireland this century. While Chapters Two, Three, and Four have been
fully revised to take account of more recent scholarship, care has been
taken to retain the core of Dr Rumpf's approach, especially in Chapter
Two, which has attracted most attention from later scholars.

Dr Rumpf's study of Ireland arose out of a general interest in the
interplay between nationalism and socialism, forces which he believes
have long impeded one another in Europe. On a more practical level,
he was encouraged by the presence of his brother, Dr Helmut Rumpf,
on the staff of the German Legation in Dublin. He conducted research
in Ireland for almost a year, and was able to interview many participants in Irish revolutionary politics who have since died. Among
scholars who assisted him, he expressed particular thanks to the late
Dr Proinseas O Suilleabhain, to Professor T. Desmond Williams of
University College, Dublin, and to his supervisor at Heidelberg, Professor Johannes Kühn.

My own involvement in this volume developed from my research into
the changing climate of grass-roots Irish nationalism in the period of
the First World War and after. It seemed to me that Dr Rumpf had
evolved a way of analysing the sort of problems I was interested in which
had almost no parallel in the writing of Irish history and politics. I am
grateful to Professor K. B. Nowlan of University College, Dublin, and
Dr J. H. Whyte of Queen's University, Belfast, who encouraged me to
take up the project, and especially to Professor Basil Chubb of Trinity
College, Dublin, who kindly made his translation available to me.
Much of the work for this edition was carried out during my tenure of
a Leverhulme Senior Research Fellowship at the Institute of Irish
Studies, Queen's University, Belfast. Professor E. R. R. Green, Director
of the Institute, gave his time generously to discuss plans for publication,
and commented on a number of chapters. I am grateful also to the
Institute's founder, Professor E. E. Evans, for discussing with me the
presentation of the maps, and to my former colleague Mr A. B. Cooke
for his particular insights into Northern Ireland politics. Professor D.
B. Quinn of the University of Liverpool, and Dr Cornelius O'Leary of
the Queen's University of Belfast, read the entire typescript and made
a number of valuable suggestions. My debt to the published work of
scholars is, I hope, fully indicated in the footnotes, but a special obligation must be acknowledged to Professor Basil Chubb, Professor F. S.
L. Lyons, Professor James Meenan, and my colleague Professor J. L.

McCracken. Without their work, the present volume could not have appeared.

The formidable resources of the National Library of Ireland were made available to both Dr Rumpf and myself, while the encouragement of the staff and the facilities of the building made the Northern Ireland Public Record Office a model archive. The staff of Liverpool University Press were generous with time and helpful suggestions at every stage in the work. The maps, all of which except numbers 4, 36, 37, 38, and 39 were conceived by Dr Rumpf, were drawn for this edition by Bernard Crossland Associates, Thame, Oxon.

My lack of facility in the German language was bolstered by Jim and Ilse Brown of Coleraine, and by my sister-in-law, Joy Savage. My wife spent many patient hours re-drafting the maps, for which a number of unexpected opportunities to get to know the shops of Liverpool, at times when the M6 or the Irish Sea were calling urgently, provided doubtful recompense.

A. C. HEPBURN

The New University of Ulster
Coleraine, Northern Ireland

CHAPTER ONE

The Historical Background

TO THE GREAT FAMINE

Ireland, it has often been said, was England's first colony. The Anglo-Norman invasion of Ireland in the twelfth century, however, was but one aspect of the general expansion of feudal Latin Christendom in the high medieval period. As a venture it achieved neither the clear-cut success of the extension of Germany into the lands west of the Elbe, nor the equally decisive failure of the crusades in Syria and the Holy Land. The English presence in Ireland was not extinguished but, for several hundred years, it was not consolidated either. The significance of the bridgehead for the future of Anglo-Irish relations did not become fully apparent until the Tudor period. From then onwards a whole series of incidents, from the appearance of the Yorkist pretender, Perkin Warbeck, in Cork in 1491, the Spanish schemes for an invasion of Munster in Elizabethan times, the Irish uprising of 1641 and the campaign of the dethroned King James II, down to the French landing in Co. Mayo in 1798, brought the situation into increasingly sharper relief. Pitt's famous declaration on the necessity for amalgamating Ireland in a union with Great Britain seemed to summarize 300 years of accumulated English political wisdom: 'Ireland is like a ship on fire. It must either be extinguished or cut adrift.'[1]

England's deep entanglement with Ireland was thus primarily a by-product of her developing great-power status in the early modern period.[2] In such a context it was always necessary to demonstrate that Ireland lay within the English sphere of influence. A second factor, overlapping at points with the first, was the political instability of Eng-

1. Cited in O. MacDonagh, *Ireland* (Englewood Cliffs, New Jersey, 1968), p. 4.
2. The best general survey of Ireland in the early modern period is J. C. Beckett, *The Making of Modern Ireland, 1603–1923* (London, 1966).

land itself in the early Tudor period, and, more especially, throughout
the seventeenth century. Henry VII and Henry VIII had hoped to control Ireland as easily and cheaply as possible, by winning the Old English and a proportion of the native landowners to their side. But after
the final breach with the great Earl of Kildare in the 1530s, the Tudor
monarchy gradually found itself committed to a policy of full military
conquest. The coincidence of this development with the spread of the
Reformation in England added religion to the existing barriers of geography and culture which divided the two countries. In the seventeenth
century Ireland was squeezed by James I, on account of its leaders'
dalliance with the Spanish cause; by the Earl of Strafford, as part of his
effort to finance English government without parliamentary taxation;
and finally by Cromwell, in order to prevent the island becoming the
centre of opposition to the parliamentary cause. Charles II never felt
sufficiently secure to relax the Cromwellian grip on the country. The
career of James II, reviving as it did in English minds the inclination to
equate Roman Catholicism with political disaffection, set the final seal
of bitterness on Anglo-Irish relations. During the ensuing century and a
half of struggle by Catholics to dismantle the paraphernalia of religious
repression, the modern phenomenon of Irish nationalism was born.

It is therefore possible to describe Ireland's troubled relationship
with England in purely political terms. Certainly the primary motives
of British governments before the Union were political ones. Nevertheless it was the social and economic effects of British policy during this
period which provided the mainspring for the subsequent successful
appeal of nationalism. There was an important connection between
England's political requirements and her social and economic policies,
for in the absence of a large standing army, those who helped to keep
Ireland within England's political orbit were paid for their services in
expropriated Irish land. This was equally true of the large estates which
were granted to such people as the Cromwellian 'adventurers', and the
smaller holdings offered to attract English yeomen to Munster in the
1580s. Although this last scheme was a failure, the idea had more success a generation later, when lowland Scots farmers were drawn to
Ulster on account of the depressed conditions in their own area. The
effect of this policy on traditional Irish society was to dispossess native
landowners who attempted to resist English expansion and, especially
after 1690, to engender a more general discrimination against the holding of landed property by Catholics. By the beginning of the eighteenth
century most Irish land was owned by Protestant Anglo-Irishmen, who
were frequently absentees. The policy had been directed primarily
against native landlords rather than their tenants, and Catholic tenants
still predominated almost everywhere except in the area of the Ulster
plantation. But, particularly after the devastation of the Cromwellian

period, many thousands of tenants chose to follow their old landlords who, as 'delinquent proprietors', were transplanted to the rough lands west of the Shannon. In this way a grim pattern was established, lasting until the twentieth century, whereby the density of the Irish rural population was in inverse proportion to the quality of the land on which it was settled. In the planted counties of Ulster, where Protestants were in a majority or near-majority, conditions were somewhat easier. But even here there existed a microcosm of the national situation, for Protestants dominated the more prosperous valley lands while Catholics remained in a majority in the mountainous districts.[3]

Towards the end of the eighteenth century it appeared that Ireland's condition might improve. In the 1770s, the policy of encouraging the dismemberment of Catholic-owned estates was reversed, apparently in order to attract into land the capital being accumulated by a small Catholic commercial middle class. This class, in turn, benefited from the generally improved condition of Irish agriculture and industry, especially the production of linen, wool, cotton, and beer, brought about by protective measures, tax concessions, and the enormous expansion of demand for military supplies following the outbreak of the French revolutionary wars. The new confidence which was instilled by the creation of an independent Irish parliament in 1782 may also have played some part.

But within a few years the trend of events—political, economic, and social—turned Ireland once more very sharply in a downhill direction. In the aftermath of the 1798 rising, William Pitt set the Irish policy of the British government on yet another new course with the passage of the Act of Union in 1801, but he was prevented by both royal and cabinet opposition from granting Catholic emancipation, which had been promised as a *quid pro quo*. Later, as part of the general depression which followed the conclusion of the French wars in 1815, Ireland's economic expansion came to a halt. Unfortunately, the remarkably rapid increase in the marriage and birth rates which the expansion had induced was less easily halted. The Irish population began to expand from a fairly static level about 1760, reached five million by 1801, six and a half million by 1821, and seven and a half million by 1831, before attaining its peak of over eight million at the census of 1841.[4] This rate of demographic growth, on such a slender economic base, was sustained by the continued subdivision of holdings and a heavy dependence on the dietary qualities of the potato. After the first partial failure of the potato crop in 1817, it became clear how precarious this situation was. When

3. Even today there is a remarkable similarity between the religious-demographic and the topographical contour lines (see below, p. 165).

4. Recent research suggests that population growth was beginning to level off before 1845. F. J. Carney, 'Pre-famine Irish population: the evidence from the Trinity College Estates', in *Irish Economic and Social History*, ii (1975), 34–45.

the crop failed completely, in 1846–7, the ensuing disaster was no more
or less than the culmination of a 'rural crisis' which had been sapping
the structure of Irish society for a generation. Only steady emigration,
a high mortality rate and, some historians argue, a declining marriage
rate during the 1830s, postponed the catastrophe for so long.[5] Eastern
Ulster, where from the 1820s the revived and mechanized linen industry provided the basis for a new industrial, society, was to some extent an exception to the gloomy story.[6]

THE CHARACTER OF IRISH NATIONALISM

The prevailing economic orthodoxy of the 1840s dictated a stern response to the famine by the British government.[7] It was thought that
Irish rural society had broken down because there were too many people
in the country. A side effect of the collapse had been the economic destruction of the traditional landlord class. The policy implemented was
thus a two-fold one. Large-scale emigration was regarded as inevitable,
which meant discouraging the distressed peasant from remaining on his
land, while legislation was introduced to facilitate the transfer of the
great bankrupt estates to a new class of solvent 'capitalist' landowners.
The 'Gregory clause' obliged poor law guardians to refuse famine
relief to a peasant until he had reduced his landholding to less than a
quarter of an acre. The land was thus effectively cleared, but the price
was a deeply implanted feeling of bitterness against the apparent harsh-
ness of the government. This feeling was intensified by the conduct of
the new landlord class, for although the easing of population pressure
made the 1850s a decade of relative peace and comfort, the new landlords were not really progressive farmers, but land speculators who had
taken advantage of low post-famine prices. Their interest was in a good
return from the land, which meant high rents, promptly paid. For this
reason they tended to encourage the expansion of the larger grazing
tenants and give little sympathy to the small man who fell behind on his
rent. Because it was more business-minded, the new landlord class was
in fact harsher than the old, though it brought little or nothing in the
way of new farming methods to the land.

5. For a more detailed introduction to the debate on the economic and social
condition of Ireland before the famine, see F. S. L. Lyons, *Ireland since the Famine*
(2nd edn, 1973), pp. 34–42; L. M. Cullen, *An Economic History of Ireland since 1660*
(London, 1972). Cullen, p. 118, stresses a declining death-rate as a factor in the
population explosion, and it must be admitted that the demographic debate is by
no means resolved.
    6. The intense specialization implicit in the Industrial Revolution meant that
English competition quickly stifled Irish cotton and wool production after 1815. But
the same process worked to the advantage of the Ulster linen industry.
    7. For an analysis of this policy see R. D. C. Black, *Economic Thought and the Irish
Questions, 1817–70* (Cambridge, 1960).

The wave of revolutionary fervour which swept Europe in 1848 found Ireland too depressed to make an effective response. The parliamentary nationalist movement, which had flourished for a while after the political emancipation of Catholics in 1829, was in disarray following the death of its leader Daniel O'Connell and the split with the romantic nationalist Young Ireland movement. This latter group did attempt a rising in 1848, but its members were mostly literary men, and the movement was based neither on practical revolutionary skills nor on the material grievances of the people. The rising was a fiasco. Its only achievement was to throw up from its rank and file a new generation of rather more hard-headed leaders.

The new movement, the Fenian Brotherhood or IRB,[8] was as purely nationalist and devoid of social theory as its predecessor. But its stance on the national question was more determined and less woolly—Ireland was considered a 'republic' which was permanently in existence, but temporarily occupied by the enemy—and while Fenian views about social problems were naïve, the movement was none the less very efficient at enlisting in its support a stratum of society previously untouched by purely political activity.[9] Its most active leader, James Stephens, despite his Bohemian image and a cosmopolitan revolutionary background acquired in Paris in the 1850s, was able to recruit perhaps as many as 80,000 men. To do this he spent two or three years touring the Irish countryside, and was particularly effective in the south and south-west, and later in Dublin.

Another new characteristic which the Fenians brought to Irish nationalism was the American connection, firmly rooted in the bitterness of many thousands of emigrants who had settled in cities such as New York, Boston, and Philadelphia after the famine. The most important contribution which Irish-America made to the nationalist movement, financial assistance, did not disclose its full potential until the next generation. But the emigrants' other main characteristic, impatience with the progress of the movement at home, was revealed at once. Despite years of earnest preparation, the Fenian uprising never really happened. It was hamstrung by its lack of money and guns, and perhaps by the absence of a really suitable opportunity for a rising. In

8. It was not entirely clear at this time even to its members whether IRB stood for Irish Republican Brotherhood or Irish Revolutionary Brotherhood. The confusion over names stems partly from the secret character of the movement, and partly from its more or less autonomous existence on either side of the Atlantic. 'Fenian', the term most commonly used by historians, was derived by John O'Mahony, leader of the American wing of the movement, from 'Fianna', the warriors of the folk hero Finn McCool.

9. A good introduction to Fenianism is a series of radio talks edited by T. W. Moody, *The Fenian Movement* (Cork, 1968). Professor Moody lists 'small farmers and labourers, soldiers, schoolmasters, clerks, shop assistants and urban workers generally' as forming the backbone of the movement (p. 106).

one important sense the Fenians were as big a failure as the Young Irelanders. Their significance, and their greater historical stature, is attributable partly to their success in enlisting mass support for an avowedly violent movement, but also in large measure to the posthumous credit they received through being acknowledged as spiritual parents by the successful revolutionaries of 1916–21.

In the intervening half-century, such success as was won by Irish nationalists came on the constitutional front. The year 1867 is doubly significant, for it witnessed not only the final collapse of the Fenians, but also the passing of a large measure of parliamentary reform in Great Britain, which heralded a new dynamic era of parliamentary politics. Gladstone's disestablishment of the Episcopalian Church of Ireland in 1869 and his Irish Land Act of the following year seemed to offer Irish nationalists new hopes of success at Westminster.[1] During the 1870s a strangely heterogeneous group of Irish MPs were gathered together into a new party by Isaac Butt, an ex-Tory barrister who had made a nationalist reputation by his powerful speeches as defence counsel for some of the Fenian prisoners. The national demand of the party was realistically moderate: 'home rule' for Ireland, with a Dublin parliament within the United Kingdom.

Butt's leadership became very spasmodic, however, and the party did not begin to make effective progress until two further developments occurred. The first was the replacement of Butt by Charles Stewart Parnell, a *declassé* Protestant landlord heading a party composed increasingly of lower middle-class Catholic shopkeepers and farmers, with a few country solicitors. Parnell and his colleagues soon devised a series of procedures in the House of Commons which seriously impeded the passage of government business and won the party valuable publicity. Aided by the further extension of the parliamentary franchise in 1884, which quadrupled the Irish electorate, Parnell was also able to increase the size of the home rule party, while making its personnel more radical and more subservient to his authoritarian style of leadership.[2] At the same time, by the so-called 'new departure' of 1878–9, Parnell was able to convince the main stream of the remaining Fenians that this style of constitutional politics was worthy of its support. He thereby secured for his movement a far wider range of financial backing in America than any other constitutional movement ever had.[3]

It is none the less very doubtful whether these achievements would

1. Although it was largely ineffectual in practice, the 1870 Land Act at least reversed the previous trend of land legislation by recognizing that a tenant had a legally definable interest in his land just as his landlord did.

2. The best study of the politics of the Parnellite decade is Conor Cruise O'Brien, *Parnell and his Party* (Oxford, 1957).

3. For an analysis of these developments in their American context see T. N. Brown, *Irish-American Nationalism, 1870–90* (New York, 1966).

have produced the great results they did, particularly in the area of land reform, had it not been for a second major development which coincided with Parnell's appearance on the political stage. From the early 1870s improvements in long-distance transportation, particularly the successful refrigeration of meat, brought the farmers of the Americas into direct competition with English and Irish farmers in their domestic market. When this coincided with a general economic recession, originating in the US economy and aggravated for free-trade Britain and Ireland by the adoption of protectionist policies by other countries, the outcome in Ireland was a serious fall in farm prices.[4] Then came three consecutive years of very bad harvests, 1877–9. In the still precarious condition of the Irish rural economy this meant widespread inability among tenants to pay their rent and a renewal of eviction on a large scale. The peasants' response was the Land League, which, combining the virtues of a centrally organized pressure group with the traditional methods of agitation, became a more effective force for agrarian reform than Ireland had ever seen. Although the government was able to drive the League out of existence by 1882, its vigorous agitation, embracing considerable intimidation and a fair measure of terrorism, enabled the Parnellite party at Westminster to extract a really effective programme of land reform from the Liberal government, and so bind the small farmer to the national cause in a way that had never been done before. The Land League, an agrarian organization, effectively laid the foundations for a series of successive constituency political organizations which maintained the Irish party at Westminster until the whole constitutional movement withered away during the First World War.

It became, in fact, relatively easy for the Irish politicians at Westminster to maintain their power base among the rural tenantry, for after 1885 both major British parties accepted, and worked hard to instigate, the principle of nationwide peasant proprietorship in Ireland. The future of the traditional system of land tenure seemed so unappealing in the political and economic circumstances of the 1880s that even the majority of the landlord class was willing to see it go, once the British Treasury had been persuaded to bridge the gap between what the tenant could afford to pay for the land and what the landlord could afford to accept. The policy developed slowly between 1881 and its full adoption in 1903, but progress was always steady enough to keep the Irish party secure in its political leadership at home. Thus the fai ure of the home rule movement to achieve its *national* objective in the crisis of 1886 or at any time in the following two decades hardly seemed to

4. E. Strauss, *Irish Nationalism and British Democracy* (London, 1951), makes some interesting, though not always entirely convincing, causal connections between economic and political developments.

undermine its position at all. The party in the hands of Parnell's successors became a group of highly accomplished and professional leaders,
backed by a well-drilled rank and file, which fitted increasingly well
into the House of Commons on the radical wing of the Liberal party.[5]
Its ultimate weakness lay in the confident assumption that its position in
Irish politics was assured. Its power base was so secure for so long among
the expanding lower middle class of peasant proprietors and aspiring
tenants that it failed to make any really serious efforts to broaden its appeal. For a nationalist party it allowed its base to become too narrow.[6]

Outside Ulster, where constant sectarian pressure caused the minority Catholic community to place its aspirations unquestioningly in the
hands of the charismatic Joe Devlin, the party was unable to attract
important sections of the urban population and, as time went on, it
became to a considerable extent an upholder of the *status quo* in many
rural districts. Its final collapse was occasioned only by the cataclysmic
events of 1912–16, but its long-term deficiencies left it ill-equipped to
cope with such crises. In the countryside it offered nothing very exciting
to younger men, and nothing at all to the younger sons of farmers and
to landless men, except the possibility of a subsidized labourer's cottage.
In the towns it pressed for the erection of working-class housing, but it
had no formal connection with trade unions, and generally its links
with employers were more apparent than its links with workers. With
the exception of Devlin its national leadership remained in the hands
of a small group of ageing men, while local leadership rested equally
firmly in the conservative hands of successful shopkeepers, publicans,
and the larger peasant proprietors. There was little to attract the
younger generation of university-educated men in the ideology of the
party, and little encouragement given to them to join it. Rightly or
wrongly, the political subaltern class in nationalist Ireland came to regard 'the party' as synonymous with wirepulling and jobbery.

Of these groups, the younger countrymen were the least sophisticated
politically, and remained politically unorganized until a new situation
arose, created by the First World War. The politics of the urban
workers were more complex, and will be dealt with below (p. 10). The
third category of dissident nationalists was clearly identifiable as a

5. The political history of these years is best followed in the biography of one of
the main protagonists, F. S. L. Lyons, *John Dillon* (London, 1968). For the organization of the party, see the same author's *The Irish Parliamentary Party, 1890–1910*
(London, 1951).

6. Joseph Devlin, a Belfast man who had charge of the party's organization from
1904 to 1918, was for a while successful in building a viable political machine on the
structure of the Ancient Order of Hibernians, a Catholic benefit society which gained
its dynamism from sectarian animosities in Ulster. But it was a brittle arrangement,
which proved incapable of resisting the expansion of Sinn Féin after 1914. See A. C.
Hepburn, 'The Ancient Order of Hibernians in Irish politics, 1905–14', *Cithara*,
x. ii (1971), pp. 5–18.

group some years before its force was effectively channelled behind a cohesive political leadership. A large number of its members were employed as national (primary) schoolteachers, or minor civil servants and clerks, while a smaller, but equally distinguishable group were doctors. A substantial part of the younger members of the priesthood fell within the same general grouping. The national ethos in which such people moved is best summarized by the term 'Irish-Ireland'. It was a new wave of nationalism, the basis of which was essentially cultural, from which the Irish party, despite occasional efforts, was never able to derive any substantial advantage. The new mood was wider and vaguer than membership of any particular organization, but a representative section of it was contained within either the Gaelic League, formed in 1893 to work for the revival of the Irish language, or the Gaelic Athletic Association, formed in 1884 to revive traditional Irish sports.[7] The latter was always frankly nationalist: it excluded policemen and soldiers from its ranks, and any one who participated in a 'foreign' sport such as Association football. The hard core of the revolutionary movement, even though most of its members were language revivalists themselves, always took more political interest in the GAA than in the League, presumably because it contained a greater proportion of vigorous young men.

Two overtly political nationalist movements were ultimately to capitalize on this new mood, though they did so very slowly, requiring the stimulus of war to develop a mass membership, and the upheaval of the Easter rising before they could merge with one another. Sinn Féin was formed in 1905 by Arthur Griffith, a journalist and newspaper proprietor. Apart from some limited success in Dublin corporation politics, the movement remained a small group of not very harmonious leaders, grouped around Griffith and his weekly newspaper, with little following, until 1916. Any wider publicity it achieved was mainly on account of Griffith's idiosyncratic political demand, which was based on an analogy between Anglo-Irish relations and Hungary's position in the Austrian Empire before 1867. Ireland, he argued, should withdraw her political representatives from Westminster, create instead a national assembly in Dublin, and call for a restoration of the independent Irish constitution of 1782, with sovereignty vested in 'the King, Lords, and Commons of Ireland'. Britain and Ireland would become, thereby, a 'dual monarchy' along the same lines as Austria-Hungary. It was a scheme easily ridiculed: by the sophisticated, who observed the ramshackle condition of the suggested model, and by the more parochial, to whom it seemed simply 'foreign'. Griffith's contribution to the theory of the post-1916 revolutionary movement was his emphasis on

7. The Gaelic League remained formally non-political until 1915, although most of its activists had for many years been prominently identified with the nationalist movement outside the parliamentary party.

abstention from British institutions and the creation of an alternative structure in Ireland itself.

More radical than Griffith, the true advocates of violent revolution were members of the secret society known as the Irish Republican Brotherhood. This group claimed direct descent from the Fenians of 1867, and John Devoy, in New York, was indeed a link between the two bodies. The main differences were that, unlike the original Fenians, the new IRB remained a small secret group working under cover of other organizations, never recruiting on a mass scale itself and, probably because of this, it was never effectively penetrated by the police.

As regards social and economic policy, Griffith and Sinn Féin were middle-class conservatives, using the arguments of the German economist Friedrich List. They called for a national policy of protection in order to create a flourishing Irish industrial and agricultural capitalism which would provide the basis for future prosperity. The IRB was probably more radical than Sinn Féin in its social as well as its national outlook. It showed no enthusiasm for Griffith's rather uncritical faith in Irish capitalism, but it usually subordinated social and economic matters so completely to the national question that it is difficult to speak of the IRB as having any formal views on such matters at all. Certainly the main difference between Sinn Féiners and IRB men is to be found elsewhere, in the area of tactics and temperament.

THE LABOUR MOVEMENT AND NATIONALISM

A comparison of the developing labour movements in Britain and Ireland offers some interesting contrasts. In Britain the movement experienced a gradual and steady build-up of industrial and subsequent political power, and was characterized in the main by cautious and moderate leadership, and by a generally harmonious and fruitful alliance at all levels between middle-class socialist intellectuals and working-class labour leaders. In Ireland the movement scarcely developed at all before the end of the nineteenth century, but when it did at last make an appearance it was a very explosive one. The leadership of Comrades Larkin and Connolly attracted far more attention from the Bolsheviks and other continental revolutionaries than did the prosaic activities of most British labour leaders. The movement in Ireland was, furthermore, based almost entirely on the trade union movement, winning very little support from intellectuals. Another difference between the two countries was that while the British movement continued to make steady advances, its Irish counterpart declined after 1920 almost as rapidly as it had previously grown.[8]

8. For detailed studies, see J. D. Clarkson, *Labour and Nationalism in Ireland* (New York, 1925) and A. Mitchell, *Labour and Politics in Ireland, 1890–1930* (Dublin, 1973).

These differences can be explained in two ways. Firstly the development of a working-class consciousness in Ireland was impeded by the special circumstances which then prevailed: the long predominance of the national question over all social questions, except that of land tenure, discouraged the development of political debate along class lines, while the pre-industrial economy of much of the country meant that there was no effective base for the steady development of unions. Only in Protestant Belfast, with 19,000 trade unionists, mainly skilled men, had the movement advanced far by 1900. Elsewhere in Ireland there was nothing on a significant scale until the development of the general west European trend towards mass unionization of unskilled workers. The second factor conditioning the development of trade unionism in Ireland was international. In all countries forming part of the western economy, the decade prior to 1914 witnessed violent industrial unrest. An all-round decline in real wages in these years produced a situation in which relatively full employment existed side by side with serious discontent. The circumstances were ideal for the growth of trade union militancy in many countries and the new style was able to make a particular impact in Ireland because it was operating in more or less virgin territory.

Both the leading Irish socialists, James Connolly and James Larkin, were prominently identified with the new syndicalist style of the international trade union movement, Connolly as one of its leading theorists,[9] Larkin as a prime example of the practical syndicalist, a manufacturer of what Sorel called 'the myth of the general strike'. Both men, equally, came to adopt strong nationalist republican positions, though by separate routes which reflected their different personalities. Larkin, the spontaneous pragmatist, had in his early days professed the usual contempt of the international socialist for nationalism.[1] Born in England, speaking with a Liverpool accent, and believed to have shaken off his Catholic background, Larkin began his Irish career organizing the English-based National Union of Dock Labourers in Belfast in 1907, and had some success with Protestants as well as Catholics. But it soon became apparent that his executive had misgivings, not just about his way of executing business, but about the general principle of committing funds contributed by English members to the support of strike action in Ireland. He was thus forced by circumstances to turn instead to the idea of a new Irish-based union, which meant in practice coming to terms with nationalism. His Irish Transport and General Workers' Union, founded in 1909, rapidly became an exclusively nationalist body

9. Connolly's concept of 'industrial unionism' was identical with 'syndicalism'. See his letter to Edward Lynch of Cork, 23 May 1912 (William O'Brien papers, National Library of Ireland, MS 13940/2).

1. The standard biography is E. Larkin, *James Larkin, Irish Labour Leader, 1876–1947* (London, 1965).

(and indeed drew much of its strength from that fact). Connolly, however, was much more typical of the socialist revolutionary in his ability
to intertwine thought and action. In a sense, his attempt to convert a
nationalist revolution into a socialist one by getting into the driving
seat was equally pragmatic, but the theoretical justification for his
changes of position was always carefully worked out. Thus in 1897,
when he was endeavouring to carve a niche in nationalist politics for
his tiny Irish Socialist Republican Party, he wrote: 'If you remove the
English army tomorrow and hoist the green flag over Dublin Castle,
unless you set about the organization of the socialist republic your
efforts would be in vain. England would still rule you through her
capitalists, through her landlords, through her financiers. . . .'[2] Almost
twenty years later, when Connolly had already committed himself to
participation in a rising planned by 'bourgeois nationalists', he argued
that, 'The cause of labour is the cause of Ireland, the cause of Ireland
is the cause of labour. They cannot be dissevered. Ireland seeks freedom.
Labour seeks that an Ireland free should be the sole mistress of her own
destiny, supreme owner of all material things within and upon her
soil. . . .'[3]

The dynamic force which Connolly and Larkin brought to labour
politics in Ireland was, as we shall see, captured effectively by the republican wing of the national movement. If the ITGWU as it operated
between 1909 and about 1918 is subtracted from the Irish labour movement, what is left is not only smaller, but also very much more like a
backward form of its English counterpart. A separate Irish Trades
Union Congress had come into existence in 1894 but, plagued by fears
of a split between its members on national/religious lines, its progress
had been modest. The Athlone congress of 1906 witnessed a particularly
bitter debate leading to the defeat of a republican motion. A total
membership of 60,000 in 1900 had risen only to 70,000 by 1910:[4] in
1918 there were as many members in the ITGWU alone. The development of a political wing caused particular anxieties, for such a body
would scarcely be able to avoid adopting one or other position on the
national question. Not until 1912, when the movement had been somewhat gingered up by Larkinism and, probably more important, convinced of the urgency of the situation by the apparent imminence of a
home rule parliament, did the congress agree to reconstitute itself as
'The Irish TUC and Labour Party'. As the name suggests, the TUC
controlled the party. There were no constituency organizations apart
from regular trade union branches, and no candidate could stand for
election under the party banner unless he were a trade union member
himself and sponsored by a trade union in his candidature. While such

2. *Shan van Vocht,* January 1897.   3. *Workers' Republic,* 8 April 1916.
4. Clarkson, *Labour and Nationalism,* ch. 7.

an arrangement was primarily intended to prevent fraudulent use of the 'labour' tag, it also had a constricting effect on the development of the party, which could in any one area only be as strong as were the local trade unions. The party, mindful that its only industrial base was in Protestant Ulster, stood aloof from the synthesis which Connolly was forging between the ITGWU and nationalism, and at its 1916 congress passed a neutral resolution on the subject of the recent Dublin rising.

The various nationalist movements reacted to the emergence of Labour in a number of ways. As we have seen, the left wing of the IRB-republicans displayed some traits of social revolutionary thought themselves, maintaining that 'there is little doubt that the English empire . . . provides more opportunities for the parasites than would be the case in an Irish republic'.[5] These elements supported the strikes of 1911 and 1913, and were not afraid to declare that sweated labour could exist under nationalist employers as well as unionist ones[6]—especially if the nationalist employers were supporters of the constitutional movement. There was further common ground between the republicans and the socialists in the mutual belief that there should be an armed uprising in Ireland in the event of a European war. On the other hand, left-wing republicans much preferred to justify their social radicalism in the vague terms of Gaelic 'co-operativism' rather than the overt language of Marxism. The attitude of Sinn Féin towards the labour movement was very different. Griffith strongly criticized the strikers of 1913, both as men of violence and as would-be destroyers of the precious growth of Irish capitalism which he saw as the only real basis for future independence. The leaders of the Irish parliamentary party, though they emphasized the political rather than the economic dangers of Larkinism, took up a position which was in practice very similar.[7]

We can recognize in this division of the national parties over the 1913 strike a trend that recurred in Irish politics right down to the 1930s: radical nationalism tended always towards socialism, while usually remaining distinct from it. The more moderate the nationalism, the more conservative was its attitude towards the existing social system.

THE CATHOLIC CHURCH AND NATIONALISM

The purpose of the penal laws of the seventeenth and eighteenth centuries had been to stifle the emergence of a modern Catholic élite in Ireland to replace the defeated native aristocracy. One unexpected out-

---

5. *Irish Freedom*, a paper operated by the IRB, 1910–14, cited in Clarkson, *Labour and Nationalism*, p. 287.
6. Ibid.
7. See especially the views of John Dillon, Lyons, *John Dillon*, pp. 335–7.

come, however, was the relative strengthening of the position of the priests in Irish Catholic society. For many years French and Spanish seminaries were virtually the only establishments which offered an education to Catholic Irishmen. By the end of the eighteenth century a number of upper- and middle-class Catholics were attending Trinity College, Dublin, but for large numbers of rural Irishmen the only educated man with whom they came into any regular contact was the parish priest, who, after 1795, probably received his education from the new seminary, St Patrick's College, at Maynooth, Co. Kildare. In a countryside where the landlord was regarded increasingly as an alien, this was a fact of immense significance.

The first political manifestation of the new situation came when the priests led their flocks to the polls, in the late 1820s, to vote for Catholic emancipation in opposition to the landlords' candidates. This was an ironic reversal of the traditional deference vote which in England continued to dominate rural elections for another century. But Catholic and national interests were not always so obviously linked as in this case. At many stages in the nineteenth century, particularly when agrarian disorder or talk of violent revolution was in the wind, the church as a body did not seem to be in sympathy with the national demand at all. Cardinal Cullen, Archbishop of Armagh, and later Dublin (1852–78), is the best example of this. The measures which he took to improve Roman discipline within the Irish church caused the Fenian journal, *The Irish People*, to complain ruefully that 'Dr Cullen *is the hierarchy*'.[8] Among the bishops, only Archbishop MacHale of Tuam resisted his efforts to deny the sacraments to practising Fenians. Half a century later, the Bishop of Cork refused to sanction the activities of the IRA as legitimate warfare.[9] But the expression of such attitudes by the Irish hierarchy, though very important, did not prevent many members of the clergy from actively encouraging the national cause. Father Patrick Lavelle, the Fenian supporter of the 1860s, was a relatively isolated figure, but priests who worked alongside the land agitators of the 1880s were more common, even though almost all of them subsequently worked for the removal of Parnell from the leadership of the national movement in 1890–1.[1] By 1918, even though most of the hierarchy were either supporters of constitutional nationalism or else neutral, and despite the fact that the leading Sinn Féin priest, Michael O'Flanagan, was severely disciplined for his platform activities, the

8. Cited in E. R. Norman, *The Catholic Church in Ireland in the Age of Rebellion, 1859–73* (Cambridge, 1965), p. 5.

9. Pastoral letter, December 1920, cited in W. A. Phillips, *The Revolution in Ireland, 1906–23* (2nd edn, London, 1926), p. 177.

1. For this period see two articles by E. Larkin, 'The Roman Catholic hierarchy and the fall of Parnell', part i in *Victorian Studies*, iv (1961), and part ii in *Review of Politics*, xxviii (1966).

great majority of the younger priests who took any interest in politics at all were active in the cause of Sinn Féin.

In the last half-century of the union, then, the Catholic church gave useful support to the prevailing nationalist orthodoxy of the day. But the bond between the church and nationalism in fact went far deeper. As well as the attitude of the church towards national aims, there was the important psychological role which the church played in voicing the individuality and independence of the Irish people. Despite the efforts of the Gaelic League and the emphasis of the leaders of the revolutionary generation on the language revival, religion remained, and still remains, the real badge of nationality in Ireland. National consciousness and Catholic faith indeed have interrelated in such a way as to make cause and effect more or less indistinguishable. Not only has Catholicism strengthened Irish nationality, but Irish nationality has also strengthened Catholicism. It is argued that Ireland cared little for Rome so long as England was Catholic.[2] Had not the Pope invested Henry II with the sovereignty of the country? The extraordinary intensity of religious life in Catholic Ireland, even today, among all classes of the population is, in part at least, a legacy of the solid 'national' front created in the days of British rule, though the moral austerity, sometimes called Jansenist, which so surprises continental Catholics, is a product of rural social and economic conditions over a long period, rather than directly political in origin. Even among those whom the church has punished for their participation in revolutionary or terrorist activities, there has been very little turning away from the faith altogether. Remarkably, in an authoritarian Catholic country, there has never been an overtly anti-clerical party in politics. It is debatable whether the Marxist wings of the IRA in the 1930s and again in the 1960s were even *implicitly* anti-clerical.

One general reason for this phenomenon is fairly obvious, and is another outcome of the interrelationship between religion and nationality. The Catholic church in Ireland in modern times has never been established, nor ostentatiously rich. The higher clergy could never be bracketed with the aristocracy as defenders of the old regime. It is almost a truism to say that the church in Ireland was a peasant church, its pastors drawn from the same small farming stock as its flock. Certainly this is the main reason why the majority of priests found no difficulty in supporting a very radical policy on the land question in the 1880s and afterwards. Even when condemning agrarian crime the bishops took care to distinguish clearly between social justice on the one hand and the excesses provoked by injustices on the other.

But this attitude on the land question is in sharp contrast to the attitude adopted by the church towards the socialist labour movement

2. Phillips, *Revolution in Ireland*, p. 11.

in the years down to 1914, and, indeed, for many years afterwards. A clergy which could readily understand the need for rural radicalism took a much less sympathetic attitude towards urban problems, although once again there were many individual exceptions to this rule.[3] Between 1911 and 1914, especially, the Irish hierarchy directed a blistering attack at Larkinism and socialism which not infrequently amounted to a denunciation of labour political organization altogether. It seems clear that the church sincerely regarded the new movement as a danger to its flock. Yet socialism in Ireland was no more than 'a phantom';[4] had it really managed to sink any roots among the people, the church would scarcely have been able to take the extreme stand which it did. In England, where probably the majority of the faithful were working-class Irishmen who supported the Labour party, the Catholic hierarchy found very little difficulty in coming to terms with 'the new socialism'.[5] None the less, there is no doubt that the long-term antipathy of the bulk of the Irish population to even the milder forms of socialism, which certainly handicapped the Labour party at least until the middle of the twentieth century, was the product of church influence in the years down to 1914.

THE ULSTER CRISIS, THE WAR, AND THE RISING

Following the two general elections of 1910, the Irish parliamentary party at last achieved the goal it had been striving towards for almost a quarter of a century: the balance of power at Westminster. It gradually became clear, however, that an ironic corollary to the Liberal government's dependence on Irish votes to stay in office was total Irish dependence on that government to further its aspirations. It was a game of double bluff, and as the Conservative party became increasingly involved with Unionist resistance to home rule in Ulster, it became apparent whose bluff was the more vulnerable. Between the summer of 1912 and the spring of 1914 the Liberals' resolve to introduce home rule for a united Ireland steadily withered away until it seemed that they were unwilling to enforce anything more than home rule with the permanent exclusion of six Ulster counties. What the outcome would have been if the new constitutional arrangements of 1911 had not given the House of Lords power to delay the passage of the Home Rule Bill for two years is a matter for speculation. In the event, the inevitable delay gave Ulster Unionists plenty of time to recruit, train, and arm 100,000 Protestants pledged to resist home rule.

3. See E. Larkin, 'Socialism and Catholicism in Ireland', *Church History*, xxx (1964), 462–83.
    4. Ibid, p. 481.   5. Ibid.

The peculiar position of the six counties of the north-east must[6] be explained in terms of the history of both the seventeenth and the nineteenth centuries. The bulk of Ulster Unionists were descended, or believed themselves to be descended, from English and Scottish settlers of the seventeenth century. But by the end of the nineteenth century the Industrial Revolution and accompanying urbanization had reinforced the ethnic myth with a new series of differences. In Ulster there was now a prosperous middle class, almost entirely Protestant except for a few Catholic lawyers and doctors, and rather more shopkeepers and publicans. There was, too, a large industrial working class, also mainly Protestant but for a large proportion of Catholics among the unskilled labourers. The relationship between these two classes of Protestants, both after their fashion staunchly Unionist in politics, has not yet been investigated satisfactorily.[7] Assertions have been made by historians of both red and green persuasion that the Unionist working class is a dupe of the landed and capitalist ascendancy, or alternatively that it is a *petit bourgeois* 'fascist' class. Both these views, unsupported by serious social analysis, are scarcely less brittle than the Orangeman's view of Protestant solidarity as a case of 'all loyalists together'. None the less, it was made unequivocally clear in 1912–14, and remains true today, that almost all Ulster Protestants object to the prospect of being governed by an all-Ireland parliament in which they would form a permanent minority, for one or all of three reasons: because the majority are Catholic; because they are economically less advanced than the north-east; or because they object to any formal ties with Great Britain. The only occasion since 1798 when Ulster Protestants and Catholics have participated in a struggle on the same side was a short period in the summer of 1907 when the then unknown Jim Larkin succeeded in calling a series of industrial strikes which momentarily divided the city of Belfast on class rather than religious lines.[8] The ease with which such new loyalties were brushed aside when the elections of 1910 brought the national question back into the centre of politics is a clear indication of the enduring strength of sectarian feeling.

The apparently successful Ulster resistance to the 1912 Home Rule Bill seriously undermined the position of the Irish party by exposing a

6. Really more like three and a half counties, for Counties Tyrone and Fermanagh both had small Catholic majorities, while the southern parts of Counties Armagh and Down were solidly Catholic.

7. But see P. Gibbon, *The Origins of Ulster Unionism* (Manchester, 1975), which appeared while this work was in the press.

8. In 1932 Protestant workers in the Shankill Road district rioted on one occasion in support of Catholic strikers who were receiving stern treatment at the hands of the police on the adjacent Falls Road. See I. Budge and C. O'Leary, *Belfast: Approach to Crisis* (London, 1973), p. 151. Earlier, in the 1850s, the Tenant League had for a while provided a common platform on the land question for Ulster Protestants and southern Catholics. See J. H. Whyte, *The Tenant League and Irish Politics in the Eighteen-Fifties* (Dundalk, 1966).

fatal hollowness at the centre of parliamentary nationalism. At the same time the focus of this resistance, the Ulster Volunteer Force, the first of the private armies which were to dominate the politics of many European countries for the next generation, offered the nationalists the example and stimulus of an alternative mode of procedure.[9] The Irish National Volunteers were the outcome of this stimulus. Although the intention of most of their founders was simply to make a forcible demonstration of public opinion, and although they were taken under the control of a reluctant parliamentary party for a while during 1914, this force ultimately proved to be the front organization which the real revolutionaries of the secret IRB needed in order to mount a large-scale rising. The outbreak of war in August 1914 gave another powerful boost to the position of this group, for resistance to recruiting provided a common policy around which all the more extreme nationalists, and the socialists, could unite, and had the additional attraction of widespread popularity. Under John Redmond's leadership the parliamentary party gave unintended assistance to the development of this policy by committing itself, and attempting to commit the entire volunteer force, to wholehearted support of the war. The party's declaration that it would resist conscription for Ireland lost much of its credibility in face of enthusiastic appearances by many of its MPs on recruiting platforms.

The Dublin rising of Easter 1916 was the third and final setback for constitutional nationalism, and established in outline the character of the movement which would replace it. Yet the planning of it was bungled; by its very nature it was doomed to failure from the start, and its participants were greeted with jeers by the Dublin crowds after their surrender. Irish nationalists were everywhere opposed to conscription, and in the rural districts, where wartime pressure for the expansion of tillage created something like full employment on the land, were against voluntary recruiting as well. But they were not in principle opposed to the war effort. Indeed one of the main impediments to the expansion of the revolutionary movement in 1914–16 appears to have been the propensity of some of its more hot-headed members to shout 'Up the Kaiser' as they marched along. At least 100,000 Catholics from Ireland served in the British Army during the war,[1] and while there can be little doubt that unemployment, or underemployment and very low wages, were the most powerful recruiting agents, such personal commitment to the war effort was scarcely compatible with intense anti-British sentiments. Dublin is said to have been the first city in the

9. For an account of the UVF, see A. T. Q. Stewart, *The Ulster Crisis, 1911–14* (London, 1967).

1. The number of Irish Protestants involved was somewhat over 70,000. (Until his death in March 1918 John Redmond received copies of the official monthly recruiting statistics. Redmond papers, National Library of Ireland, MS 15259.)

United Kingdom where German property was attacked in the wave of fury which followed the Kaiser's invasion of Belgium in August 1914.[2]

None the less, even though nationalist Ireland did not support the rising, and would probably not have given its support to a subsequent one, it gave its political backing almost totally to the legitimate heirs of the rising. The swing of public opinion away from the parliamentary party and in favour of the developing republican coalition was a steady process, spread over the two and a half years between the rising and the general election of December 1918. But it was already clear by the summer of 1916 that Irish politics were undergoing a more drastic upheaval than at any time since the rise of the Parnellite party forty years earlier. The initial stimulus for this change seems to be the one normally identified by the hagiographical school of nationalist historians: national revulsion against the wave of executions which followed the rebels' surrender, reinforced at the local level by sweeping and somewhat indiscriminate arrests of known republicans. All nationalist political movements, except the parliamentary party, were in fragments at the end of the rising. It was the new radical public opinion, inarticulate though it was, which knew what is wanted and provided the sense of urgency which the disparate factions needed to bind themselves together. By the time the old Sinn Féiners, the Volunteers, the Irish Nation League, and a number of smaller bodies had come together (in October 1917) in support of de Valera's compromise formula—that the new Sinn Féin should work for 'the international recognition of . . . an independent Irish republic' after which the people 'may by referendum freely choose their own form of government'—public opinion was already solidly behind them.[3]

The participation of the working class in the Easter Rising had been symbolized formally by the presence of Connolly and his Citizen Army, 300 strong at the most. In fact, as British cabinet ministers noted afterwards, many of the rank and file of the non-socialist Volunteers were also products of the Dublin slums. The action of the military government after the rising, in arresting a large number of trade union leaders, especially those associated with the ITGWU, is a further indication of the presumed link between socialism and the rebellion. But the Irish TUC, even after the event, took care not to associate itself directly with the revolutionaries.[4] The real truth is contained in the famous remark attributed to Connolly, in prison awaiting execution: 'The socialists will not understand why I am here. They forget I am an Irishman.'[5]

2. Personal interview with Mr Kevin O'Shiel of Dublin, former member of the Irish Land Commission, who was active in Irish politics during this period [E. R.].

3. For an account of these developments see M. Laffan, 'The re-organization of Sinn Féin in 1917', *Irish Historical Studies*, xvii (1971), 353–79.

4. Irish TUC and Labour party, *Annual Report, 1916*, p. 41.

5. Cited in N. Mansergh. *The Irish Question, 1840–1921* (London, 1965), p. 242.

Just as, ultimately, Connolly's socialism was subsumed within his nationalism, so also was the entire labour movement devoured. If 1913 marked the beginning, then 1916 marked the end of social revolution in Dublin. Henceforward, while the membership of the trade union movement, notably that of the ITGWU,[6] grew bigger and bigger throughout the country, its political influence grew less and less. This, then, was one important outcome of the rising. Another was the all-but-accomplished destruction of the parliamentary party, which further weakened Labour's relative position by flooding the new Sinn Féin with ex-Redmondites at the local level. The most important political result, already discussed, was the regrouping of the national forces in the new Sinn Féin, which amounted to a radical rethinking of aims so far as the old Sinn Féiners were concerned, coupled with an apparent modification in the view of the militant Volunteer element as to how those aims were to be attained. One certain fact was that as the new national front increased in external unity, so social tensions were glossed over as much as possible, and appeared in the following years only occasionally, and in attenuated form.

SOCIAL UNREST AND THE EXPANSION OF SINN FEIN

Although the labour movement after 1916 lost its leading role in the national struggle, it continued to co-operate with Sinn Féin, and tacitly acknowledged that party's leadership in political matters. In the early spring of 1918, for instance, Sinn Féin instigated a series of measures, with at least one eye on publicity, against the rumoured danger of a 'famine' in Ireland. The party discouraged and even sabotaged attempts to export food from the country. In these measures it received the general support of the Labour party and vital co-operation from the ITGWU and certain other unions. The ITUC also submitted an application in 1917 for admission to the international labour movement as an independent national unit. At the same time, however, it refused a Sinn Féin request that it sever all its connections with the British TUC, on the pragmatic grounds that 'we can work for freedom and we will, but at the same time we will claim our share of patrimony when and where opportunity offers'.[7] There remained within the labour movement political militants who, even in 1918, publicly voiced the view that a dominant Sinn Féin party would become simply 'another political mouthpiece of the capitalist class in this country'.[8] The Volunteer movement reciprocated this suspicion, for although its rank and file in

6. Police estimated the membership of the ITGWU at 85,000 at the time of the treaty negotiations (in which Labour took no part) in October 1921 (Public Record Office, CO 904/158/5).
7. R. M. Henry, *The Evolution of Sinn Féin* (Dublin, 1920), p. 273.
8. Irish TUC and Labour party, *Annual Report, 1918*, p. 106.

the towns was predominantly working class, its programme betrayed little socialist influence and it was widely held that national aims should not be blurred by the introduction of social issues.[9]

A major grievance in rural districts in 1917–18 was the government's alleged failure to enforce its own compulsory tillage regulation, by which all farmers, including the large graziers, were called on to till a minimum of 10 per cent of their land or else rent it out to labourers and small farmers who would do so. Sinn Féin was quick to appreciate that a resort to direct action to implement the government's tillage order was an ideal way of attracting the support of the rural proletariat. All over the south, west, and midlands of Ireland, and especially in Counties Clare and Sligo, in the early months of 1918, Sinn Féin clubs, previously devoid of an agrarian policy, marched out of their villages with spades in order to commandeer grazing land 'in the name of the Irish republic.'[1] This new phase of the movement, originating very much at the local level, served an important purpose in spreading the party into areas of the west where it had previously had little influence. For a while even 'pure' nationalists like de Valera were not averse to a little agrarian radicalism,[2] and it seems that at least two members of the party's standing committee favoured the permanent adoption of such a policy.[3] But the majority quickly grew anxious about the potentially divisive social effects of the agitation, and the order soon went out to Irish Volunteers not to participate in cattle-driving and ploughing, 'as these operations are neither of a national nor a military character'.[4] Nationalist historians customarily cite such instructions as evidence that the Volunteer movement was capable of giving Ireland responsible government, while socialists tend to perceive in them the seeds of betrayal. The answer is that the Sinn Féin leaders, inexperienced men projected rapidly into the forefront of national politics, were guided by short-term political motives. In the circumstances of 1918, the development of an agrarian policy seemed at first to be a good idea. Then, as it expanded so rapidly under its own momentum with very little effort from headquarters, it came to appear less of an aid to party recruitement than a threat to the party leadership.

It is therefore evident that while Sinn Féin's support was often socially radical, its social programme, national leadership, and (in many areas) local leadership, was very moderate. A split along class lines did

9. E. O'Malley, *On Another Man's Wound* (Dublin, 1936), p. 59.
1. D. Macardle, *The Irish Republic* (4th edn, Dublin, 1951), pp. 240–1.
2. In speeches at Boyle, Co. Roscommon, and Castlefin, Co. Donegal, in February 1918, de Valera told the people to keep up their Volunteer organization, as it would be needed to resist conscription *and divide the land among the people* (Monthly police reports. Report of the Inspector-General, February 1918. PRO, CO 904/105).
3. D. Figgis, *Recollections of the Irish War* (London, 1927), p. 186.
4. Macardle, *Irish Republic*, p. 241.

not seem impossible in the early months of 1918. One important factor at this time which worked in the opposite direction, in favour of national unity, was the threat of conscription into the British Army. It was an immediate and real issue, yet it contained no class connotations at all, it had no political antecedents which might discourage any section of national opinion from supporting it and, perhaps most important from the electoral point of view, it was instrumental in winning over a large proportion of the Catholic clergy to the Sinn Féin camp. In its role as the main organizer of resistance to the conscription threat, Sinn Féin gained credibility as the new party of majority national opinion.[5]

THE WAR OF INDEPENDENCE

A series of by-elections in 1917–18 was the first official indication that Sinn Féin had replaced the old parliamentary party as the standard-bearer of Irish nationalism. Sinn Féin claimed six of the nine seats which fell vacant during that time. The parliamentary party held only two seats in Ulster where, thanks to Joe Devlin's organization and influence, it had managed to maintain its general position, and one in Waterford City, where John Redmond's personal bailiwick was narrowly retained by his son. The general election, which followed closely on the end of the war in December 1918, fully confirmed the new situation. There is evidence to suggest that the near-predominance in some towns of families with members serving in the British forces may have accounted for the smaller Sinn Féin majorities in constituencies with sizeable urban populations. But over-all the swing to Sinn Féin was immense, and nationwide.[6] Of 105 Irish seats, the new party won 73, the Unionists 26 (all but 3 of them in the six counties), and the Irish parliamentary party, which at the dissolution had held 68, was reduced to 6. Waterford City was once again its only success outside Ulster, and in 25 southern seats it was unable to mount a candidate at all. After protracted negotiations with Sinn Féin and debate within itself, the Labour party decided not to contest the election. The influence of most of its leaders was thrown, more or less explicitly, behind Sinn Féin, though one of the reasons given for its decision not to contest was that a significant proportion of the rank and file of the trade union movement was still sympathetic towards the parliamentary party. Had the Labour party stood in the election it would have been obliged to take up a position for or against abstention from the British parliament, and would thus have been thrown into disarray over a national rather than

5. I am currently preparing a more detailed study of the respective roles of social and national issues in the growth of support for Sinn Féin, 1914–18 [A. C. H.].
6. See map 12, p. 56.

a social question. Its reason for backing down, therefore, was as much to avoid splitting itself as to avoid splitting the national front.[7]

The annihilation of the parliamentary party was a predictable outcome of its ineffectiveness over the previous six years. Without this strong negative factor in its favour, Sinn Féin's sweeping victory would have been a puzzling one. Resistance to conscription, and therefore to the war, was a major basis of its support, and the somewhat sudden conclusion of the European conflict removed an important plank from its platform. There was no doubt about the popularity of the main national objectives of the party, but it is by no means clear that the majority of its leaders or its supporters at the end of 1918 were united behind a strategy which they were confident would secure those objectives. Of course the Irish Volunteer element favoured some sort of military resistance to British rule, but there was none of this in the election programme. There was much talk of an 'appeal to the [Versailles] peace conference' and the appointment of plenipotentiaries, but there was no indication that such a policy would have any success, and indeed the parliamentary party sought to counter it with talk of an approach to President Woodrow Wilson, accompanied by much waving of the Stars and Stripes at election meetings. The real distinguishing feature of Sinn Féin, apart from its glossed-over links with the Volunteers, was its policy of abstention from Westminster and the accompanying pledge to create a national assembly, Dáil Eireann, in Dublin. Only after the election did it become clear that the Volunteers, now renamed the Irish Republican Army, had replaced the politicians as the dominant force in the country.[8]

When the new assembly met in Dublin, in January 1919, its attendance numbered a mere twenty-seven. Thirty-four of its members were in prison, while another eight were on various missions. The two most experienced leaders, de Valera and Griffith, were both absent, and what proved to be a gathering of historic significance took place hurriedly and in circumstances of some confusion. Thus the provisional constitution which was ratified embodied a less equivocal statement on the republic than de Valera might have thought prudent, together with a very radical statement of intent on social matters, the 'democratic programme'. It was a programme owing more to Pearse's style than to Connolly's, but it implied none the less more drastic changes in the

7. B. Farrell, 'Labour and the Irish political party system: a suggested approach to analysis', *Economic and Social Review*, i (1970), 477–502, includes a well-documented account of Labour's decision to withdraw from the election.

8. Inasmuch as the IRA was the national army it was assumed to be responsible to the Dáil, the national parliament. But not until late in 1920 did the Dáil formally take responsibility for IRA actions, and there is some doubt about whether it ever achieved much real control. See K. B. Nowlan, 'Dáil Eireann and the army: unity and division', in T. D. Williams (ed.), *The Irish Struggle, 1916–26* (London, 1966), pp. 67–77.

social order than had ever previously been proposed by representative politicians in Ireland. Among other things, it was resolved that:

the nation's sovereignty extends not only to all men and women of the nation, but to all its material possessions; the nation's soil and all its resources, all the wealth and all the wealth-producing processes within the nation and . . . we reaffirm that all rights to private property must be subordinate to the public right and welfare.

The programme was drafted by Thomas Johnson, leader of the Labour party, and in its original form was apparently more radical still, but it had been toned down following a meeting of IRB leaders on the evening before the assembly. Michael Collins is said to have advocated the scrapping of the programme altogether.[9] At all events it remained simply a form of words which may have served a useful short-term political purpose so far as relations between national and Labour leaders were concerned, but which never at any stage bore much resemblance to the social policy actually pursued by Sinn Féin.

The revolutionary Dáil, as it developed its underground bureaucratic structure between 1919 and 1921, was much more concerned with maintaining the morale of a united national movement. In practice this meant not interfering with existing social policies, except in so far as they were generally identified with 'alien' British rule. The essential conservatism of the revolutionary regime is nowhere indicated more clearly than in its agrarian policy. Traditionally, Irish nationalist movements were at their most radical in this area, but with the widespread establishment of peasant proprietorship, the social base of the forces calling for change had narrowed down to landless men and uneconomic smallholders. During the winter and spring of 1919–20, when more active agitation developed in the west than had been seen on the land for many years, Sinn Féin responded very sharply indeed, maintaining that 'the mind of the people was being diverted from the struggle for freedom by a class war'. In a number of cases, judicial officers appointed by the Dáil brought in verdicts in favour of landlords and against the agitators, such judgements subsequently being enforced by the local IRA, who were thus in effect working to protect existing landed interests against the land-hungry.[1] Historians of the left have frequently contrasted such a policy with the intentions voiced previously in the Dáil's democratic programme.[2] Sinn Féin's purpose was to demonstrate its ability to provide responsible and respectable government, to seek

9. For a more detailed account of these events see P. Lynch, 'The social revolution that never was', in Williams (ed.), *Irish Struggle*.

1. K. R. O'Shiel, 'Some recent phases of the land question in Ireland', in *Manchester Guardian*, commercial supplement, 10 May 1923.

2. See E. Strauss, *Irish Nationalism and British Democracy* (London, 1951); C. D. Greaves, *Liam Mellows and the Irish Revolution* (London, 1971); D. R. O'Connor Lysaght, *The Republic of Ireland* (Cork, 1970).

to dispel the alarm created by IRA violence against 'British' institutions by showing that in all respects other than that of national sovereignty, nothing in the new Ireland would be changed. In the context of 1919–20, it seemed especially important to most Sinn Féin leaders, anxious for the support of American and world opinion, to distinguish themselves clearly from the Bolshevist uprisings which had occurred in a number of European countries—a distinction which the British government, with publications such as 'Bolshevism and Sinn Féin',[3] was intent on confusing for the same reason. Any manifestation of social revolutionary tendencies in Ireland after 1918 was, therefore, rapidly suppressed.

Far from being disaffected by these developments, the Labour party and trade union movement in fact concurred in them. The Labour movement itself had more or less dropped its old Larkinite-syndicalist image by 1919 and re-emerged as a rapidly expanding trade union bureaucracy with a broad social democratic base. The struggle for self-determination was presented in very general terms to the labour movements of the rest of the world as a battle between imperialism and nationality, between rich and poor. In Ireland itself the movement played a wholehearted supporting role in the national struggle. When Sinn Féin and IRA prisoners went on hunger strike in April 1920 to secure prisoner-of-war status, they were supported by a general strike throughout the south of Ireland.[4] At about the same time, transport workers refused to handle any military goods. When the railwaymen found that they got no support in this from the English section of their union, they seceded, and joined the ITUC as a separate group.[5] The Irish labour movement outside Protestant Ulster thus fully identified itself with the republican cause. Its reward came in the form of fulsome tributes from de Valera, as president of the underground republic:

When we wanted the help of labour against conscription, labour gave it to us. When we wanted the help of labour in Berne, labour gave it to us and got Ireland recognised as a distinct nation. When we wanted labour to stand down at the election and not divide us, but that we should stand four square against one enemy, labour fell in with us. I say labour deserves well of the Irish people; the labour man deserves the best the country can give.[6]

With its facile confusion of 'labour' meaning the political party and 'labour' meaning simply the working class, no better illustration could be found of the general ambivalence of Sinn Féin towards the labour movement.

Just as the threat of military conscription had brought about a national front of parties opposed to the British connection in 1918, so

3. *Intercourse between Bolshevism and Sinn Féin*, HC 1921 [Cmd. 1326], xxix. 489.
4. Clarkson, *Labour and Nationalism in Ireland*, p. 340.   5. Ibid., p. 414.
6. Cited in Macardle, *Irish Republic*, p. 286.

in 1919–21 the predominant political emotion of 'national resistance' to 'British repression' enabled Sinn Féin once again to smother all other parties under the national blanket. Indeed, the campaign of military and political resistance offered by the IRA and Sinn Féin to British rule was truly remarkable. Its success, coupled with the increasingly brutal reprisals which it elicited from the British forces, helped to harden Irish feeling against any compromise settlement, so that when a truce at last came, in July 1921, it proved extremely difficult for the Sinn Féin negotiators to give ground on either of the two main issues: sovereignty and unity. But the British government, a coalition dominated by Conservatives, and led by a Liberal, Lloyd George, felt itself to be equally limited in its freedom of action by the pressures of party politics.[7] For two months in the autumn of 1921 treaty negotiations between the two sides continued almost daily.[8] Neither side was very optimistic about the possibility of agreement. The policy of the Irishmen was, if necessary, to 'stage the break on Ulster', so that Britain's determination to dismember their country would appear as the cause of the renewed conflict. Lloyd George briefly considered the advantages of such a break for his own future,[9] but ultimately settled for a maximum offer of dominion status within the Empire, or else 'immediate and terrible war'.

It seemed for a while that the question of Ulster's future would remain the sticking-point, but by the time the negotiations reached their climax on 6 December 1921 that issue had been temporarily removed from the stage by what seems, in retrospect, a simple piece of duplicity. The British delegation proposed that the contended six counties of Ulster—Antrim, Armagh, Derry, Down, Fermanagh, and Tyrone—be excluded from the settlement pending the appointment of a boundary commission to review the proposed border. The Sinn Féiners accepted, with surprising credulity, having been led to believe that the commission would revise the boundary so drastically that the northern state would be too small a unit of government to survive. The newly established regime in Belfast, however, concurred with the proposal on the completely opposite, and correct, assumption that the commission would confine itself to revisions of detail in the immediate neighbourhood of the border.[1]

7. For some indication of these pressures see Lord Beaverbrook, *The Decline and Fall of Lloyd George* (London, 1963); M. Cowling, *The Impact of Labour* (London, 1971).

8. F. Pakenham (Earl of Longford), *Peace by Ordeal* (London, 1935), remains the best account of these negotiations.

9. It might have been a good issue on which to leave his Conservative allies in the coalition and re-emerge as the leader of British radical opinion. See Cowling, *Impact of Labour*, p. 123.

1. The Northern Ireland government, nevertheless, refused to nominate a representative when the commission was at last set up, in 1924.

The Sinn Féin delegation, having been offered what they chose to regard as a guarantee of unity, reluctantly agreed under tremendous pressure from Lloyd George to accept his proposals for a treaty. They signed away their demand for full sovereignty without making the telephone call to de Valera and his colleagues in Dublin which they knew would have resulted in a veto of their signatures. Their decision very shortly brought the national front to an end.

CHAPTER TWO

The Social Structure of Irish Nationalism and Republicanism, 1922–3

The nature and social structure of Irish nationalism was revealed more clearly in the post-treaty split than in any other episode in modern Irish history. Concealed undercurrents, hidden differences in the hopes and aspirations of various sections of Irish society, became suddenly and sharply apparent. The causes of the civil war must be sought in Ireland's historical heritage and social structure, as well as in the feverish political manoeuvres of the spring of 1922 and the prolonged debate over the treaty. The war of words, however, makes a suitable starting point for the inquiry.

THE TREATY AND 'DOCUMENT NO. 2'

The rejection of the Anglo-Irish treaty of December 1921 by de Valera, and almost half the Dáil, split the national movement into two hostile camps, became the central issue in Irish politics for the next fifteen years, and provided an apparently permanent basis for the Irish party system. De Valera's utmost concession was his 'Document no. 2', which sought to establish a compromise between the dominion status of the treaty and the irreconcilable republicanism of its opponents by means of an 'external association' of Ireland with the British Commonwealth. A comparison of the two schemes will illustrate both the language in which the issue was debated and the narrow margin which divided the formal demands of the two sides.

Article 1 of the treaty guaranteed Ireland essentially the same relationship to the imperial parliament as that enjoyed by the Dominion of Canada. In contrast to this, de Valera's document emphasized that fundamental sovereignty rested with the Irish people, though conceding that 'for purposes of common concern, Ireland shall be associated with the states of the British Commonwealth' (article 2). 'Matters of common concern' were deemed by the document to include defence, peace and war, political treaties, and whatever else was currently regarded as being of common concern by members of the Commonwealth. In respect of these points there should take place 'such concerted action founded on consultation as the several governments may determine' (article 4).

The treaty symbolized the link between Ireland and the British Commonwealth by an oath of fealty, to be taken by members of the Free State parliament, 'to His Majesty King George V, his heirs and successors by law, in virtue of the common citizenship of Ireland with Great Britain and her adherence to and membership of the group of nations forming the British Commonwealth of Nations' (article 4). De Valera on the other hand had urged some form of words such as 'I do swear to bear true faith and allegiance to the constitution of Ireland and the Treaty of Association . . . and to recognize the King of Great Britain as head of the associated states.'[1]

Otherwise there was little essential difference between the two documents: Ireland would assume its share of the United Kingdom's public debt (article 5 of the treaty and article 13 of the document); the Irish army would be no larger in proportion to the total population of the state than was the British army to the population of the United Kingdom (articles 8 and 10 respectively); and although, on the question of Britain's retention of naval bases in Ireland, Document no. 2 was slightly more explicit concerning Ireland's right to terminate the arrangement after five years, the issue was never at the centre of the debate (articles 6–7 and 7–9 respectively). So far as the right of Northern Ireland to secede from the Free State was concerned, there was no practical difference between the two documents at all.

The text of the treaty none the less drew forth many different interpretations, because nowhere was the status of a dominion precisely defined. The flexible vagueness which was held to be the great strength of the British constitution was felt by both Britain and the dominions to be a vital ingredient in an imperial relationship which was always adapting itself to changing circumstances. Many Irish Republicans, however, saw only the wording of the text, and feared a narrow, literal interpretation.[2] They pointed to the constitution and government of Canada as defined in the *Canadian Year Book, 1914*:

The Canadian parliament consists of the King, the Senate, and the House of Commons . . . All military and naval forces are under the command-in-chief of the sovereign . . . The King may disallow any act passed by the parliament

1. See D. Macardle, *The Irish Republic* (4th edn. Dublin, 1951), p. 579 and (for the full text of both documents) pp. 953–63.
2. See the columns of the anti-treaty journal, the *Republic of Ireland*.

of Canada . . . The final court of appeal [is] . . . the judicial committee of the Privy Council in England.[3]

In the view of anti-treaty Republicans, such provisions contained the seeds of continued British hegemony in Ireland.

Supporters of the treaty on the other hand could point out that the position of the monarchy in the dominion constitutions was in fact only symbolic, and that in practice no use was made of the rights of veto and command over armed forces. Furthermore, it could reasonably be anticipated that the general trend within the Empire towards further loosening of the ties would continue. The dominions, it was argued, were striving like Ireland for more and more independence, and therefore the admission of the Free State to dominion status brought Ireland powerful allies in its struggle. Indeed, so far as formal allegiance was concerned, the oath which Free State representatives were required to take made a far more discreet reference to the source of imperial authority than did those of the other dominions. A member's first loyalty was to the Free State constitution. In the opinion of Michael Collins, the treaty 'gives us freedom, not the ultimate freedom that all nations desire and develop to; but the freedom to achieve it'.[4] Arthur Griffith believed that it guaranteed all Ireland's fundamental interests, and that if it were to be rejected Ireland would lose the sympathy of the world.[5] In one sense, perhaps, the treaty had also a moral advantage over Document no. 2, in that it was signed under pressure from Lloyd George,[6] and might therefore in the long run be construed as less binding than de Valera's voluntary offer.

De Valera believed that it was necessary, whatever the cost, to be free to call the new state a republic.[7] Although the two documents agreed on all practical clauses, the treaty retained the forms of British constitutional law (it was not, in fact, a treaty, but 'articles of agreement') whereas Document no. 2 was more in the style of an international treaty. The differences were formal and ideological. As it turned out, the Canadian precedent was followed so that the Governor-General was appointed on the suggestion of the national government, with automatic ratification from London. The right of the Crown to veto Irish legislation was never exercised, and the Free State soon demonstrated its independence in a practical way by joining the League of Nations. Distrust of England, however, was so deeply rooted in historical experience, the English king was so much a symbol of foreign rule, that many Republicans could not accept this compromise as

3. *Canadian Year Book, 1914* (Ottawa, Department of Agriculture), p. 8.
4. F. Pakenham (Earl of Longford), *Peace by Ordeal* (London, 1935), p. 367.
5. Macardle, *Irish Republic*, p. 610.
6. Pakenham, *Peace by Ordeal*, pp. 296–7.
7. Ironically, what was denied to de Valera in 1921, a republic associated with the Commonwealth, was granted to India and Pakistan in 1947.

the minor concession it really was. Thus, extreme Republicans such as Cathal Brugha could liken the difference between the treaty and Document no. 2 to that between 'a draught of water and a draught of poison'.[8]

These formal differences were also important to British politicians, as the treaty negotiations had made clear. Lloyd George made one concession after another—only in regard to the question of the Crown and the oath was he obliged to stand firm if he was to remain at the head of a government which could carry the settlement through. Britain had not been defeated in the field, as Michael Collins in particular was aware. In these circumstances, her willingness to settle on the terms offered seemed to pro-treaty Irishmen a remarkable development beside which complaints about 'the Republic' were mere carping:

The greatest empire of modern times, at the height of its power and strength, went down on its knees to a little nation and begged for terms. There is no parallel to that in ancient and modern history. ... To grasp the whole magnitude of it one has only to compare the terms of the Irish truce with the armistice which Germany accepted at the close of the great war. ... She was treated as a vanquished enemy. Whereas we ... were treated as England's equal....[9]

THE POST-TREATY SPLIT

The dispute between the supporters and opponents of the treaty was bitter from the very beginning. Although the Dáil debate continued for almost a month, the split among the Sinn Féin parliamentarians, and, most important, within the IRA, was apparent from the very first day. On 7 January 1922 Dáil Eireann approved the treaty by the slender margin of 64 votes to 57, and immediately the minority withdrew in protest at the decision. De Valera resigned the presidency and was replaced by Griffith, and the pro-treaty majority began to set up a provisional government under the terms of the London agreement. Their opponents maintained that the second Dáil, elected in May 1921, and the government of the Republic which was responsible to it, was the only legitimate source of authority in Ireland, and had no power to abolish itself in favour of a Free State within the British Empire. The bulk of the population, weary of the long struggle, hoped that order would be quickly restored in conditions of de facto independence, and the rapid release of prisoners and withdrawal of British troops encouraged such hopes. But from April 1922 onwards, violent clashes occurred more frequently between the two wings of the IRA, provoked mainly by Republican opponents of the treaty seeking to strengthen their position by the occupation of barracks and bases.

8. Macardle, *Irish Republic*, p. 640.
9. P. S. O'Hegarty, *The Victory of Sinn Féin* (Dublin, 1924), p. 63.

Griffith and Collins could not permit the existence of an armed opposition indefinitely if they were really intent on establishing the new regime. Their political and military position was so precarious, however, that for a while they dared not intervene, but made a number of efforts to preserve the *status quo*. The general election of June 1922 was generally expected to be a national referendum on the treaty. But in May Collins and de Valera, in an attempt to avoid civil war, made a pact by which the two factions of Sinn Féin nominated a coalition panel of candidates in the same proportions as the original vote on the treaty. The intention was to provide the basis for a coalition government in the third Dáil. In practice, however, the successful entry into the election of the Labour party and the Farmers' party, along with a number of independent candidates, destroyed the basis of the pact and gave voters an opportunity of expressing preferences for or against the treaty. In the election of June 1922, first-preference votes were cast as follows: pro-treaty 239,193; anti-treaty 133,864;[1] Labour 132,511; Independents 63,641; Farmers 51,074.[2] The proportion of explicitly anti-treaty voters was therefore less than 22 per cent of the whole.[3] The victory of the pro-treaty party considerably strengthened its position. For this reason, and because of increasing pressure from the British government, the provisional government shortly afterwards called for the surrender of the Four Courts in the centre of Dublin, which had for almost three months been occupied by IRA forces hostile to the treaty. The rejection of this ultimatum and the consequent attack marked the beginning of a civil war of remarkable bitterness, if relatively few casualties, which continued until April 1923.

One of the most remarkable aspects of the Irish struggle for independence is the way in which the national unity, which had characterized the 1918–21 period, broke up amidst such violence. It is hard to believe that the bitter hostilities of 1922–3 sprang simply from the almost academic differences between the treaty and Document no. 2. The remainder of this chapter will examine the social background of the supporters and opponents of the treaty, and consider whether social unrest in any way determined the character of the struggle. By tackling these questions it may be possible to establish the nature of Irish nationalism in this period and clarify the relationship between national and social aspirations. The investigation will lead us from personal to general factors, from the role of the individual temperament to the impact of impersonal social forces.

1. This figure included 3,148 votes for Dan Breen, whose name appeared on both panels, but who later opposed the treaty.
2. D. O'Sullivan, *The Irish Free State and its Senate* (London, 1940), p. 62.
3. The minor parties were all pro-treaty in the sense that their candidates were willing to take their seats in the Free State Dáil. For the position of the Labour party, see below, pp. 62–67.

The republic of 1919–21, though its achievements were substantial, had not been a thoroughly organized state. It was essentially an underground organization which, with the backing of public opinion, was able to exercise a number of the functions of government in certain districts at certain times. Its main task, however, was to provide propaganda and moral and financial support for the IRA.[4] In the first and second Dáils passionate speeches were made and applauded; representatives were selected according to their prominence in the fight against England, with little regard for their political or administrative abilities; and the executive governed in the absence of official opposition, though with its authority restricted in practice by the autonomous existence of bodies such as the IRB.[5] The habit of unquestioning acceptance of parliament's decisions had not yet been established. Lacking the circumstances of a real state, men had pledged themselves to the idea of a republic which existed quite independent of reality.

Ever since the Fenian period extreme nationalists had asserted the myth of an inviolable, indestructible republic. On top of this tradition came the heady excitement of three years' guerrilla warfare, which created what one contemporary called a 'mystical, hysterical, neurotic worship of "The Republic" and "The Army" ', stifling by its intensity even the traditional Irish sense of humour. The Republic had come to be 'worshipped for its own sake, without reference to the meaning of the word or the condition which would establish its meaning'.[6] In the absence of an acceptable political system, many had pledged themselves to symbols which they were not prepared to sacrifice even when the real essence of their demands was granted.

Viewed in these terms the division of opinion over the treaty was to a great extent a matter of temperament, and analysis can proceed no further. The same is true of another factor which influenced many of the protagonists, the question of personal friendship and loyalties. Even before the truce certain rivalries had already become apparent. Collins and Mulcahy, the military leaders, are said to have scorned de Valera's views. because he was not well informed about the military situation.[7] Arthur Griffith developed a strong personal antipathy towards Erskine Childers.[8] Quite early on in the struggle against the British, Cathal Brugha and Austin Stack had come to resent the rapid rise to power and prestige of Collins, a younger, and perhaps more able and hard-

4. P. S. O'Hegarty, *A History of Ireland under the Union* (London, 1952), p. 761.
5. Ibid., p. 762. The IRB, the secret society which had planned the 1916 Rising, continued its existence until at least 1922. Almost inevitably its activities are ill-documented, but it seems clear that its members, who included Michael Collins, regarded it as having first call on their allegiance until such time as an Irish republic was fully and openly established.
6. Ibid., p. 781.
7. E. O'Malley, *On Another Man's Wound* (London and Dublin, 1936), p. 288.
8. T. de Vere White, *Kevin O'Higgins* (London, 1948; Tralee, 1966), p. 60.

working man. Collins never expected that these men would support a settlement for which he took responsibility.[9] The majority of the IRB, on the other hand, although it was traditionally the most extreme republican organization, remained loyal to Collins, its president, until the end, accepting his interpretation of the treaty as a 'stepping-stone' on the road to a republic.[1] De Valera's political opponents, at least, have alleged that his personal declaration of opposition to the treaty proposals caused many of the political rank-and-file, who might otherwise have been inclined to vote 'yes', to adopt a more intransigent position.[2]

An analysis of the treaty split must start with the participants in the political process, the members of the Dáil. It has often been pointed out that all six women members voted against the treaty.[3] The primary motivation for four of them at least may well have been the bereavements they had suffered at the hands of the British authorities. Furthermore, it is remarkable how many of the most irreconcilable figures were not of purely Irish origin. Erskine Childers was, in his own words, an Irishman by choice.[4] Cathal Brugha's family were from Yorkshire. De Valera, though he had grown up in Ireland, was born in New York of a Spanish father. M. P. Colivet's family were from the Channel Islands. Constance Markievicz's roots were firmly in the Anglo-Irish ascendancy class. Going outside the Dáil, Maud Gonne was of English origin, Patrick Pearse had an English father, while Roger Casement and Tom Clarke were both of Ulster Protestant background.[5] This phenomenon, the extreme fervour of the convert, is found in religious denominations and nationalist parties in many countries.

The Sinn Féin politicians elected in 1918 and 1921 came predominantly from the lower stratum of the urban and small-town middle class.[6] Table 2.1 indicates how the main occupational groups divided on the treaty question in January 1922. There seems to have been a predominance of professional people and possibly white-collar workers on the pro-treaty side, while more businessmen were to be found in the opposite camp. The distinctions are not sufficiently clearcut, however, to permit any general conclusions to be drawn. One noticeable characteristic of the Dáil as a whole was its youth,[7] but there is no

9. M. Forester, *Michael Collins: The Lost Leader* (London, 1971), p. 212.
1. F. O'Donoghue, *No Other Law* (Dublin, 1954), pp. 186–95.
2. O'Hegarty, *Victory of Sinn Féin*, p. 72.
3. See for example, ibid., ch. 19, 'The Furies'.
4. Macardle, *Irish Republic*, p. 901.
5. Sean MacStiofain, chief of staff of the Provisional IRA, 1970–2, grew up in London as John Stephenson.
6. J. L. McCracken, *Representative Government in Ireland: A Study of Dáil Eireann, 1919–48* (London, 1958), p. 34.
7. McCracken, *Representative Government*, p. 30. Of the Dáil elected in 1921, 38 per cent were under 35, 75 per cent under 45.

TABLE 2.1

Voting in the Dáil, 7 January 1922

Occupational group	Pro-treaty	Anti-treaty
Professional (including teachers and journalists)	32	19
Business	8	16
Farmers	9	7
White-collar workers	8	3
Artisans	3	—
Others (including not known)	4	12
Total	64	57

Note: It has not been possible to obtain information on all members. The main sources for the table are *Thom's Irish Who's Who, 1923*; *Irish Independent*, 30 December 1918; and the personal recollections of Mr A. McCabe, TD for Sligo in the second Dáil.

indication that age was a determining factor in voting on the treaty. Young and old were found on both sides in approximately equal numbers.

As far as the IRA was concerned, de Valera's opposition to the treaty was certainly not the sole cause of the division within its ranks. His decision had little influence on its radical wing, for men like Rory O'Connor had from the beginning viewed the negotiations with distaste, knowing that only a compromise could result. These men were the spiritual successors of those Fenians who had maintained that England only understood the language of force, and that to negotiate at all was tantamount to betrayal. De Valera could have done nothing to persuade this group to accept the treaty, and indeed was later to separate from it, when, in 1926, he withdrew from Sinn Féin to establish Fianna Fáil.

An analysis of the split within the IRA reveals two main trends. One is geographical, and will be discussed below (pp. 38–50). The other is a vertical one within the command structure of the army, indicating that among the lower echelons there was more opposition to the treaty than at the top. Nine out of thirteen members of the general headquarters staff supported the treaty;[8] eight of the nineteen divisional headquarters reported a majority in favour of acceptance;[9] while at the brigade level there was an anti-treaty majority of 70 to 80 per cent.[1]

8. O'Donoghue, *No Other Law*, p. 208.

9. *An t-Óglach*, the Free State army newspaper, 24 April 1922, gave the number of pro-treaty divisions as twelve. The figure given here is from Macardle, *Irish Republic*, p. 964.

1. Because the situation was so confused and observers so partisan, the sources for this information are inaccurate and contradictory. The structure of the IRA was necessarily somewhat haphazard: one division might consist of a few hundred men, another of several thousand. O'Donoghue, *No Other Law*, p. 221, an anti-treaty source, estimates that of 71,250 officers and men of the IRA, 63 per cent, took the Republican side in March 1922.

Further analysis of the two IRA factions reveals few broad differences. On both sides officers and men were very young. They came mostly from poor homes, and many were unemployed, although there was also, especially at officer level, a large lower-middle-class element.[2] They had become popular heroes, celebrated everywhere, and consequently many of them took a somewhat elevated view of the importance of their political opinions.[3] An additional complication is that the ranks of the IRA expanded enormously after the truce of July 1921, so that during the civil war the number fighting on the Republican side alone was probably many times greater than the number who had fought against the British.[4] It is, however, probably true to say that the sons of the larger farmers were to be found on the Free State side, while the sons of small farmers and the landless men were more likely to be Republicans. For arguments in support of this theory, it is necessary to analyse public opinion in general.

The southern Unionists were numerically a small group but possessed, then as now, considerable economic power and influence, and had for some years accepted the fact that a certain degree of Irish independence from Britain could no longer be avoided. In 1918 they had not been prepared to go any further than a moderate measure of devolution, but after the events of 1919–21 the treaty seemed to them to be the least of evils, and they supported it unequivocally. Republicans were not slow to turn this to their advantage, and it was frequently alleged that those who had opposed the struggle for independence were now among the most prominent supporters of the treaty.[5]

The most prosperous Catholics, whether or not they had previously given support to the independence movement, now generally shared this desire for stability. Any material grievances which still troubled the business community had been met by the agreement to transfer complete control of tariffs and the economy to the Free State. The debates in the Dáil, and the vast number of resolutions passed by chambers of commerce and local government bodies, made it abundantly clear that the commercial middle class stood mainly on the side of the provisional government.[6] Alongside them stood the Farmers' Union, representing the more prosperous elements in the farming community. The newspaper press, which had in the main gone over from the moderate home

2. P. Beaslai, *Michael Collins and the Making of a New Ireland* (Dublin, 1926), ii. 372; O'Hegarty, *Victory of Sinn Féin*, p. 66.

3. O'Malley, *On Another Man's Wound*, p. 59; W. A. Phillips, *The Revolution in Ireland, 1906–23* (London, 1926), p. 176; personal information [E. R.].

4. Beaslai, *Michael Collins*, ii. 405; O'Hegarty, *Victory of Sinn Féin*, p. 124. Both these sources, admittedly, are strongly pro-treaty.

5. Macardle, *Irish Republic*, pp. 633–4. For a detailed study see P. J. Buckland, *Irish Unionism: The Anglo-Irish and the New Ireland, 1885–1922* (Dublin, 1972).

6. J. D. Clarkson, *Labour and Nationalism in Ireland* (New York, 1925), p. 450; *The Republic of Ireland*, 21 January 1922.

rule policy of the old parliamentary party only when the electoral victory of Sinn Féin became an accomplished fact, was equally solid in support of the treaty. The *Republic of Ireland,* a slim, low-circulation weekly, was the only national newspaper in the hands of the Republicans.

Although there was a significant amount of support for the Republicans among the lower clergy, the Catholic church as a body supported the treaty side as strongly as it could. The hierarchy condemned the killing of Free State soldiers by Republican forces as murder, and absolution was officially refused to members of the 'irregular' forces:[7] a sanction more respected in Ireland than in many Catholic countries. An attempt was made by the Republican leaders to lessen clerical opposition by an appeal to Rome, but to no avail.[8] The Catholic church had almost always followed rather than led the national movement in Irish history, and had certainly always taken the majority and, if possible, the more moderate side in any split. In the circumstances of 1922, with the pro-treatyites having a parliamentary majority and the Republican opposition being essentially military in nature, the position adopted by the church was both sensible and predictable.

Where, then, did Republican support come from? Socialist writers claim that small farmers and the industrial workers of Dublin and Cork were ready to channel their social discontent into support for the party of intransigence, and that the Republican leadership, had it not been held back by its essentially lower-middle-class character, could have ensured political success by inscribing revolutionary social aims on its banner.[9] They further maintain that social discontent among the small farmers was in fact a major cause of the civil war in the western districts. Certainly it would be surprising if the less privileged elements in the population were not more open to radical slogans than those better off. It is also true that the growing number of unemployed and the landless sons of small farmers provided an inexhaustible reservoir of recruits for the IRA.[1] But the extent to which this was an indication of social radicalism within the Republican movement is open to question. The social and geographical background to the split requires closer investigation before such questions can be answered.

7. E. Neeson, *The Civil War in Ireland, 1922–23* (Cork, 1966), pp. 327–8.
8. Ibid., p. 330.
9. Eg B. O'Neill, *The War for the Land in Ireland* (London, 1933), p. 106, and preface by Peadar O'Donnell; E. Strauss, *Irish Nationalism and British Democracy* (London, 1951), pp. 265 and 271.
1. Irish Labour party and TUC, *Annual Report, 1922,* p. 78.

A SOCIAL-GEOGRAPHICAL ANALYSIS
OF THE NATIONAL STRUGGLE, 1918–21

It is not an easy matter to produce an accurate map of the centres of military activity during the war of independence. The IRA was not an orthodox army seeking to conquer and occupy territory in the traditional manner, but a series of underground guerrilla units whose object was to promote a breakdown in British authority in as many places as possible. Small groups of badly equipped men—sons of small farmers, labourers, shop assistants, clerks, and artisans—sought to bring the British administration of Ireland to a standstill by attacking and destroying isolated police barracks, by ambushing military columns, by shooting individual British soldiers, spies, and informers, and by a general policy of bombing and sabotaging enemy installations and the property of enemy sympathizers. This campaign was answered to an increasing extent on the British side by reprisals which consisted in the main of the destruction of houses of prominent Sinn Féiners and of community-owned institutions like the co-operative creameries.

It seems reasonable to assume that the amount of destruction carried out by British forces in a district (map 1) reflects approximately the extent of national resistance in that district.[2] But since British forces were temporarily driven out of some districts altogether by the intensity of IRA activity, and would therefore have been unable to administer revenge, it is useful to check the information this map contains against the number of IRA incidents recorded in the Chronology of the Bureau of Military History (map 2). In general the two maps confirm one another. Cork features a little more prominently in the second map, Clare a little less. Mayo seems to have been slightly more active than map 1 would suggest. Only in the north-west, in Leitrim, Longford, and Sligo, does it appear that reprisals were significantly out of proportion to the extent of IRA activity.[3] Another source of information, though less specific, is the number of incidents attributed by the police to Sinn Féin and the IRA. From the beginning of 1919 to 31 March 1920, 1,089 disturbances were reported, including 588 in Munster, 269 in Leinster (mainly in Dublin), 137 in Connaught and 95 in Ulster.[4] Ernie O'Malley, who acted as national organizer for the IRA, later recollected that Waterford and Kilkenny fought very little and that

2. It should be noted, however, that in the disturbed conditions of the time there was probably quite a high degree of inaccurate reporting.

3. It is not unlikely, however, that the peak period of IRA activity in the north-west midlands area was in the second half of 1920, and is not therefore included in the figures for map 2. See Macardle, *Irish Republic*, p. 388, and Seán MacEoin's account of 'The battle of Ballinalee', *With the IRA in the Fight for Freedom* (Tralee, nd), pp. 101–14.

4. Parliamentary Papers 1920, xl. 799. The *Irish Bulletin*, organ of Dáil Eireann, maintained, 2 February and 4 April 1920, that these figures were greatly exaggerated.

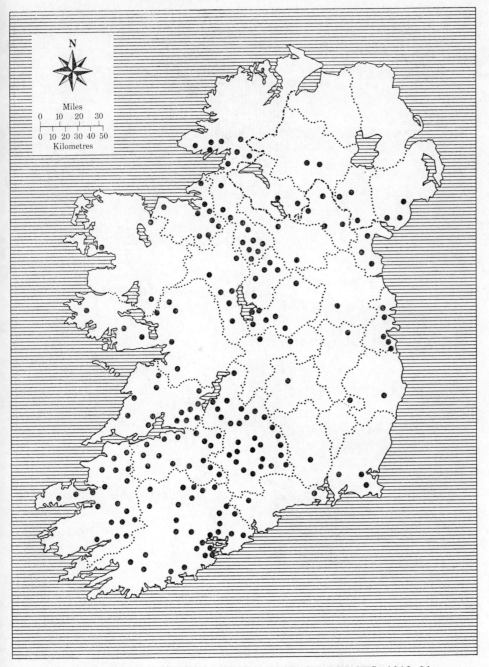

1. REPRISALS CARRIED OUT BY BRITISH FORCES, 1919–21

Each dot indicates a town or village in which buildings were destroyed between September 1919 and July 1921. *Source:* Dáil Eireann Information Bureau (National Museum of Ireland, Dublin).

(39)

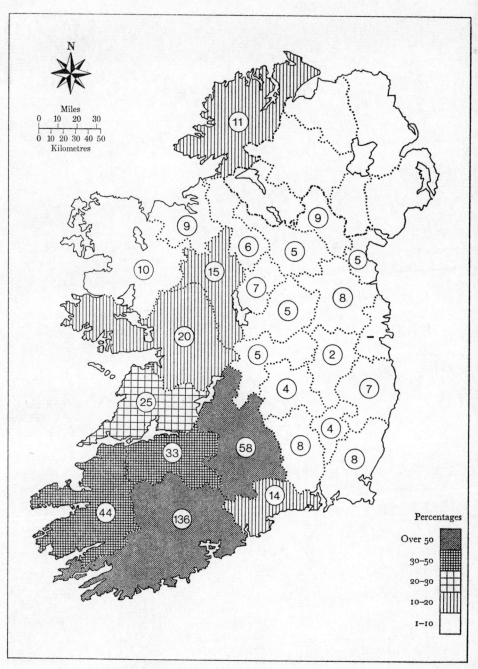

2. SIGNIFICANT IRA OPERATIONS, 1919–21

The map shows the number of operations conducted between 1 September 1919 and 30 June 1920, and between 1 January and 30 April 1921. Dublin city and county are omitted from consideration, as being the headquarters of both British and IRA organization. Information for Northern Ireland is not available. *Source: Chronology of the Bureau of Military History, 1913–21* (Dublin).

Donegal was good for nothing.[5] Another indication of the scale of disturbances is the fact that on 4 January 1921 a state of martial law was proclaimed in Cork, Kerry, Limerick, Tipperary, and Clare.[6]

A compilation of thirty-eight reports by IRA veterans on their operations in various districts, called *With the IRA in the Fight for Freedom*, contains eleven reports referring to Co. Cork, six to Co. Dublin, five to Clare, four to Kerry, three to Co. Limerick, and nine to the remaining twenty-one counties which later made up the Free State. All these sources tend to confirm the general impression that five counties in the south-west (the province of Munster, excluding Waterford) were by far the most militant districts. A secondary centre of activity was in Sligo, Longford, and Roscommon. Donegal and Mayo, considering their relatively large size and population, appear to have been as inactive as some of the eastern counties. Conversations with a number of former participants and their contemporaries confirm all these impressions, with the exception that Co. Mayo was considered by some to have played a more active role than is apparent from these maps.

The style of warfare conducted by the IRA required determined support from a substantial proportion of the local population, so we can deduce that areas of high IRA activity were areas of strong IRA support. Cork, for instance, 'is a small city, where many people are known to one another. The IRA leaders were known by name and appearance to thousands, but they were never betrayed.'[7] Such unanimity was a precondition for success. Where it was lacking, where a considerable section of the population was indifferent or opposed to the IRA, then its actions were necessarily sporadic. In Trim, Co. Meath, the IRA on one occasion 'were actually hampered [by the civilian population] . . . when making preliminary arrangements to occupy their positions'.[8] In Loughrea, Co. Galway, a town which for some years had been torn by rivalries between Sinn Féin and supporters of the old parliamentary party, posters appeared in March 1921, purporting to come from 'The Anti-Sinn Féin Society', forbidding any men aged between 17 and 40 to enter the town.[9]

Although military activity could flourish only in districts where it had the backing of the population, other questions must be asked before the pattern of IRA activity can be fully explained. The usual answer given by those who participated in the struggle is that local leadership was all-important, that effective IRA units developed in areas where enthusiastic and efficient men came forward to organize them. Certainly this was necessary: without effective leaders there could be no

5. O'Malley, *On Another Man's Wound*, pp. 94 and 218.
6. *With the IRA in the Fight for Freedom*, p. 34.
7. Ibid., p. 33.   8. Ibid., p. 89.
9. Chronology of the Bureau of Military History, Dublin, 1913–21, iii. 311.

recruits. But why were leaders to be found in some districts and not in others? The historian must admit that there is an element of chance in such things. But more important, and more readily explained, is the political and social climate of the various districts. As an IRA organizer, Ernie O'Malley was very clear about this:

Each county was different; the very map boundaries in many places seemed to make a distinction. The land seemed to determine the nature of the people often enough; weather, pasture, grazing, tillage good or bad, nearness to the sea, whether remote from towns and cities, hilly, mountainous, or undulating. Sometimes I came to a townland where there was a company of twenty or thirty men and boys. Tall, well set up and lanky, eager, lithe, willing to learn and anxious to take risks. Six miles away across the barony the people were cowed; the men had no initiative. They were irresolute. The captain of the company sometimes made the difference, sometimes the men themselves, but in part it was the nature of the land and the long struggle against odds that had told.[1]

In the early days of the struggle, officers were mostly elected. Frequently a prominent farmer or sporting hero was chosen rather than the man most likely to do an effective job. O'Malley considered many such choices to be indications of moral cowardice, with 'extenuating under-currents of a candidate's influence, position, or power'.[2] These factors were probably influential sometimes even when officers were not elected. In some districts the IRA is said to have been under the direction of local businessmen who cared more for the preservation of peace and order than for bold action and the risk of British reprisals against property.[3] In a rural society where habits and customs, views and standards were as firmly rooted as in most parts of Ireland, the question was not so much whether a potential local IRA leader existed as whether the nature of local society would permit him to operate effectively. Or, to put it another way, it was a question of whether the social class from which leadership had to come was sufficiently inspired by the fighting spirit to undertake the risks of leading a guerrilla war.

It can be seen from maps 1 and 2 that the general gradient of increasing IRA activity from east to west of the country corresponds inversely to the extent of anglicization. The eastern side of Ireland was subjected to English influence more intensely, and for a much longer period, than the western area (map 3). British planters settled in the east, where retired officers and civil servants sought estates, and the 'Pale', around Dublin, had been more or less effectively under English control since the time of Henry II. The submission of the west on the other hand did not take place until the late seventeenth century, and even then, owing to the poor quality of the land, was not penetrated in the same way as the east. It was also in the west that the Irish language

1. O'Malley, *On Another Man's Wound*, p. 129.   2. Ibid.
3. Personal information [E. R.].

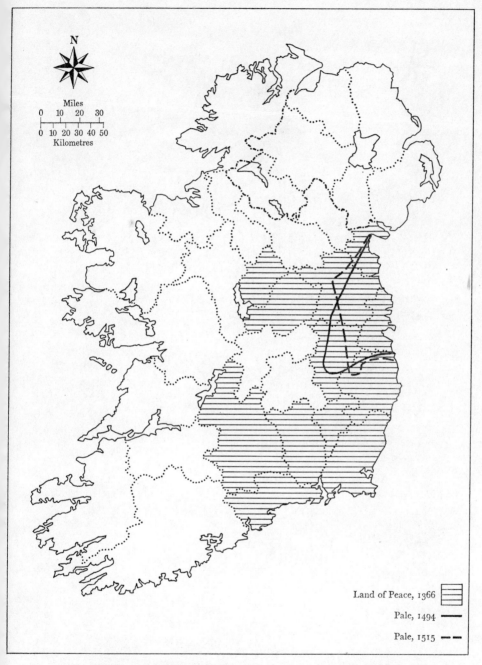

Miles
0 10 20 30

0 10 20 30 40 50
Kilometres

Land of Peace, 1366

Pale, 1494

Pale, 1515

3. THE 'LAND OF PEACE' AND THE 'ENGLISH PALE'

The shaded and delineated areas indicate the furthest extent of English influence in the pre-modern period. *Source:* T. W. Freeman, *Ireland* (London, 1972), p. 90.

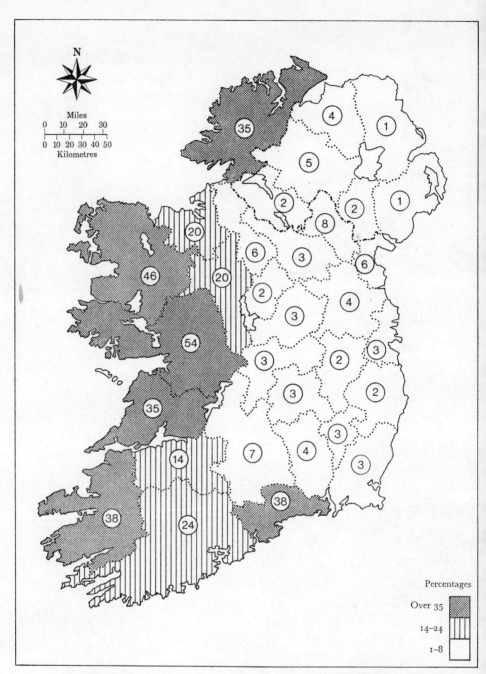

4. DISTRIBUTION OF IRISH LANGUAGE SPEAKERS, 1911

By county, this map shows the percentage of the total population claiming to be Irish language speakers at the time of the 1911 census. *Source:* Thom's *Irish Directory*, 1928.

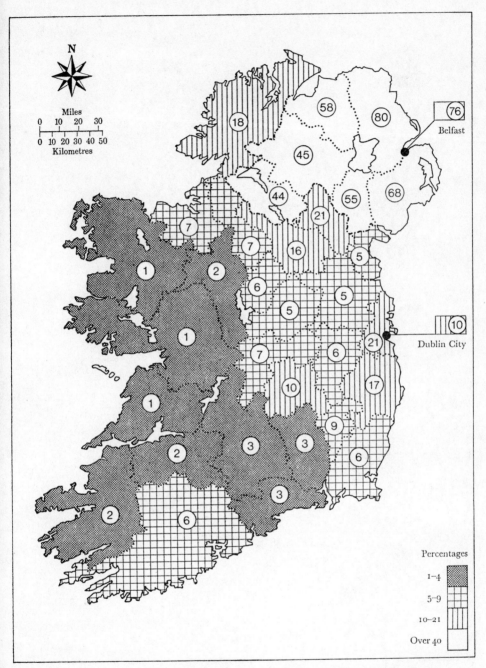

5. THE NON-CATHOLIC POPULATION, 1926

The figures are given in percentages, by county. *Source: Irish Free State Census, 1926; Census of Northern Ireland 1926.*

(45)

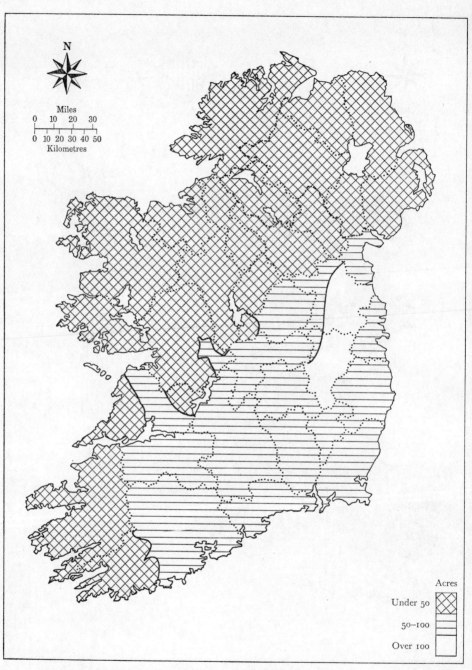

Acres	
Under 50	
50–100	
Over 100	

6. AVERAGE SIZE OF FARMS, 1936

Source: T. W. Freeman, *Ireland* (London, 1972), p. 186.

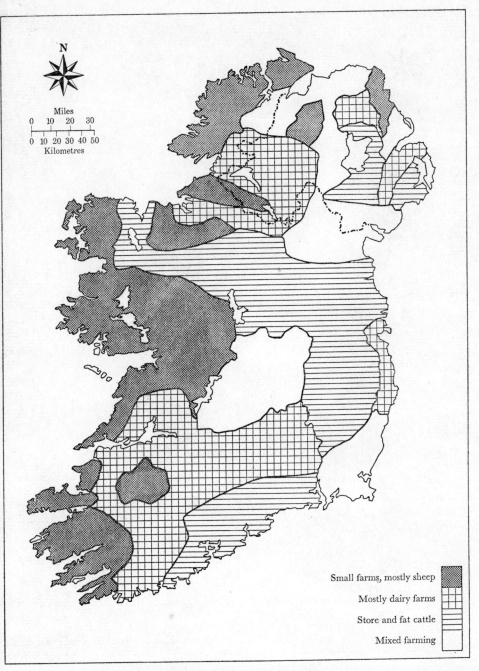

N

Miles
0 10 20 30

0 10 20 30 40 50
Kilometres

Small farms, mostly sheep

Mostly dairy farms

Store and fat cattle

Mixed farming

7. MAIN FARMING TYPES

Source: Adapted from T. W. Freeman, *Ireland* (London, 1972), p. 195.

(47)

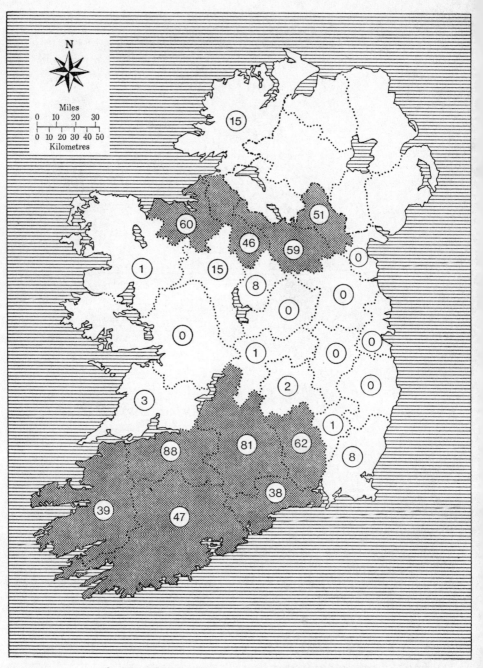

8. CO-OPERATIVE DAIRY ORGANIZATION

The figures show the percentage of all milch cows in each county which were supplying creameries in 1926. Figures for Northern Ireland are not available. *Source:* L. Dudley Stamp, *An Agricultural Atlas of Ireland* (London, 1931), p. 47.

was preserved long after it had been replaced elsewhere by English (map 4). The proportion of non-Catholics in the population provides a further indication of the degree of English penetration, and the same east–west gradient is confirmed (map 5).

The question arises as to whether there is any discernible relationship between the economic structure of a region and the extent of its participation in the independence struggle. Map 6 shows the average size of farms in different parts of the country. The large farmers of the east and south-east were better off than the small farmers of the west and north-west even before land purchase. Once the land reform programme had been carried through, their material grievances against Britain were completely removed, and any further dislocation of relations constituted a threat to the basis of their trade, for over 90 per cent of their major product, cattle, went to the English market. The position of the small western farmer was different. Even when cattle were the basis of his farming he sold them as very young steers to the east, and was therefore isolated from any direct economic link with Britain.[4]

The situation in Tipperary, Limerick, east Clare, and Co. Cork is more difficult to explain. Here much of the land was in the hands of relatively strong farmers, yet the area was none the less in the forefront of the fight against England, so it is not enough to consider the size of farms alone. Maps 7 and 8 indicate the distribution of different types of farming, and demonstrate that the centres of IRA activity coincided to a considerable extent with the main dairy-farming areas, especially the areas where co-operative creameries were the basis of organization: Counties Limerick, Cork, Tipperary, Kerry, Leitrim, and Sligo. Though founded by a Unionist,[5] the co-operative movement had always enjoyed the support of Sinn Féin, partly because its self-help doctrines accorded well with Sinn Féin teaching. The parallel breaks down in the cases of Clare and Longford, which were active in the struggle but which had little co-operative organization, and in Cavan, Kilkenny, and Waterford, where there was a considerable number of co-operatives but relatively little IRA activity. On the other hand this thesis does offer some explanation for the surprising absence of disturbance in Donegal, Galway, and Mayo, three western and strongly Gaelic counties. The preconditions for co-operative dairy organization are developed dairy farming, combined with a fair degree of rural wealth, community spirit, and organization. It seems, therefore, that these

4. C. Arensberg and S. T. Kimball, *Family and Community in Ireland* (Cambridge, Mass., 1940, 1968), p. 29.
5. Sir Horace Plunkett (1854–1932), younger son of the 16th Baron Dunsany, sat as Unionist MP for south Co. Dublin, 1892–1900. He founded the Irish Agricultural Organization Society in 1895, and became a supporter of dominion home rule for Ireland in 1917.

factors had to be present in a farming community in order to stimulate active participation in the national struggle. Map 9, which indicates the density of population on the land, confirms this impression (the densely populated areas around Dublin and Cork must be discounted, as not strictly 'rural').

Another factor which must be taken into account is the presence or absence of a strong tradition of militant nationalism in the various parts of the country. Tipperary and Limerick, for instance, had for centuries been regarded as centres of resistance to British rule. A study of the number of outrages recorded by police during the land war of 1880–2 (map 10) indicates clearly that many of the areas which led the way in this struggle were also most strongly Republican in the 1918–23 period, at least so far as voting was concerned.[6] The relationship between Land League incidents and later IRA military activity is less close, and must be explained in terms of the general development of the land question.

THE LAND QUESTION AND THE NATIONAL STRUGGLE[7]

Did traditional Irish land-hunger play a significant part in the struggle of 1919–21, or had the great programme of agrarian reform begun by Gladstone in 1870 diverted the course of Irish nationalism in any way? Map 11 shows the now familiar gradient from east to west, but the effects of reform were perhaps the opposite of what Gladstone in his early years might have expected. Tenant purchase had by 1923 proceeded most rapidly in the districts of the west and south-west, where the agrarian situation had been most desperate. Yet some of these districts were now those most disturbed by militant nationalism. It was in Munster especially that the raising of living standards by means of British legislation had been most effective. The landscape of whole districts in Counties Cork and Limerick had been changed by measures like the Labourers' Acts as early as 1903.[8] Ernie O'Malley reported that in those parts of Tipperary where land reform had progressed furthest people were more independent and assertive, and therefore more nationalist, than people in other districts.[9]

In the western counties the situation was more complex. To make the tenant farmer the owner of his land did little or nothing to moderate the craving for land on the part of men without land, or with an in-

6. There is a very high correlation between the amount of support for the Republican Sinn Féin party in the general election of 1923 and the number of agrarian outrages reported in the various counties for the period 1879–82. See P. Pyne, 'The third Sinn Féin party, 1923–26, part II', *Economic and Social Review*, i. ii (1970), 255.

7. See also Appendix 1, pp. 224–31.

8. R. J. Kelly, 'The agricultural labourers of Ireland', *New Ireland Review*, xx (1903), 298.

9. O'Malley, *On Another Man's Wound*, p. 150.

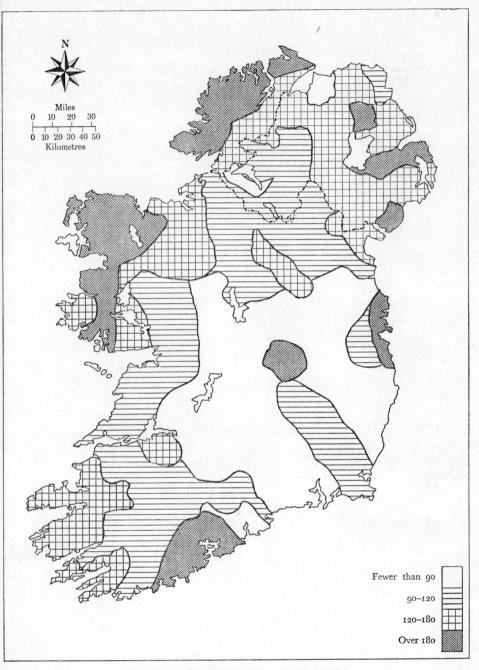

Miles
0   10   20   30

0 10 20 30 40 50
Kilometres

	Fewer than 90
	90–120
	120–180
	Over 180

9. DENSITY OF POPULATION, 1936

The map shows the number of persons per square mile of improved land in 1936. *Source:* T. W. Freeman, *Ireland* (London, 1972), p. 186.

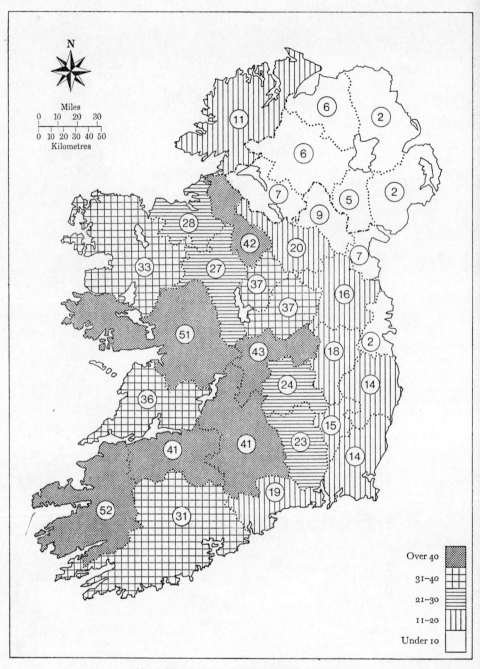

10. AGRARIAN OUTRAGES, 1880–2

The number of reported outrages by county are shown per 10,000 of the population. The city populations of Dublin, Belfast, Cork, Limerick, and Londonderry have been excluded from the calculations. *Sources:* County police inspectors' returns of agrarian offences, in *Parliamentary Papers*, lxxviii (1881), p. 619; lv (1882), p. 1; lvi (1883), p. 1.

sufficient amount of it; on the contrary, it tended to stimulate demand. This was the most intractable aspect of the land question in the west of Ireland. As the Congested Districts Board[1] had discovered, there was an innate conflict between the economic and social requirements of the situation. The Board had authority over much of Connaught and the western fringes of Munster, which contained a number of large (if often bankrupt) estates, together with a multitude of tiny uneconomic holdings. It aimed to create more viable economic units by redistributing among small farmers the good estate land previously rented on short leases to large graziers. Its task was near completion by 1915, when shortage of money brought its operations to a halt.[2] Western agriculture had been established on a more realistic economic basis, while the social structure was also healthier, in the sense that a rural middle class had been created. But the total number of farms was, if anything, reduced, since the craving for land could not have been fully met without once more splitting up the land in an uneconomic way.

The Board had always known that there was insufficient land for everyone, but it had never been able to persuade the mass of the people that this was so. Two problems proved intractable: on the one hand ownership of land remained the main indicator of social status in the west of Ireland, while on the other the problem of emigration recurred with each generation. So in spite of the Board's great achievements there remained substantial agrarian discontent in the western counties. This had erupted into serious disturbances in 1898–1902 and 1907–8, and did so again in 1918 and 1920. As Ireland's first Minister of Agriculture once observed, 'the Irish countryman believes that nature intended him to be a farmer, and there is an idea that there is enough land for all'.[3] The remarkable intensification of national feeling in Ireland after the end of the nineteenth century, though fed from sources quite different from a desire for land distribution, undoubtedly contributed to the growth of a craving for land by fostering the belief that the place for an Irishman was at home. The will to avoid emigration was very strong among young people in the pre-independence period, a trend greatly intensified by the total halt to emigration during the First World War. The result was greatly increasing pressure on the land at a time when agrarian reform was forced to come to an almost complete standstill.[4]

1. Created by the British government in 1891 to give specialist attention to the social and economic problems of the poorest western districts. It was merged into the Irish Land Commission in 1923.

2. J. E. Pomfret, *The Struggle for Land in Ireland, 1800–1923* (Princeton, 1930), p. 311.

3. Patrick Hogan, 'The Irish land question and its future', *Manchester Guardian*, 10 May 1923.

4. Kevin O'Shiel, personal interview. See also O'Shiel's article, 'Some recent phases of the Irish land question', *Manchester Guardian*, 10 May 1923.

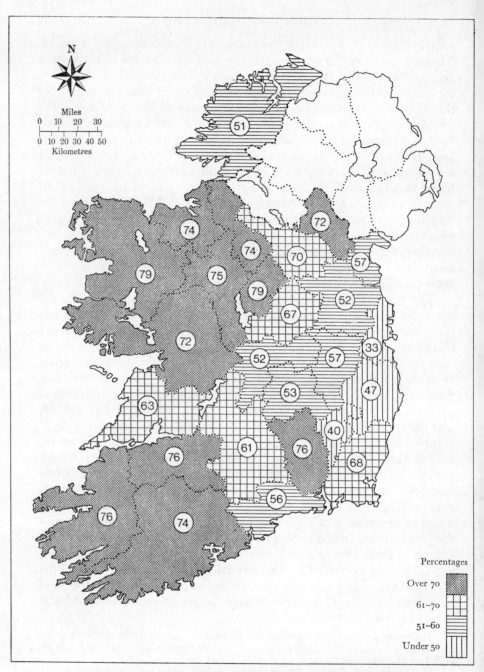

11. THE PROGRESS OF LAND PURCHASE TO 1923

The map shows the percentage of the total acreage of each county purchased by tenants under the Land Acts of 1881–1909. *Source: Report of the Irish Land Commission*, 1951, p. 29.

Thus, in the winter and spring of 1920 the hunger for land sought to associate itself once more with the independence movement. Unrest began in Kerry, and spread throughout most of Connaught, as well as Tipperary, Westmeath, and Offaly. Galway, Mayo, and Roscommon were especially disturbed. The Sinn Féin leadership, however, had already come across this problem two years earlier, and had set itself against any encouragement of agrarian revolution. It appealed for national self-discipline and, ultimately, at the request of western landlords who were in despair over the apparent powerlessness of the British authorities, land courts were set up under the aegis of Dáil Eireann. In this way, ironically, an important agency of the national underground government had its origins in the anxieties of a class which had stood aloof from the national movement in all its phases. These courts dispensed justice according to existing British law. Frequently, therefore, the decision went in favour of a landlord, in whose interests the judgement of the court would be upheld by the local IRA. When these courts were forced undercover by the British, independent land committees sprang up which sometimes assumed a more radical character, though they were often also the tools of one individual's greed.[5] The decisions of such committees were very often reversed as soon as the Dáil courts could re-establish themselves.

What then was the relationship between the land question and the war of independence? The districts where the most violent agrarian unrest occurred during this period were not the centres of the national struggle. The social aspirations of landless men were not primarily expressed in terms of hostility to the British administration. To a certain extent such aspirations were directly excluded from the national struggle, for the spirit which dominated the IRA leadership at all levels inculcated a deep suspicion of any attempt to mix social aims with the pure cause of the national struggle.[6] The social condition of many areas of the west was not favourable to an active national fight. The main national resistance was concentrated in more prosperous districts, just as de Tocqueville noticed was the case in the French Revolution, and as was also true of the German peasants' wars.

This analysis, however, is not incompatible with the fact that, on the one hand, IRA volunteers were often recruited from very poor rural districts, and on the other that western counties were solidly Republican. The poorer classes of a relatively prosperous county often responded very differently from the poor classes of a poor county. In the former case there existed a leadership to channel the militant instincts of the rural proletariat, in the latter such leadership was either very

5. One such exploiting committee was the Cragg land committee in south-west Roscommon. See also *The Constructive Work of Dáil Eireann*, no. 2, pp. 8–23.

6. See, e.g., O'Malley, *On Another Man's Wound*, p. 59.

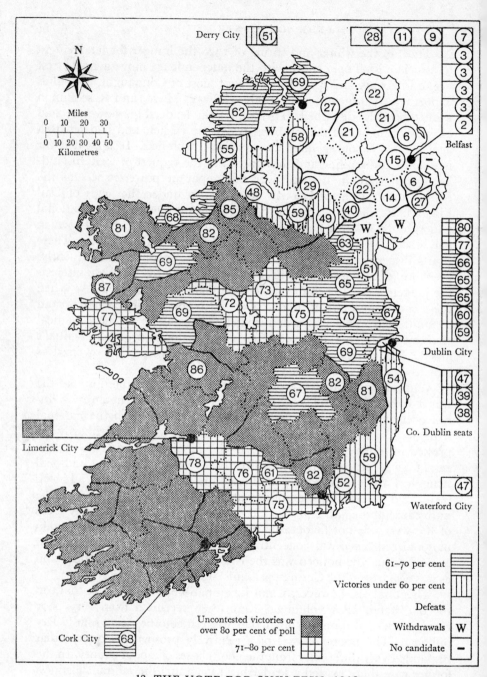

12. THE VOTE FOR SINN FEIN, 1918

The figures show the votes cast for Sinn Féin candidates in the general election of 1918, as a percentage of the total poll, by single-member constituency. The party won all seats except those not shaded. The main opponent of Sinn Féin outside Ulster was the Irish parliamentary party, which had sought for forty years to win home rule by parliamentary agitation. In seven Ulster seats a pact operated between these two parties to prevent Unionist victories on a split vote. Most of the other seats in the area which became Northern Ireland were won by Unionists against opposition from both Sinn Féin and the Irish parliamentary party.

weak or entirely lacking. Thus many districts, especially in the west, could express strong sympathy with the national struggle, as they did at the general election of 1918 (map 12), without ever taking a prominent part in that struggle. The preconditions for active participation were therefore twofold: vigorous leadership, backed by strong popular support. In the western districts the Republican spirit was often in evidence, but local leadership was insufficiently developed. In many eastern districts the leadership potential was strong, but the active support of a broad segment of the population was missing. In the main centres of national resistance, especially in the south-west, both elements were fully present.

A SOCIAL-GEOGRAPHICAL ANALYSIS
OF REPUBLICANISM, 1922–3

The civil war was essentially a controlled retreat on the part of the Republicans. Most of the fighting took place in Munster and Connaught. In mid July 1922 the IRA (the pro-treaty forces were by then known as the 'National' or 'Free State' Army) held a line from Waterford to the Shannon, but this front was soon outflanked, especially in the east, and in August the last town in Munster fell into the hands of Free State troops. The struggle continued as guerrilla warfare, mainly in southern mountain districts, although the centre of the conflict shifted to the west in September, as Ballina in Co. Mayo was temporarily reoccupied by the IRA. But as the struggle dragged on through the winter of 1922–3 the desire for peace became most apparent in those parts of the country where the fight had been most violent, and the IRA lost much of the sympathy and support which it had at the beginning of the conflict. In May 1923 the Republican leadership allowed the war to peter out.[7]

Areas where the IRA opposed the treaty were mainly those areas which had fought most actively against the British forces earlier (map 13). Only in Connaught and in the Waterford–Kilkenny area was there a noticeable increase in military activity in 1922. The change in the south-east is probably explained by the replacement of half-hearted IRA leaders by stronger men during the truce.[8] But over-all, the correlation between the maps is too close to be explained simply in terms of the attitude of a few IRA commandants. The fact that anti-British and subsequent anti-treaty activity went together indicates that the animosities developed during the earlier campaign produced a deep-rooted spirit of intransigence in these areas.

7. Two detailed narratives of the civil war have been published recently: E. Neeson, *The Civil War in Ireland* (Cork, 1966) and C. Younger, *Ireland's Civil War* (London, 1968).
8. Personal information [E. R.].

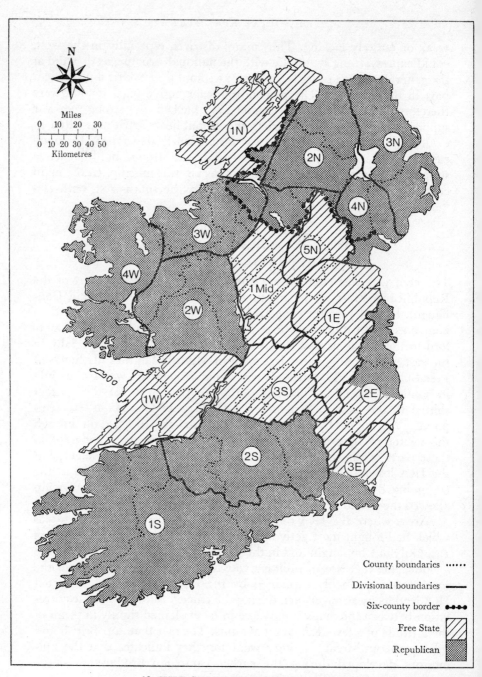

13. THE SPLIT IN THE IRA, 1922

The map indicates the attitude to the treaty taken by each IRA division in the spring of 1922. (*Note.*
The circled figures and numbers identify the IRA division in each area.) *Source:* F. O'Donoghue,
No Other Law (Dublin, 1954), frontispiece.

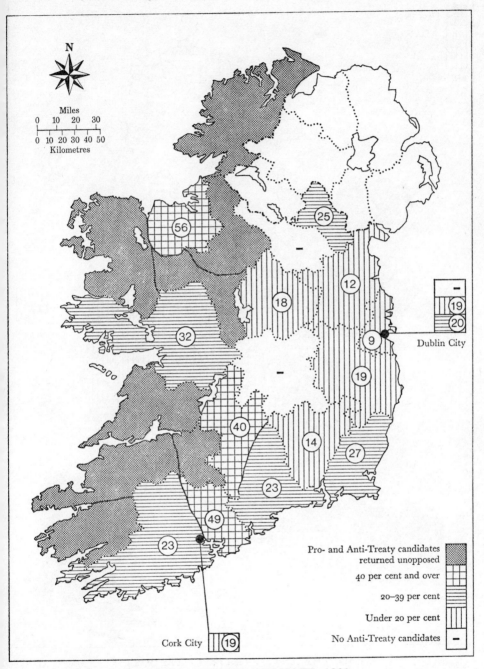

14. THE ANTI-TREATY VOTE, 1922

The map shows the percentage of first-preference votes cast for Republican candidates in the 1922 General Election, by multi-member constituency.

(59)

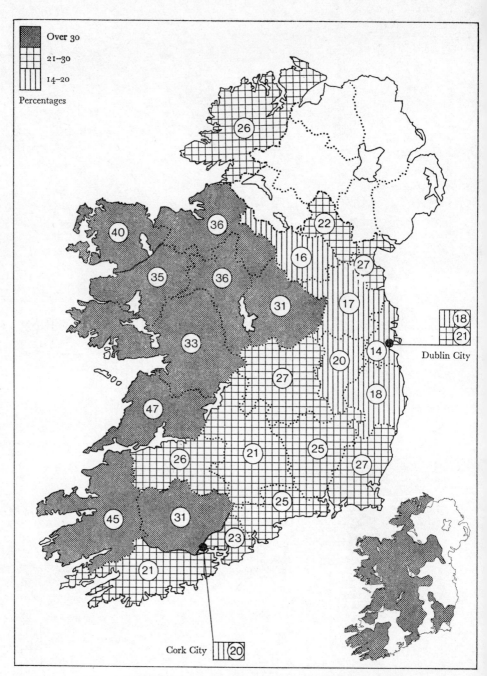

15. THE ANTI-TREATY VOTE, 1923

Percentage of first-preference votes cast for Sinn Féin (Anti-Treaty) candidates in the 1923 General Election. The inset shows the areas in which over 70 per cent of the working population were engaged in agriculture at the 1936 census. *Source:* T. W. Freeman, *Ireland*, 1st edn (London, 1950), p. 137.

Against this, the 1922 general election figures suggest that the attitude of the local IRA is not necessarily an accurate guide to public opinion (map 14). Interpretation is complicated by the large number of uncontested seats. Probably this was partly the result of IRA intimidation, though it seems reasonable to assume that Republican support was above average in such areas. None the less, it is clear that the concentration of Republican votes lay less in the south than in the west. In many parts of the south the policy of the anti-treaty IRA no longer reflected the views of the majority of the population. In the more prosperous farming districts of Munster the desire for peace and order, even if it had to be 'within the empire', was stronger than the desire for a republic at all costs. The general election of August 1923, the first held under peaceful conditions, indicates even more clearly the shift of opinion in the south (map 15). The small-farming districts of the west, on the other hand, demonstrated their continuing commitment to Republicanism. There is also a strong correlation between areas where Republicans did well and the portion of the country in which over 75 per cent of the labour force worked on the land (map 15, inset). It was in the area of the Gaeltacht and the old Congested Districts Board that Republicanism retained its strength.

The question arises as to whether post-treaty Republicanism and agrarian revolutionary instincts went hand in hand. One contemporary source, admittedly sympathetic towards the Free State side, certainly maintained that this was so, especially in Galway and adjacent counties:

Irregularism and land grabbing go together, so much so that many of the shootings and burnings are due more to economic than to political motives. When the Free State government began to take active steps a month or two ago, Ireland was nearer to a recrudescence of the land war than it had been for a generation.[9]

Most Republicans, however, would have strongly denied the importance of such motives. The main stream of Republicanism, at any rate, had not embraced such radical social goals—or indeed any social goals. As had happened in 1918 and 1920, it is probably true that certain grass-roots radical elements were seeking to convert the Republican movement to their own purposes, but de Valera and his followers kept aloof from such aims because they did not want their ideal of a republic, which had assumed an almost spiritual significance, to be blurred by material issues. A few Republican intellectuals thought very differently, but they were unable to make their voice heard at all until the late 1920s, and then with only slight effect.

None the less, the split between the pragmatism of the Free Staters

9. *Manchester Guardian*, 15 March 1923.

and the romantic idealism of the Republicans did coincide with certain lines of social division within the population. The small farmers of the west owed the preservation of their traditional Gaelic outlook to a remote situation and economic backwardness; they were in a sense sheltered from the worldly pressures which inclined other parts of the country to take a more practical view.

Another factor which it is difficult for the historian to evaluate is the question of local rivalries. In Kerry, for instance, a vendetta raged for generations between the O'Sullivans and the Murphys. Supporters of the O'Sullivans tended to be of Norman or Anglo-Saxon origin, from the more propserous sections of the community, while the Murphyites found their strength among the smaller, Gaelic-speaking farmers. In some parts of Kerry the split of 1922 closely followed the lines of this distant and quite irrelevant family feud.[1] This phenomenon, old animosities feeding on a new crisis, is found in civil wars everywhere, and probably intensified the struggle in many parts of Ireland in 1922.

THE LABOUR MOVEMENT AND THE SPLIT

The official attitude of the Labour party and the trade unions to the civil war was one of neutrality. But since they did not expressly announce their opposition to the treaty, and in fact showed themselves willing to co-operate with the provisional government, they were *de facto* a pro-treaty party, and were regarded as such. Their policy was to attempt to focus public attention on social problems and so force the national issue from the centre of the stage:

With the signing of the treaty one more chapter of the still uncompleted story of Ireland's struggle for national freedom has been closed. Tomorrow the struggle for the freedom of Ireland's men and women begins anew. . . . Henceforward the struggle which you, the worker, must perforce engage in shall be plainly and openly a struggle against capitalism. . . . Whatever form of government may be established, whatever name it may assume, Free State or Republic, unless it realises these aspirations it is not a Republic in the eyes of the workers. . . . Royalist sycophants when kings were in the ascendent, we now discover . . . seeking favours of the Republic. . . . Do not allow yourselves to be drawn into opposing camps.[2]

As a result of the long struggle, but also because of the general post-war situation in Europe, social distress had increased considerably in Ireland since 1918. The number of unemployed had reached 130,000 by 1922 and a wave of wage-reductions was under way.[3] The provisional

1. Personal information [E. R.]. A few years earlier, the factions had taken opposite sides in the struggle between the Irish parliamentary party and the followers of William O'Brien for control of the national movement in Munster. See, especially, the East Kerry elections of 1906 and January 1910.
2. Irish Labour party and TUC, *Annual Report, 1922,* pp. 19–21.
3. Ibid., p. 15.

government gave little priority to social reforms, except in so far as it alleviated unemployment incidentally by recruiting an enormous army during the civil war. Unable to control militant Republicans on one side, the government was anxious not to alienate conservative and former Unionist elements on the other. Again and again the trade unions complained that 'the new Irish treasury is more reactionary that what our experience of the British has been', and that 'international experience shows that the decisive factor is not the nationality of the government but the system'.[4]

All this, however, was not sufficient reason for the Labour party and the unions to transfer their support to the Republicans. It is true that the *Voice of Labour*, official organ of the Irish Transport and General Workers' Union, the largest and most radical Irish union, opened its columns to the Republicans as an experiment, but this advance, if such it was intended to be, was short-lived. The Republicans were simply not prepared to inscribe a radical social programme on their banners. The *Voice of Labour* maintained that the arguments which Republicans used to win the workers away from the government could be applied equally against the Republicans themselves, that Document no. 2 offered the working class no more than the treaty did: 'When all is said and done, the Republican opposition will find that out of the very necessities of the case it will be driven back upon the workers' republic before the full aims of Irish Republicanism are gained.'[5] But the Republican party made no concessions towards the radical wing of the Labour movement, and in return received no co-operation from it.

Other unions were even more reserved in their attitude towards the Republicans. The TUC resolved in 1922 that 'we not only think that the political aims of the Republican party are unreasonable but we must also condemn the methods most severely'.[6] It objected to a 'rule of revolvers and bombs' by any side, and regretted that 'the army is becoming an end in itself'.[7] A general strike against militarism of all kinds took place on 24 April 1922, while in Cork city violent trade union protests were made against the anti-treaty military authorities, who had ordered coercive measures to be taken against workers giving assistance to the Free State.[8] Its support for Free State 'law and order' made the Labour movement an opponent of the Republican militants. It attempted to maintain a position of neutrality by making various offers of mediation, but they aroused little enthusiasm, and the TUC subsequently complained that it was not sufficiently consulted by the new government.[9] The Labour party was never able to win for itself the

4. Ibid., p. 166; Irish Labour party and TUC, *Annual Report, 1923*, p. 27.
5. *Voice of Labour*, 7 January 1922.
6. Irish Labour party and TUC, *Annual Report, 1922*, p. 39.   7. Ibid., p. 23.
8. Ibid., p. 141; Macardle, *Irish Republic*, p. 701.
9. Irish Labour party and TUC, *Annual Report, 1922*, p. 18.

role of referee and the political advantages which such a position would
have brought.

None the less, the party did achieve some success in the general
election of 1922. Seventeen out of its eighteen candidates were returned.
J. D. Clarkson, a writer very much in sympathy with the Labour movement, extracted the maximum of political significance from this result:

Aside from the issue of peace or war, the election returns cannot be construed
as expressing confidence in the provisional government. In the few cases in
which it was possible to vote against the pro-treaty panel without voting for
an avowed representative of capital on the one hand or a protagonist of
metaphysical formulae on the other, the electorate expressed its want of confidence in the social ideals of the Free State party.[1]

Up to a point this is correct. But subsequent developments belie the
underlying implication that more people would have voted Labour had
they had the opportunity to do so. At the general election of 1923,
when the party ran forty-four candidates, the number returned dropped
to fourteen.

A remarkable characteristic of the Labour party and TUC in this
period is the moderate policy which it pursued in practice, compared
with its theoretical attachment to revolutionary formulas and its frequent declarations of solidarity with revolutionary movements in other
countries. The Irish deputies to the Berne International Labour Congress of 1919 had sided with the minority which declared for the
dictatorship of the proletariat as against parliamentary democracy,[2]
and the party pressed the provisional government in 1922 for famine
relief and trade agreements with Soviet Russia.[3] The main expressed
aim of the Labour party remained 'to win for the workers of Ireland
collectively, the ownership and control of the whole produce of their
labour'.[4] Despite all these gestures, the party under Thomas Johnson's
leadership firmly embraced parliamentary democracy and repudiated
any attempts to provoke a social revolution.[5] Indeed, apart from a few
heady days in 1913 and 1916, few had ever thought that the workers
would respond to a revolutionary call. Congress was clear that the wise
policy was to tread softly and concentrate on expansion of the membership.[6] Johnson, especially, was very much aware of the fact that if
Labour were ever to succeed at the polls it would require votes not only
from urban workers but also from small land-owning farmers.[7]

Within the sphere of industrial organization this policy was highly
successful. Membership of the TUC grew from 100,000 to 300,000 be-

1. Clarkson, *Labour and Nationalism*, pp. 458–9.
2. Ibid., p. 328.   3. Ibid., p. 447.
4. Irish Labour party and TUC, *Annual Report, 1922*, supplement.
5. Clarkson, *Labour and Nationalism*, p. 456.
6. See, for instance, Irish Labour party and TUC, *Annual Report, 1918*, p. 135.
7. Ibid., p. 136.

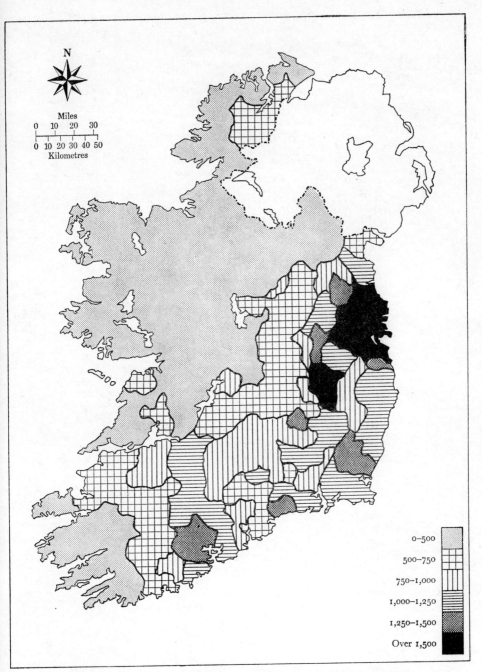

16. FARM LABOURERS PER THOUSAND FARMERS, 1936

Source: J. Meenan, *The Irish Economy since 1922* (Liverpool, 1970), p. 114.

(65)

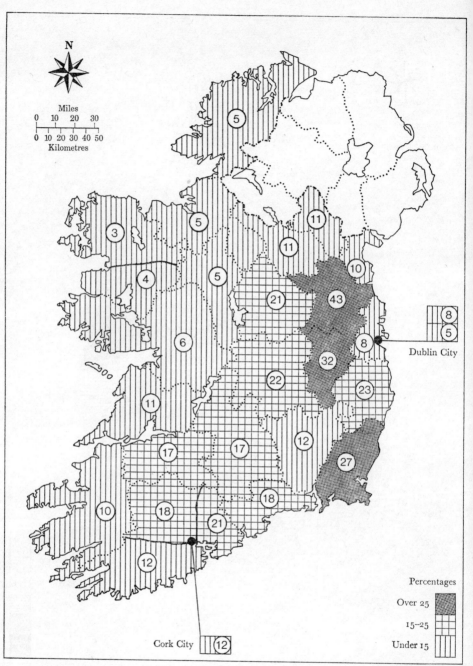

17. FIRST-PREFERENCE VOTES FOR LABOUR CANDIDATES, 1923

The following votes cast for Independent Labour candidates have been incorporated in the above General Election figures: Cork East 21 per cent; Dublin North 5 per cent; Dublin South 3 per cent; Leitrim-Sligo 2 per cent; Longford-Westmeath 13 per cent; Mayo South 4 per cent; Tipperary 1 per cent.

tween 1917 and 1921. But despite the close bond between the TUC and the Labour party, the party was unable to convert this industrial support into political support. Election results show that the Labour party was surprisingly weak where one would have expected it to be strong, in the cities of Dublin and Cork. A comparison of maps 16 and 17 suggests very strongly that Labour's votes came first and foremost from farm labourers in the eastern and south-eastern counties. It was from within this area, especially Waterford and Wexford, that during the first months of 1922 a spate of violent agitation against farmers by their labourers was reported, leading in some cases to the establishment of dairy and farm soviets.[8] But these disturbances were made possible by the general state of disorder and the administrative vacuum as the new regime struggled to establish its authority. Although they flared up once more in the early summer of 1923 they received little encouragement from the political leaders of the Labour movement, and had no further impact on the political situation. Unlike the western disturbances, which were based on the old hunger for land, these eastern upheavals were essentially movements for higher pay and better working conditions.

The response of urban workers to the treaty split is not easy to determine. We have seen that they did not vote Labour in large numbers in 1922, and in 1923 the party, now badly split by the return of Jim Larkin from America,[9] did very much worse, especially in Dublin. Although in the circumstances of 1922 Labour's modest performance came as no surprise, it is remarkable that it fared much less well in 1923, when the national issue was receding from the forefront of politics. Some commentators on this period, especially those from the left, maintained that industrial workers as a body favoured the Republican party. The election figures provide no support for such an assertion. Republican support was below average in the cities, whereas support for the pro-treaty wing of Sinn Féin was above average.[1] It seems clear that the 'working class' as such had no identifiable voting preference in these elections. Then as now, class consciousness (as distinct from status consciousness) was not an important factor in Irish politics or Irish society.

SUMMARY

The original Sinn Féin party was recruited mainly from the middle class, especially the intellectuals. After 1916 a link with more radical

8. *Voice of Labour*, 25 February, 4 and 18 March 1922; Clarkson, *Labour and Nationalism*, p. 445.

9. See Appendix 2, 'Workers' Union of Ireland'.

1. Pyne, 'The third Sinn Féin party', p. 236.

elements was established, and time and again we find attempts being made to combine social aspirations with the new national awakening. In the early stages of the war of independence it was the younger and poorer elements in urban and rural society who supported the combatants. As a consequence of the increasing severity of British military policy and of the successes of the IRA and the Dáil, the more prosperous sections of nationalist society, and in 1922 a section of the southern unionists, came over to the Sinn Féin side.[2] This conservative influx widened the Sinn Féin front, but at the same time softened the character of the movement.

The war of 1919–21 was concentrated in the south, where a strong national tradition coincided with a modicum of prosperity among the farmers. The east had been under British influence for too long, the west was too poor and depressed to produce effective local leadership. In the dispute over the treaty, Irish social divisions became visible in the form of differing national demands. The shift in the central focus of Republicanism from south to west is the clearest proof that the social background to the struggle of 1919–21 differed from that of the civil war which followed. With the passing of the treaty, the comfortable farmers of the south were satisfied. The small farmers of the west, with their more primitive subsistence economy and traditional Irish culture, were less open to practical economic considerations, and adhered rigidly to the ideal of a republic. Their tendency to hold radical ideas on some social questions is not an indication that conscious social motives played any direct part in shaping the character of post-treaty Republicanism. On the other hand, radical social ideas which were not closely embedded within the national idea met with little approval, even among small farmers and landless men. The Labour party therefore remained in the background of politics.

2. Southern unionism divided in 1918 on the question of whether home rule should be accepted as 'inevitable'. The Irish Unionist Alliance maintained its traditional position until the end. The unionist Anti-Partition League, which split from it in 1919, involved itself in the background to the treaty negotiations, and worked for inclusion of 'safeguards' in the Free State constitution. A small group, led by Lord Mayo, made a brief attempt to establish a pro-treaty political front of ex-unionists, farmers' unions, chambers of commerce, and pro-treaty Sinn Féin clubs. See P. J. Buckland, *Irish Unionism: The Anglo-Irish and the New Ireland, 1885–1922* (Dublin, 1972), p. 273.

CHAPTER THREE

The Conservative Period 1922–32

THE IRISH FREE STATE UNDER CONSERVATIVE LEADERSHIP

Neither of the pro-treaty leaders, Arthur Griffith and Michael Collins, survived the civil war, the first dying of a heart attack, the second in a Republican ambush. William T. Cosgrave, regarded by Churchill at least as 'a chief of higher quality than any who had yet appeared',[1] assumed the leadership of the pro-treaty wing of Sinn Féin, and subsequently took office as first President of the Executive Council of the Irish Free State. In the spring of 1923 his party was reconstituted under the name Cumann na nGaedheal. Cosgrave's was the first fully operative administration in independent Ireland. Faced with a legacy of distress and destruction, in an atmosphere charged with intense political passion, yet almost totally lacking in political experience, the government's task was formidable.

The heady days of revolution over, the work of reconstruction had to begin. For a people educated for generations in a nationalist faith, who had come to assume, almost without question, that a golden age would follow the ending of British rule, who expected to see old Ireland rise from her chains a beautiful young woman, political reality could only be a very sobering experience. In the past, all social and economic grievances had been laid indiscriminately at the door of the alien ruler. It was, to say the least, questionable whether any government could in the circumstances meet the expectations which had been raised. Yet, following the terrible events of 1919–22, there was quite clearly a longing for peace and order among many sections of the community. This, as the election results of 1922 and 1923 demonstrated, was to give a tremendous political impetus to the forces of moderation. No other

1. W. S. Churchill, *The World Crisis: The Aftermath* (London, 1929), p. 349.

democratically elected government in Europe during the inter-war years was to enjoy the decade of uninterrupted power which Cosgrave's did.

In Belfast the recently established parliament of Northern Ireland voted promptly to exclude the six north-eastern counties from the new state, as it was entitled to do under the terms of the treaty. The Boundary Commission, which was subsequently appointed by the three governments concerned to adjust the frontier 'in accordance with the wishes of the local population', chose to interpret its terms of reference in the narrowest sense, so that instead of taking opinions over a considerable portion of the north of Ireland (in which case large areas of Fermanagh, Tyrone, south Armagh, and south Down might have been transferred to the Free State) it restricted its inquiries to a narrow strip of land on either side of the border and consequently recommended only minor adjustments, one of the most significant of which would in fact have transferred a prosperous section of east Donegal from the Free State to Northern Ireland.[2] The Free State representative promptly resigned from the Commission, and shortly afterwards his government concluded an agreement with Britain under which the Boundary Commission clause in the treaty (article 12) was revoked, in exchange for which the Free State was released from its obligations in respect of British war debts (article 5).[3] The view was widely held in Dublin that the large nationalist minority contained within the existing boundaries of Northern Ireland constituted the best possible guarantee of a united Ireland at some future date. On the other hand, the financial settlement was not entirely favourable, for it committed Ireland to the payment of about £4 million in compensation to victims of the troubles of 1919–22.[4]

In other aspects of its dealings with Britain, however, the new government was more successful. The Free State was able to make rapid progress towards equal rights within the Commonwealth, and to define 'dominion status' in its own sense. At the Westminster Conference of 1926 it was the Irish delegation which forced the pace in the first moves towards transforming the Empire into the British Commonwealth of Nations. The dominions, including Ireland, now became 'autonomous communities', 'equal in status', and 'freely associated' with Britain.[5] Constitutional practice, ironically, had drawn very close

2. The broad outlines of the proposal were leaked to the *Morning Post*, 7 November 1925, but the full document, kept secret for many years, is now available as *Report of the Irish Boundary Commission, 1925*, ed. G. J. Hand (Dublin, 1969).

3. For the text of this Financial Agreement, 3 December 1925, see D. Macardle, *The Irish Republic* (4th edn, Dublin, 1951), p. 977.

4. Ibid., p. 892.

5. This conference, and Ireland's general role in the history of the dominions, 1921–31, is fully described in D. W. Harkness, *The Restless Dominion* (London, 1969). See especially, ch. 6.

to de Valera's discarded concept of 'external association'. At the same time it was agreed that the imperial representative, the Governor-General, would in future be appointed by the king on the advice of the dominion government concerned, and would no longer be in any sense a representative of the British government.[6] Indeed, in 1927 the Governor-Generalship was given to an Irish citizen, James McNeill, a Catholic and a nationalist.[7] In the following year the Irish government appointed its own ambassador in Washington. Earlier, in 1925, General Richard Mulcahy, the Minister of Local Government, and Thomas Johnson, leader of the Labour party, had asserted before an interparliamentary congress in Washington the right of the Free State to remain neutral in case of a war involving the United Kingdom.[8] In 1929 the state sought to emphasize its sovereignty by putting itself under the jurisdiction of the Permanent Court of International Justice at The Hague, without the qualification entered by other dominions that disputes between members of the British Commonwealth were not international disputes.[9] A year later the Irish representative was elected to a seat on the Council of the League of Nations.[1] Even de Valera admitted that in 1921 he had not considered such progress possible.[2]

In face of such favourable developments in the imperial relationship, it is scarcely surprising that the 'stepping stone to the Republic' attitude to the treaty, advanced earlier by Michael Collins, faded into the background in government circles. Griffith's approach, that there was no objection to membership of the British Commonwealth so long as Ireland retained her practical sovereignty, came more and more to dominate government thinking. Ernest Blythe, Minister for Finance, declared in January 1927 that 'if we could get a republic for the Free State by holding up a finger, I would not hold up that finger'. The prospects for a reunited Ireland would in such circumstances disappear, he argued, yet there would be no compensating increase in freedom or security.[3] The government did not often extol the British connection so unequivocally, however. Its customary imperial policy was to steer a middle path which would avoid alienating more than necessary both the prosperous and influential unionist minority and the main stream of nationalist opinion.

6. Ibid., pp. 108–9.
7. His brother Eoin had founded the Irish Volunteers in 1913 and narrowly escaped a death sentence in 1916, before becoming a member of the first Irish cabinet and Free State representative on the Boundary Commission.
8. J. Hogan, *Elections and Representation* (Cork and Oxford, 1945), p. 340.
9. Harkness, *Restless Dominion*, pp. 141–2.
1. *Round Table*, xxi (1930–1), 147. The Irish correspondent of *The Round Table* throughout this period was J. J. Horgan, a Cork solicitor and former Redmondite Nationalist. I am grateful to Dr Cornelius O'Leary for this information [A. C. H.].
2. *Dáil Eireann Debates*, xxx, col. 792, cited in Harkness, *Restless Dominion*, p. 29.
3. *Round Table*, xvii (1926–7), 586.

Against all expectations, a Unionist party did not reappear in Free State politics after the civil war, though in Dublin and certain border constituencies there appeared from time to time independents who were in fact thinly veiled 'Protestant' candidates. One possible reason for this was the numerical decline of the Protestant and unionist population in the Free State. After the treaty they withdrew in very large numbers from administrative and governmental positions, many of them transferring to the newly created Northern Ireland civil service. The census of 1926 showed that only 9·4 per cent of males employed in defence and the public service of the Free State were non-Catholics: a mere 1 per cent more than their proportion of the whole population. At the lower levels of the public service the Local Government Appointments Commission sought to ensure that merit, rather than social influence, became the sole criterion for appointment, with the result that here, too, the Catholic proportion of employees increased rapidly. Along with this went the almost total withdrawal of British Army and associated civilian personnel and a significant proportion of Protestant landowners, so that the number of non-Catholics in the Free State area dropped between 1911 and 1926 by 32 per cent.[4]

Those Protestants who chose to remain under the new regime do not appear to have suffered any material disadvantages—though it is not clear whether this is evidence that those who departed were unnecessarily alarmist or whether those Protestants who remained were by and large those who felt that their economic positions were unassailable. While the non-Catholic proportion of the Free State population had fallen to 8·4 per cent in 1926, 28 per cent of all farmers with over 200 acres were Protestants, as were 18 per cent of the entire professional class. In 1936, the proportion of employers and top management in business and commerce who were not Catholics was between 20 and 25 per cent.[5] While the proportion of non-Catholics in the Dáil remained very low, former Unionists were generously represented in the Senate. On the High Court bench, Protestants outnumbered Catholics by six to three, a greater imbalance than had existed during the last years of the Union.[6]

Perhaps because it experienced no economic disadvantages, the non-Catholic population which remained in the Free State after 1922 showed no lack of loyalty towards the new regime. It was thus all the more natural that the moderate, pro-treaty wing of Sinn Féin, as it transformed itself into Cumann na nGaedheal, began to shift to the right. Opposition to the new government came not from the right but

4. *Irish Free State Census, 1926*, iii. 113.
5. Some of the higher figures were: bank officials 53 per cent non-Catholic; commercial travellers 39 per cent; lawyers 38 per cent.
6. O'Sullivan, *The Irish Free State and its Senate*, p. 75.

almost exclusively from the left. The continued terrorism of the IRA and the recalcitrance of the Republican party encouraged this shift to the right, for the followers of Collins, the radical wing of the pro-treaty party, who had only accepted the treaty on the assumption that it would end bloodshed, tended to drift away when it became clear that this was not to be the case. The re-entry of de Valera into the Dáil, at the head of Fianna Fáil, in 1927, encouraged the government trend towards conservatism. Cumann na nGaedheal's basic attitude differed little from that of the British Conservative party between 1895 and 1905: a well-governed Ireland would receive positive economic benefits from its association with Britain, and quickly forget old passions and hatreds.

For a while these policies seemed to meet with unequivocal success. There was a marked decline in general hostility towards Britain: British newspaper sales in Ireland increased dramatically, while the number of national Irish newspapers fell from seven to three; the British Legion, the association of First World War veterans, whose Irish members had at one stage been compelled by public opinion to secede from the main body, was by 1925 able to conduct large-scale armistice celebrations in the Free State.[7] Very shortly the Commonwealth quarterly journal, The Round Table, felt able to declare that so far as Ireland was concerned 'the wave of emotional nationalism has been shattered upon the reef of political fact'.[8]

In its economic policy the Cosgrave administration gave no indication that it wished to alter the traditional role of Ireland as the agricultural complement to industrial England. On the advice of a Fiscal Inquiry Committee, and later of a Tariff Commission which was strongly dominated by men of conservative economic views, any general move in the direction of protectionism was firmly rejected.[9] Agriculture, it was felt, would be strangled by the high tariffs which new industries would require. While no one denied that a full return to laissez-faire all round would have a disastrous effect on existing industry, strong emphasis was placed on the need for efficient management, and it was made plain that the state was not at all inclined to bale out businesses which failed to withstand the blast of British and other foreign competition. As if to underline its point, the government soon allowed a whole series of unsuccessful concerns to go out of production.[1] On the other hand, it felt obliged to take the initiative in certain cases

7. Round Table, xvii (1926–7), 586.   8. Ibid., p. 33.

9. Irish Review and Annual, 1931 (supplement to the Irish Times), p. 27; see also Tariff Commission Report, 1926.

1. D. R. Gwynn, The Irish Free State, 1922–27 (London, 1928), p. 249. The new Fianna Fáil party, which made great play with the point, estimated the number of factories which had closed at 117 (see the party's quarter-centenary publication, Fianna Fail, 1926–51 [Dublin, 1951], p. 12).

where private enterprise did not come forward for what were regarded as necessary undertakings. In this way, Cosgrave's government set in motion the Free State's greatest and most far-sighted industrial undertaking, the Shannon hydro-electric system. Traditional liberal economic thinking was clearly apparent in the decision to bring the income tax down below the standard British rate, in the hope of attracting British capital, enticing rich emigrants to return, and generally encouraging private enterprise.[2] This measure, which brought direct benefit to only 15,000 of the population, not surprisingly drew a violent attack from the Labour party. It was pointed out that while the annual tax revenue had been reduced by around £3 million since 1920, increases in social benefits had been quite negligible.[3] Thus, although the Cosgrave administration did attempt to steer some sort of middle course in economic matters, it was attacked from all sides: the Farmers' party complained that there were too many tariffs, Fianna Fáil and the Republicans said there were too few, while Labour railed against the all-round lack of interest in dismantling the *laissez-faire* capitalist system. Even within the cabinet, rival voices spoke up loudly on behalf of both free trade and protective tariffs.[4]

The tension within the Irish economy is not simply between industry and agriculture but also within agriculture, between tillage and cattle-rearing. The latter issue, just as much as the former, was intertwined with the national issue, since it involved the nature of Ireland's economic relationship with Britain. The strengthening of industry by means of protective tariffs was opposed by farmers, and while the expansion of tillage at the expense of cattle production might mean greater economic independence, equally it would bring about a serious reduction in the gross national product. Cosgrave's government developed an economic policy in harmony with its foreign policy: collaboration with Britain became the guiding principle as far as possible. There was to be no burdening of agriculture, which was the mainstay of 70 per cent of the population, with state-protected industries, and no limitation of cattle production in favour of wheat-growing, the profitability of which was in any case doubtful.[5]

So far as land tenure was concerned, Irish traditions and conditions demanded that a faster pace be set along the path which had been laid down by a British Conservative government in 1903. A new Land Act in 1923 introduced the threat of general compulsion to hasten the end of landlordism and the conversion of the remaining tenant farmers into peasant proprietors. Already two-thirds of the tenants had purchased, so the problem of tenure was well on the way to solution. The govern-

2. Gwynn, *Irish Free State*, p. 266.   3. *Round Table*, xvii (1926–7), 134.
4. W. Moss, *Political Parties in the Irish Free State* (New York, 1933), p. 23.
5. *Round Table*, xix (1928–9), 378.

ment was much less willing, however, to accede to the more radical demand for the break-up of the larger grazing 'ranches' and their distribution among local 'landless men'. The medium-sized and larger farmers were good friends of both the national exchequer and the governing party: it was to be expected that in such circumstances the government would put economic and political considerations above questions of broad social principle.[6]

The social policy of the government was cautious, to say the least, and attracted constant attack from the Labour party. It was alleged at the Trades Union Congress as early as 1924 that 'while up to the present no action whatever has been taken in regard to high prices . . . the government have given direct encouragement to drastic reductions in wages'.[7] Cumann na nGaedheal activity in the areas of old age pensions and sickness insurance was noticeably less generous than corresponding legislation being undertaken in Great Britain and in Northern Ireland. Another TUC delegate commented, sourly, that 'one of the things this alleged freedom has brought to Ireland is the most desirable freedom to scrap everything calculated to benefit or improve the condition of the working classes'.[8] But during a decade when free trade and rugged individualism were battling for survival throughout the western world, it was scarcely to be expected that an Irish government, with its power-base firmly established among instinctively conservative and prosperous middle-class elements of society, would be in the forefront of the fight for a new social and economic order.

An analysis of the regional distribution of support for Cumann na nGaedheal shows some surprising results (maps 18 and 19). Contrary to what one might have expected in view of the heavily western orientation of Fianna Fáil[9] (maps 25 and 26) there was no predominance of Cumann na nGaedheal votes in the south and east. Its support was fairly evenly spread across the whole country. For an explanation of this apparent lack of profile we must turn to the election performances of the other parties (maps 20–22). Fianna Fáil, the Labour party, the Farmers' party,[1] and the independents had a social profile which

6. For a more detailed discussion of agrarian questions, see Appendix 1, pp. 224–31.
7. Irish Labour party, *Annual Report, 1924*, p. 30.   8. Ibid., *1922*, p. 252.
9. De Valera led the more moderate elements out of Sinn Féin in 1926, on the issue of participation in Free State politics, to form Fianna Fáil ('Warriors of Destiny'). See below, p. 100.
1. A number of short-lived parties appeared during the early years of the Free State which cannot be discussed in a work of this nature. The Farmers' party was the most successful of them. Like the Labour party, it originated with a number of occupational associations, the county Farmers' Unions, which had come together under a central administration in Dublin in 1919, primarily to assist the more substantial farmers in opposing the wage-demands of their labourers. Like the Labour party, the party faded, after a hopeful beginning, in face of the continued domination of the national question in politics. It ceased to exist in 1932. Most of its former supporters joined the new Fine Gael party in 1933.

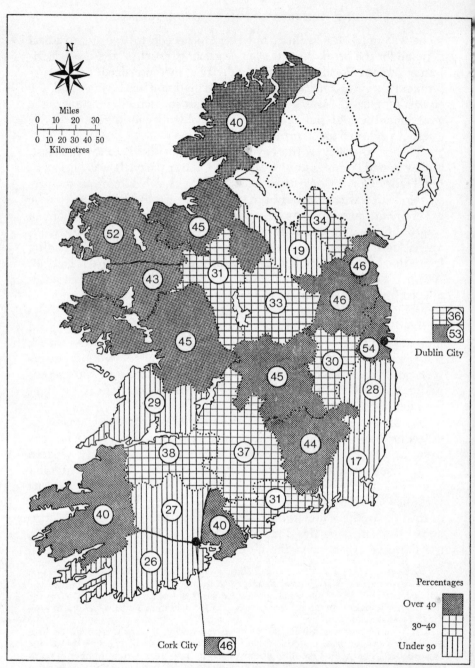

18. FIRST-PREFERENCE VOTES FOR CUMANN NA NGAEDHEAL CANDIDATES, JUNE 1927

(76)

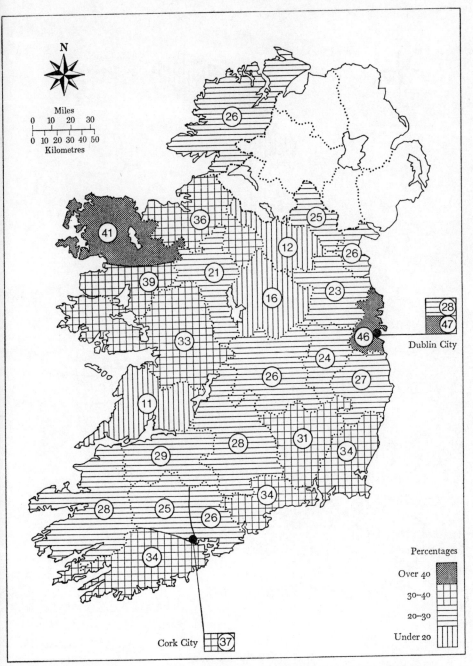

Miles
0 10 20 30

Kilometres
0 10 20 30 40 50

Dublin City

Cork City

Percentages

Over 40

30–40

20–30

Under 20

19. FIRST-PREFERENCE VOTES FOR CUMANN NA NGAEDHEAL CANDIDATES, 1933

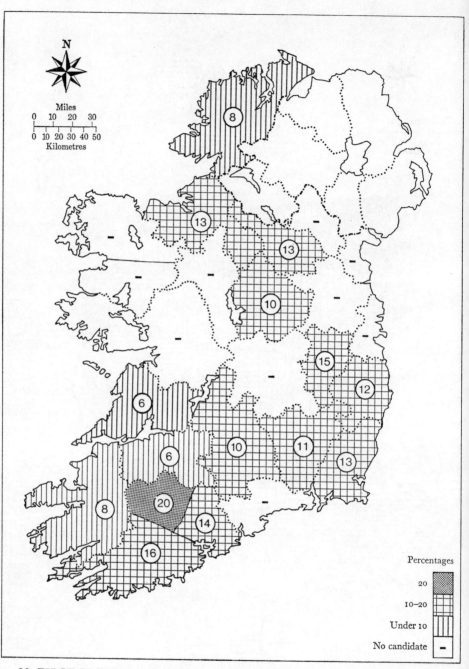

20. FIRST-PREFERENCE VOTES FOR FARMERS' PARTY CANDIDATES,
SEPTEMBER 1927

(78)

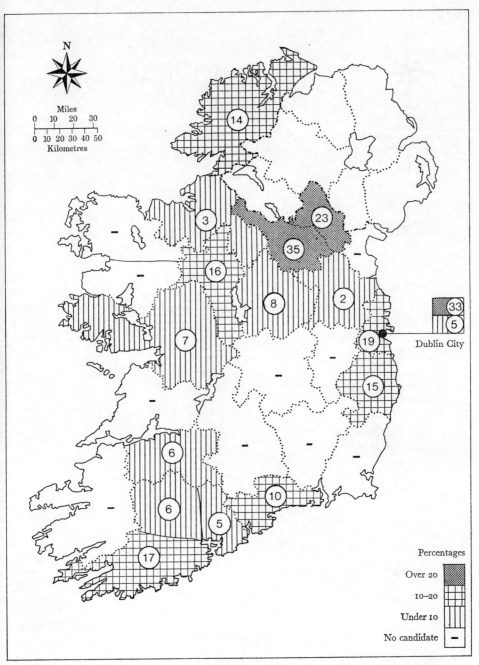

**21. FIRST-PREFERENCE VOTES FOR INDEPENDENT CANDIDATES,
SEPTEMBER 1927**

(79)

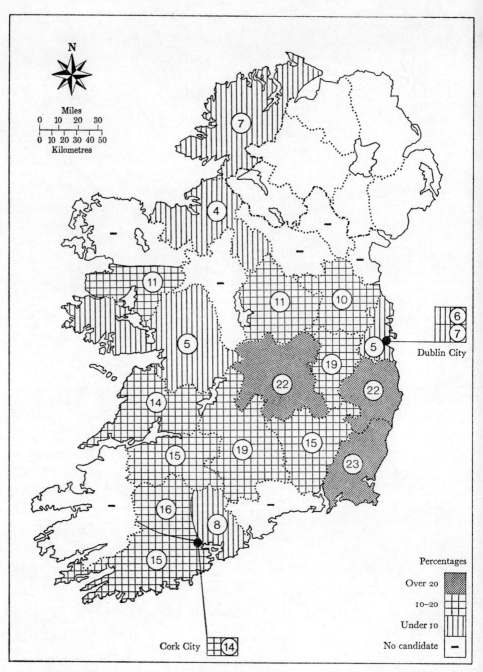

22. FIRST-PREFERENCE VOTES FOR LABOUR CANDIDATES,
SEPTEMBER 1927

may be deduced to a large extent from the geographical distribution of votes: Labour party strength was greatest in the areas with the largest population of agricultural labourers, the Farmers' party was most powerful in districts with a preponderance of larger farms, and the independents attracted support mainly in areas where there was a substantial Protestant vote (map 5). The Cumann na nGaedheal profile was essentially the negative of all these groups. Wherever a minor party could attract the support of an identifiable group in a particular region, then Cumann na nGaedheal was the loser, even though the area was not one with a strong Republican or anti-treaty reputation. This is the explanation of the rather surprising fact that some of Cumann na nGaedheal's best results came from the same western constituencies that were also the strongholds of Fianna Fáil. In these districts neither the Labour party nor the parties representing large farmers and Protestants could hope to arouse any response from the electors. In such areas, therefore, the national question inevitably remained in the forefront of politics, as the voters chose between the two parties which had fought the civil war. Studied in this light, the maps indicate the essentially defensive nature of the Cumann na nGaedheal position after 1927.

THE LABOUR PARTY IN THE NEW STATE

From 1922 to 1927 the Labour party filled the role of official opposition in the Free State Dáil. The Republicans and, initially, Fianna Fáil, refused to take their seats, maintaining that to do so would have involved swearing an oath of allegiance to the British Crown. This situation, and a feeling of disillusion in the country with both participants in the civil war, seemed likely in the earliest years of the state's existence to produce the impetus needed to propel the Labour party into the forefront of Irish political life. It gradually became apparent, however, that the success of the party in the elections of June 1922 was not to be the beginning of a steady growth in strength. The policy of Thomas Johnson, the first leader of the party in the Dáil, was always to treat the national issue as subsidiary, as a problem which had little impact on the daily lives and living standards of the mass of people. The oath was declared to be a formality, 'implying no obligation other than the ordinary obligation of any person who accepts the privileges of citizenship'.[2] The party voted to accept it under protest only, proclaiming at the same time the right of the Irish people to cancel it whenever it might become desirable to do so. But although Labour sought to distance itself from the treaty issue in this way, its resistance inevitably appeared somewhat pale beside that of the Republicans, thus confirming the popular impression that, as far as the Labour party was concerned,

2. Irish Labour party, *Annual Report, 1923*, p. 33.

national aspirations had been essentially fulfilled and remaining deficiencies did not merit any further sacrifice.

It was therefore all the more necessary for the party to make a vigorous attack on a broad range of social issues. In the provisional parliament of 1922 its proposals concerning 'the nation's primary ownership of the land and waters of the country and its rights to impose limitations on private property . . .' were voted down.[3] In other respects also the attitude of the government was unsympathetic towards the views of Labour, and the 1923 TUC conference had cause to reflect that 'the workers have to remember that the advent of an Irish parliament will be the signal for the opening of the class war'.[4] In practice, however, there was no serious thought among the Labour leaders of starting such a class war, for the workers as a whole showed little sign even of class consciousness, let alone class antagonism. The party thus turned its back, apparently finally, on the ideas of Connolly and Larkin. The report of the executive in 1924 was sober and pragmatic, advocating caution as the best policy: 'Sometimes we are liable to forget that the ever-fighting [trade] union fights itself out of existence.'[5] A reminder, perhaps, of Jim Larkin's experience in 1914, and an indication that ten years later he was not to be welcomed back into the fold.[6]

Under Thomas Johnson the party was led firmly and publicly away from the revolutionary syndicalist image which it had acquired during its early years. The Irish situation, in his view, did not call for such a policy, for which there was no popular support: 'People talked as if once they got a revolution everyone would be satisfied. . . . The issue was whether trade unionism was to be used for uplifting the common people, or making a revolution for the sake of a revolution. . . .'[7] In accordance with such a moderate line was the party's decision to send a deputation to the British Commonwealth of Nations Labour Conference of 1924. Johnson's defence of the action was as pragmatic as his socialism: 'One justification for attending . . . was that they lived close to England, and whatever was done in the Labour movement in England legislatively . . . was likely to have more effect on Irish labour than on labour in France, Germany or elsewhere.'[8] As for the division of the European socialist movement into a red Moscow International and a yellow Amsterdam International, the party sought to keep its distance, and sent no deputation to either. On the other hand, it did co-operate with the International Labour Office in Geneva.[9] The over-all change in the position of the party during the period 1919–24 is quite remarkable.

3. Irish Labour Party, *Annual Report, 1924*, p. 107.
4. Ibid., *1923*, p. 64.   5. Ibid., *1924*, p. 107.
6. For an account of the vicissitudes of Larkin's career see E. Larkin, *James Larkin, Irish Labour Leader, 1876–1947* (London, 1965).
7. Irish Labour party, *Annual Report, 1925*, pp. 177–8.
8. Ibid., p. 150.   9. Ibid., pp. 148–9.

Despite its efforts to produce practical measures for tackling the serious social problems still facing the Irish people, the decline in the Labour vote which had appeared as early as the general election of 1923 continued steadily. As one delegate at the 1925 party congress observed:

Up to the time that the election came along thousands of workers had suffered untold miseries and barbarities and horrors . . . [at the hands of] . . . the two wings of what was the Sinn Féin party. Yet with that lesson and all those facts before their eyes, the electors returned 127 of those two parties and 14 Labour representatives.[1]

It seemed that Labour could do nothing to prevent social problems being overshadowed by the national question. After the election of June 1927 it was regretted that

as in the two previous general elections the two large parties, with the almost unanimous support of the press, strove with considerable success to make the Anglo-Irish treaty once more the major issue of the election. This eminently suited parties whose economic policies and record would not bear intelligent examination.[2]

The entry of Fianna Fáil to the Dáil in August 1927 opened a new phase for the Labour party. It was reduced to the status of a minor party within the parliamentary opposition, as national issues became central to inter-party debate inside as well as outside the Dáil. But for a while its influence actually increased, even though its support was declining, for de Valera could only hope to come to power with Labour's support, and consequently sought to develop the progressive social and economic aspects of the Fianna Fáil programme: protective tariffs and the active stimulation of home industries, the extension of social security and a general expansion of state initiative in social and economic matters, were all advocated strongly by Fianna Fáil during the 1927–32 Dáil. The effectiveness of this policy may be judged by the fact that between 2 February and 6 June 1931 the Labour party voted 50 times with Fianna Fáil and only 9 times in the government lobby.[3]

In 1930 the Labour party and TUC, which had since 1912 been a single entity, separated into two distinct political and industrial bodies. This decision ended an anomalous situation, for the majority of Irish trade unionists had never in their lives voted Labour. Another reason for the change was the hope of securing better organization on the political side, for with the exception of a few constituencies in Dublin and elsewhere, there was no regular Labour party organization.[4] But the new arrangement did not strengthen the Labour party, which

1. Ibid., p. 151.   2. Ibid., *1927*, p. 41.   3. Ibid., *1931*, p. 16.
4. D. Nevin, 'Labour and the political revolution', in F. MacManus (ed.), *The Years of the Great Test, 1926–39* (Cork, 1967), p. 58.

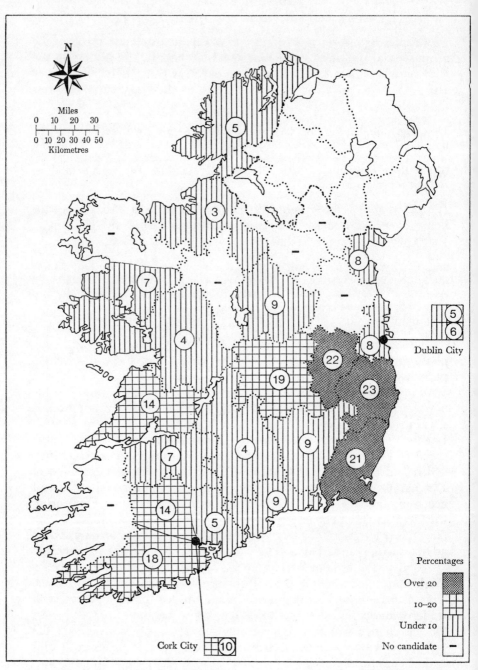

23. FIRST-PREFERENCE VOTES FOR LABOUR CANDIDATES, 1932

continued to depend for its electoral victories on the efforts and personalities of individual candidates at local level, nor did freedom from
trade union considerations bring about any new radicalization of the
party. William Norton, the new leader of the party,[5] sought to strike a
bold posture with a denunciation of the TUC as having become 'a
pettifogging reform movement',[6] but the wording of the new party
constitution revealed its position more frankly. The earlier party aim
'to recover for the nation complete possession of all the natural and
physical sources of wealth of the country', was replaced by the more
modest one of securing 'reconstruction of the social and economic
system in Ireland'.[7]

A similar penchant for moderation was displayed so far as the
national question was concerned, for despite the demands of some delegates that a more militant position be taken up, it was acknowledged
in 1931, by the decision to approve the creation of a separate labour
organization for Northern Ireland, that the unity of Ireland was still a
long way off, and could not be achieved without consent.[8] The over-all
result of these changes, however, was not more support for the party
but less (map 23), as de Valera and Fianna Fáil outmanoeuvred it on
both fronts, stressing the primacy of the national question while at the
same time stealing Labour's thunder by manifesting an apparently intense concern for social reform. Only in local elections, where the
national question played no part, was Labour able to achieve any
measure of success.[9]

During de Valera's first year in office the Labour deputies still held
the balance of power, but after the 1933 election even this vestige of influence was destroyed as the party's share of the vote dropped from 12·4
per cent to rock-bottom at 5·7 per cent. It seemed for a while that
Fianna Fáil, in adopting some of Labour's more moderate goals, had
effectively removed its *raison d'être*. But very shortly, more conservative
traits in Fianna Fáil began to manifest themselves, and while this
caused disappointment in some quarters, it at least made it easier for a
moderate Labour party to develop a credible opposition policy.
William Norton was soon pointing out that the Anglo-Irish trade war,
provoked by de Valera's decision to retain land annuity payments in
Dublin, was a heaven-sent opportunity for the introduction of a wide
measure of state socialism.[1] By 1935 the party conference was pro-

5. Norton became leader of the Labour party in 1932. Thomas Johnson had
retired following his electoral defeat in 1927 and was replaced by T. J. O'Connell,
another moderate, who in turn lost his seat in 1932.
6. Irish Labour party, *Annual Report, 1930*, p. 110.
7. Irish Labour party, *Special Congress Report, 1930*, p. 158.
8. Ibid., pp. 147–8; *Annual Report, 1931*, p. 80.
9. Moss, *Political Parties in the Irish Free State*, p. 102.
1. *Round Table*, xxiii (1933), 123.

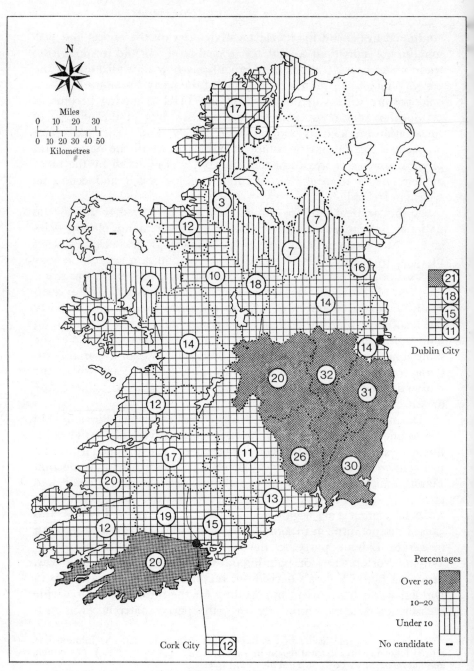

24. FIRST-PREFERENCE VOTES FOR LABOUR CANDIDATES, 1943

claiming loudly that despite all its claims and activities, Fianna Fáil had proved totally unable to alter the system of greed and usury which, it argued, still dominated Irish society.[2] The evolution of a critique of Fianna Fáil brought a dividend: the party's share of the vote grew to over 10 per cent in the general election of 1937. But the efforts proved counter-productive in the sense that as Labour campaigned for higher wages, shorter working hours, and more state control over the economy, so more and more conservatives rallied to Fianna Fáil as the only possible bastion against radical social change.[3] The result was both to strengthen and to make more conservative the ruling Fianna Fáil, and incidentally to push the Cosgrave party more firmly into the background.[4] Labour's brief effort to bang the national drum louder than de Valera, with its denunciation of the External Relations Act of 1936 for continuing to recognize the British Crown,[5] made predictably little impact on the electors, so that in 1938 Fianna Fáil was returned once again with an absolute majority in the Dáil, and stood at the height of its power.

Thus the Labour party continued to stand on the sidelines of Irish political life. Even its formal separation from the ideology of socialism, undertaken in 1940 when it accepted the advice of the Catholic church to delete the aim of establishing 'a workers' republic' from its programme, did not bring any lasting improvement in its electoral fortunes.[6] The party's share of first-preference votes did increase in 1943 to about 16 per cent, but the improvement seems to have been brought about simply by popular discontent with Fianna Fáil, and it was not maintained. Labour's support continued to depended on the popularity of a few individual figures and the support of farm labourers in the richer farming areas (map 24). The crucial task of winning over the urban working class was far from complete.

THE REPUBLICANS IN OPPOSITION

Sinn Féin

The civil war came to an end in April 1923 with the declaration of a cease-fire by the remainder of the Republican forces. There was no surrender, and weapons were put into storage for possible future use.[7] Although the ranks of the IRA were increasingly weakened by emi-

---

2. Irish Labour party, *Annual Report, 1935*, p. 19.

3. *Round Table*, xxviii (1937–8), 740.

4. For a discussion of Cumann na nGaedheal's difficulties and transformation after 1932, see below, pp. 128–34.

5. Irish Labour party, *Annual Report, 1936*, p. 18.

6. In the more liberal religious climate of 1966, the party was able to renew its pledge to 'a coherent socialist philosophy'.

7. Macardle, *Irish Republic*, p. 857.

gration after 1924,[8] thousands still retained their allegiance to its command structure, recognizing the claim of its GHQ to be the only legitimate source of military power in Ireland. The political wing of Republicanism also continued to exist, under the name Sinn Féin, which, surprisingly, had not been appropriated by the pro-treaty supporters when forming their new party. Sinn Féin did remarkably well in the general election of 1923, winning 27 per cent of the total poll and securing the return of forty-four of its candidates. Complete abstention from the institutions of the Free State remained a cornerstone of policy, however, and the party's elected representatives instead met occasionally as 'the Dáil of the Republic', claiming *de jure* legislative and executive powers.[9] De Valera remained 'the only legal president of the Republic'.

But after 1924 such a posture became increasingly unrealistic. The party's efforts to establish working agencies of the underground government, similar to those set up during the war of independence, were ineffective. A network of Republican employment exchanges functioned only briefly before collapsing through lack of funds, while attempts to create a separate judicial system failed to get off the ground at all.[1] A sharp decline in party membership in the country, a series of poor showings at by-elections, and the consequent drying-up of financial resources from the United States, brought about a crisis of confidence within the leadership. As early as March 1925 de Valera had privately come to believe that the only hope for Republicans was somehow or other to get off the hook of the abstention policy, so that 'the destiny of Ireland would be worked out in Leinster House'.[2] The inability of Sinn Féin to make any effective protest against the government's signing of the boundary agreement with Great Britain and Northern Ireland in December 1925—essentially a ratification of partition—caused other leaders of the party to adopt a similar view.[3] Thus in January 1926 de Valera set in motion a gradual process of detaching as large a body as he could of the more pragmatic Republicans from doctrinaire abstentionism. Apart from the oath, he argued, abstention was a policy rather than a principle. A special conference of the party in March 1926 defeated this proposal by the narrow margin of 223 to 218. De Valera promptly resigned as president of Sinn Féin, and shortly afterwards withdrew with his followers to found a new party, which became Fianna Fáil.[4] Such a narrow defeat, in an assembly dominated by Republican activists, held out the promise of a good reception in the country at large. The barrier of the oath remained, but now that it had

8. Macardle, *Irish Republic*, p. 883.
9. P. Pyne, 'The third Sinn Fein party', *Economic and Social Review*, 1. i (October 1969), 32–33.
1. Ibid., pp. 36–37.   2. Ibid., p. 42.   3. Ibid., p. 44.   4. Ibid., p. 46.

been isolated as the *sole* barrier to participation in Free State politics, the way was open for a further compromise in the name of pragmatism.

Secession on so large a scale weakened the influence, but not the convictions, of those who continued to sit in 'the Republican Dáil'. Mary MacSwiney, a veteran of the war of independence period, remained the driving force of the movement, while Art O'Connor, another member of the first Dáil, replaced de Valera as 'president of the Republic'. In his inaugural address, O'Connor declared that 'he did not give a fig for logic in national affairs'.[5] With the further secession of those who believed that the movement might get some wind in its sails by espousing radical social policies, Sinn Féin was distilled, or reduced, to a hard core of 'pure Republicans'.[6] By the time the most able of them, Austin Stack, died in 1929, even the police Special Branch no longer took the party seriously. Efforts to develop a new 'Republican unity' committee in the same year proved entirely unsuccessful.[7] But the hard core struggled on, entirely unmoved by such developments as the electoral victory of Fianna Fáil in 1932, the abolition of the oath, and the first steps towards the dismantling of the treaty. Sinn Féin denounced de Valera as a renegade, quoted against him his own intransigent statements from the pre-1925 period, and stood aside contemptuously from the 1933 election for 'The British Dominion Assembly of Southern Ireland'.[8] The history of the party need be carried no further in a work of this nature. A great national movement had become a political curiosity, in which condition it has been preserved until today.[9]

The IRA

The history of the IRA from the end of the civil war until 1970 bears the same tragicomic stamp as that of Sinn Féin, though its possession and sporadic use of arms, entailing spirit-breaking prison sentences and internments for its members on both sides of the Irish border, has placed the emphasis very much on the tragic side. The sharp decline in the fortunes of Sinn Féin, which caused de Valera and others to ponder on the wisdom of abstentionism, provoked the IRA leadership into a rejection of political activity altogether. At its first post-civil war convention, in November 1925, it voted to withdraw allegiance from the 'republican government', and vested sole authority in its own Army Council. The drying-up of Sinn Féin's American funds, and the fear

5. *Round Table*, xvi (1925–6), 811.   6. Ibid. xxii (1932), 498.

7. J. B. Bell, *The Secret Army: A History of the IRA, 1916–70* (London, 1970), pp. 77–78.

8. *Round Table*, xxiii (1933), 298.

9. Few would have disagreed with this judgement at the time Dr Rumpf made it in the late 1950s. In the 1970s, Sinn Féin (both Gardiner Place and Kevin Street factions), while remaining in many respects a curious political party, could no longer be adequately described as a curiosity [A. C. H.].

that the party's growing division over abstention might provoke a new split within the IRA itself, were additional factors in the Army's withdrawal.[1] Sporadic military activity henceforward became more commonplace: bank robbers and arms raiders invoked the name of the IRA for their activities, and in November 1926 a number of attacks were made on the police.[2] In the summer of 1927 Kevin O'Higgins, Vice-President of the Executive Council of the Free State, the strongest and possibly the most able member of the Cosgrave administration, was shot dead in the street. It now appears that those responsible were two young IRA men acting entirely without superior authority,[3] but the government was able to take advantage of the outcry which ensued to pass stern anti-IRA legislation. The measures met with only short-term success, however, and proved ultimately to be counter-productive, for they contributed to the government's general unpopularity and gave substance to the repressive image which Fianna Fáil sought to foist on it. By 1931 IRA terrorism was again a front-rank political issue. It was condemned only half-heartedly by Fianna Fáil, and, as another election year approached, the two bodies were to be seen side by side at the annual Wolfe Tone commemoration ceremony in 1931.[4] Very different considerations were to prevail in 1932, after the change of government, when Fianna Fáil, the IRA, Sinn Féin, and the Free State Army all made their separate pilgrimages to the martyr's grave.[5]

Given the uncompromising character of Sinn Féin and IRA attitudes, it was not unlikely that in the long run they would be no more conciliated by Fianna Fáil in power than by Cumann na nGaedheal. But the immediate IRA feeling was one of relief. The military tribunal set up in October 1931 to suppress political crime—with the power of life and death subject only to an appeal to the Executive Council—was quickly dismantled. 'We really hated those buggers, it was great to see them out', was the response of one Dublin IRA man to the departure of the Cosgrave administration.[6] In so far as it reversed the defeat, a decade earlier, of the anti-treaty forces, the 1932 election brought together the forces of Fianna Fáil with Sinn Féin and the IRA. In practical terms the parties had co-operated on a platform of 'open the gaol gates', and Fianna Fáil followed this up after the election with a gesture to mark the end of the Cosgrave era: a new reserve police force, popularly known as the 'Broy Harriers', after the new Commissioner of

1. Pyne, 'The third Sinn Féin party', p. 43.
2. Gwynn, *Irish Free State*, p. 153.
3. This is the version of events given, without source, in T. P. Coogan, *The IRA* (London, 1970), p. 79; Bell, *Secret Army*, p. 62, argues more cautiously that there is in fact no evidence available to support any of the theories offered in explanation of the murder.
4. *Round Table*, xxi (1930–1), 853.
5. Ibid. xxiii (1933), 882.   6. Coogan, *IRA*, p. 90.

Police, Eamonn Broy, was created, and drawn mainly from the ranks of ex-IRA men who were not too proud to accept patronage from Fianna Fáil.[7] Justification for raising so politically convenient a force was provided by the challenge to the new government and to democracy in general which seemed implicit in the new Blueshirt movement.[8] During the next two or three years, however, de Valera was able to turn this apparent threat to his government even more to his favour. Having brought the coercive anti-IRA legislation of 1931 to an end it would have been extremely difficult for him ever to revive it had he not been able to direct it firstly against the Blueshirts.[9] Having hostile extra-parliamentary political organizations on both his left and his right was an immense asset to de Valera in power, for he was able to apply the same legislation against each of them without appearing either repressive or partisan, and so begin the campaign to capture the middle ground in Irish politics which Fianna Fáil has continued so effectively for forty years. The IRA was not eliminated during this period (indeed the hard core of its devotees who remained were to become more bitter and desperate during the 1940s and 1950s) but its mass support was eroded to the extent that it had ceased to be a major issue in Irish domestic politics by 1938, and was not to become one again for another thirty years.

The left wing

With the secession of de Valera from Sinn Féin and the entry of Fianna Fáil into the Dáil in 1927, the left-wing element in the republican movement was at last in a position to make a serious bid for supremacy within the IRA. In November 1927 Michael Fitzpatrick, a member of IRA headquarters staff who also acted as Irish president of the Friends of Soviet Russia, led a ten-man delegation to the October Revolution celebrations in Moscow, and proclaimed that 'it will be our task to convince our fellow-workers that their hope, their salvation, is bound up with Soviet Russia'.[1] *An Phoblacht*, the IRA newspaper, grew increasingly radical in its tone, declaring that 'parliaments are for museums. They will here and forever betray revolutions.'[2] Two IRA delegates attended the foundation of the Soviet-inspired Anti-Imperialist League in Brussels in 1927, and when that body held its first meeting in Dublin a year later it was the IRA which provided the main

7. D. Thornley, 'The Blueshirts', in MacManus (ed.), *Years of the Great Test*, pp. 43–44 and 47.
8. See below, pp. 128–34.
9. T. D. Williams, 'De Valera in power', MacManus (ed.), *Years of the Great Test*, p. 36.
1. James Hogan, *Could Ireland become Communist?* (Dublin, 1935), pp. 37, 110.
2. *An Phoblacht*, 5 May 1928.

speakers.[3] Prominent IRA men were again among the delegates at the Frankfurt congress of 1929, when an imprisoned IRA man named Magennis was elected honorary president of the congress, as a gesture of sympathy 'with the Irish republicans in their struggle'.[4] In 1930 yet another Communist organization, the European Peasants' Committee, had the IRA to thank for the establishment of its first cells in a west European country.[5]

In response to the decision of an IRA convention held during the summer of 1931, another new movement was formed in Ireland itself, in the hope of re-awakening the radicalism of the small farmer. Saor Eire, as it was called, declared at its first congress: 'Long live the unity of Irish and European working farmers. Long life to the alliance of town workers and working farmers.'[6] Small farmers, agricultural workers, and urban workers were to be brought into one united Republican movement which would break the leadership of the trade unions, whose unrevolutionary character was clear for all to see. On the Republican left Saor Eire met with instant success, converting IRA units into Saor Eire branches almost overnight. The entire IRA, in the words of its most recent historian, was on the verge of 'a giant step to the left'. At its first congress, in September 1931, the new body nailed its colours to the mast with a message of greetings to Soviet Russia.[7] Collectivization was declared to be the only land policy for the nation worth considering: a daring, not to say suicidal, policy in a country of small peasant proprietors.[8]

Although Saor Eire was quickly stifled by a collusive onslaught from church and police,[9] the defeat did nothing to weaken the general influence of the left within the Republican movement, and indeed for a while may have strengthened it. Early in 1933 IRA leaders took up the case of an Irish-born American, James Gralton, who was being expelled from Ireland for spreading communist doctrines. The left-wing leaders outdid the Communist party in their concern over the issue, and although the broad stream of the movement, including the local leadership in Co. Leitrim, the area concerned, was no more than lukewarm, the result was to identify the IRA firmly with communism in the mind of the general public.[1] It was not a totally false impression, for the new constitution of the movement included proposals for the whole-

3. Coogan, *IRA*, p. 124; Hogan, *Could Ireland become Communist?*, pp. 75–76.

4. Coogan, *IRA*, p. 124; Hogan, *Could Ireland become Communist?*, p. 76; *An Phoblacht*, 10 August 1929.

5. Coogan, *IRA*, p. 125.

6. Ibid., pp. 83–84; Hogan, *Could Ireland become Communist?*, p. 88.

7. Bell, *Secret Army*, p. 81; *An Phoblacht*, 10 October 1931.

8. Ibid., 28 February 1931; Coogan (*IRA*, p. 85) records the reported response of one Co. Louth farmer to the new programme: 'Be Jasus . . . you'll not take my land.'

9. Bell, *Secret Army*, p. 88.   1. Coogan, *IRA*, pp. 104–6.

sale nationalization of land and industry, as well as agricultural market-
ing and the distribution of goods.[2]

This development by Republicans of a full-scale social and economic
programme, so different from the military posture of a decade earlier,
totally failed to produce the hoped-for improvement in the movement's fortunes. During the early months of 1934 a new split developed
on the question of forming another 'open' political organization, along
the lines of Saor Eire. At an IRA convention on 17 March the would-be
innovators were narrowly defeated, and withdrew to set up a new body,
the Republican Congress party, under the slogan 'Workers and working
farmers unite! On to the workers' republic!' Most leaders of the new
movement were well-known IRA figures, including four ex-members
of headquarters staff.[3] Appearances suggested that the split was solely
over the issue of whether the IRA should remain an undercover,
military force, or whether it should expand and concentrate on active
political propaganda and industrial agitation. It did not seem, at first,
as though the over-all left-wing emphasis of the movement would be
called into question. Indeed, the Third International for a while regarded Ireland as its brightest spot in western Europe, and was full of
praise for the IRA's work among the proletariat.[4] It seemed to some
that the victory of de Valera in 1932, with the removal of the repressive
machinery of the Cosgrave administration, had brought about a situation akin to that which existed in Russia in 1917: the Tsar (Cosgrave)
was dead; Kerensky (de Valera) was in power; the proletarian revolution was at hand.[5]

In practice nothing was further from the truth. The Republican
movement was fragmenting, because of its record of continuing failure.
Further than this, and in spite of appearances, the split was not just
about tactics; it concealed a deep division over the whole conception
of underpinning the Republican movement with socialism. Despite the
gesture towards radicalism included in the IRA's reply to the Republican Congress initiative (prompted by a hope of avoiding a split on
ideological lines), a major cause of the rift was disagreement over the
wisdom of adopting overtly Communist policies. The language of the
split may have been concerned with tactics, but a glance at the personnel shows the committed socialist element in the IRA to have been
entirely on the Republican Congress side. Although the Congress movement failed to capture the public imagination in the way it had hoped,
and in fact virtually disintegrated through lack of funds within two

2. *Governmental Policy and Constitution of Óglaigh na hÉireann* (Dublin, 1933), cited
by Hogan, *Could Ireland become Communist?*, pp. 3–13.

3. Coogan, *IRA*, p. 107; Hogan, *Could Ireland become Communist?*, pp. 18–23.

4. See its official publication, *Imprecor*, 16 March 1934, cited in Hogan, *Could
Ireland become Communist?*, p. 27.

5. *Round Table*, xxiii (1933), 126, quoting *An Phoblacht*.

years, it inadvertently made an important contribution towards the de-socialization of the IRA proper. With its bombing campaign of 1939, the IRA returned to a traditional policy of uncomplicated physical force against 'England' from which it did not deflect until the early 1960s.

If the IRA managed to extricate itself from revolutionary socialism after a series of struggles, the trade unions and the Irish Labour party had done so much earlier and with less difficulty. An Irish TUC deputation to Russia in 1926 published a report culminating in a call to Irish workers to support their Russian brothers in the fight for human progress,[6] and Jim Larkin and his Workers' Union of Ireland maintained a more steady adherence to communism after his ejection from the Transport and General Workers' Union in 1924.[7] But these were isolated cases which went against the general trend. The attendance of the trade unions at the congresses held by the Friends of Soviet Russia declined at the same time as IRA participation was increasing.[8] Efforts of Communists to enter the Irish Labour party were halted in 1934 by the resolution that 'this conference will strictly oppose any attempt to introduce anti-Christian Communist doctrine into the movement'. If the party rejected such a motion, it was argued, it would pay the penalty at the polls.[9] And so all suggestions of a 'Republican workers' truce', of a popular front of Labour and the TUC with the IRA, the Republican Congress and other left-wing groups, were rejected.[1] Holding what it believed to be the realistic view of the political consciousness of the Irish working class, the Labour party regarded proposals for such a front with far less optimism than did the Republican Congress, which thought that such a move might be extremely effective in detaching support from Fianna Fáil.[2]

How seriously should the Irish 'fellow-travellers' be taken? Was there ever any possibility of Communism winning large-scale support in Ireland? Some contemporary observers argued that the threat was a serious one. Professor James Hogan of University College, Cork, a leading political figure on the Cumann na nGaedheal side, maintained that the claim of the *Republican Congress* newspaper was essentially correct: Ireland's position was indeed analogous to that of Russia on the eve of the Bolshevik revolution. It was pointed out that in proportion to the total population, there were more active Communists in Ireland than there had been in Russia in 1917.[3] But what may have seemed the

6. *Report of the Irish Labour Delegation to the USSR* (Dublin, 1926), p. 15.
7. See E. Larkin, *James Larkin*, chs xi and xii.
8. Hogan, *Could Ireland become Communist?*, p. 111.
9. Irish Labour party, *Annual Report, 1934*, p. 113.   1. Ibid., p. 119.
2. *The Republican Congress*, 13 October 1934.
3. Hogan, *Could Ireland become Communist?*, p. 39; *Republican Congress*, 13 October 1934.

beginning of a Communist wave soon collapsed. With the possible exception of Jim Larkin, whose lifelong disregard for caution lay at the root of his failure as a politician, none of the leading Irish Marxists, whatever colours they operated under, felt that the time was ripe in Ireland for a frank avowal of the Communist faith. Their organizations masqueraded under titles like the Anti-Imperalist League, Saor Eire, or Peasants' Committees, all seemingly innocuous in the Irish context. It was quite clear to the more realistic politicians on the left that a demand for nationalization of the land might alienate the mass of country people even more than a declaration of hostility to the Catholic church. The landlord class in Ireland had been defeated during the course of the national revolution, and by the 1920s had in many cases left the country altogether, making it extremely difficult to exploit class antagonisms in the countryside to any great extent. The agitation in the west of Ireland after 1927, instigated primarily by Peadar O'Donnell, which called for the distribution of the large grass 'ranches' among local landless people, was open to the same sort of political objections as a movement based on the unemployed: it was aimed at too small a section of the community to win political power, and it was potentially divisive of the rural working class. Attempts to promote a general strike against payment of rent by western farmers during the 1920s were effectively deflated by the Fianna Fáil pledge to stop the payment of land purchase annuities to Britain. It did not become clear until de Valera was in power that the annuities, although reduced, would still be collected by the Free State government. A vital difference between post-independence Ireland and pre-revolutionary Russia was that Ireland had already been transformed, by a sweeping programme of land reform, into a nation of small peasant proprietors.[4]

The other essential difference between the two countries was the moral force of the Irish Catholic church. For historical reasons, the church in Ireland (unlike its counterpart in Russia and most European countries) had never, since the Middle Ages, been associated with the ruling orders of society. It thus retained in the twentieth century a respect and authority which it had lost almost everywhere else in Europe. There was no anti-clerical party in Ireland, because there was no class basis for it. The church's immense influence on social and economic matters was demonstrated by the annihilating effect of episcopal condemnation on Saor Eire. The hierarchy declared in October 1931 that the movement constituted a threat to the spiritual and moral welfare of the country, and within a few weeks it had collapsed.

But this high-handed power in social matters did not extend to the national question. In that field priests have had to tread with extreme care. This, very possibly, accounts for the predilection of so many revo-

4. B. O'Neill, *The War for the Land in Ireland* (London, 1933), p. 108.

lutionary socialists in Ireland for the IRA rather than any more conventional Marxist organization. On the other hand no IRA leader ever felt free to embrace openly either atheism or the full Communist creed. There was far more vague talk of 'undoing the conquest' in order to restore the alleged 'communistic' paradise of pre-Norman Ireland, than there was of Marxism.[5] As we have seen, even Connolly's thinking was not free from such contortions.[6] It is not surprising that the Third International tempered its occasional praise for the left-wing IRA with charges that the movement was too 'Mexican', too backward, undisciplined, and muddled.[7]

Indeed, most of the Marxist socialism to be found in Ireland during the inter-war period was very much a forced growth. Two Communists who stood for election to the Dáil in 1932 received a combined total of only 1,087 votes. De Valera could report to the Dáil in 1933 that there were only a handful of Communists in Co. Clare, even fewer in Counties Waterford and Kilkenny, and about 400 in Dublin. The leadership of the movement, he alleged, as if to explain the aberration, was almost entirely English or Scots.[8] Real Moscow-oriented Communism was in fact a negligible quantity. The left-wing tendencies of some sections of the IRA could really be better classified as 'national-communist'. These elements came to cling increasingly to their left-wing utopianism the more Fianna Fáil progressed towards fulfilment of national aims. It was de Valera's success with the sovereignty question that encouraged them to think of deriving new strength from a closer connection with ideals of social revolution. The enthusiasm displayed for Soviet Russia was motivated less by real admiration of Communism than by the hope of finding a political and spiritual counterweight to use against the British connection.

EAMON DE VALERA

It is now time to devote some attention to the man who has, without doubt, been the most important political figure in the history of independent Ireland. If it seems strange that a close look at de Valera has been postponed until this stage, the explanation lies in a belief that his political personality only became of crucial importance to the development of Irish history during the course of the 1920s. In spite of his major role in the independence struggle between 1916 and 1921, it seems probable that the path of the republican movement during those years would not have been essentially different without him. Only with the debate over the treaty, and more especially with the reappraisal

---

5. Hogan, *Could Ireland become Communist?*, p. 32.
6. Above, p. 12.   7. *An Phoblacht*, 18 October 1930.
8. *Dáil Eireann Debates*, xlviii, col. 2057 (July 1933).

of republicanism between 1923 and 1927, does his role in events become so crucially important as to justify special treatment in a work
devoted essentially to an analysis of general trends.

Who was the man who emerged from ten years in the political
wilderness in 1932 to serve for twenty-one of the following twenty-seven
years as head of the Irish government, followed by two seven-year
terms as head of state? Eamon de Valera was born in 1882, in New
York City. His father was a music teacher of Spanish descent, his
mother a recent emigrant from Ireland. He thus shared with a number
of other prominent figures of the revolutionary generation the distinction of being only half Irish. But from early childhood he was brought
up by his uncle, Patrick Coll, in Bruree, Co. Limerick. It was not surprising that it was this west-of-Ireland rural background, rather than
the Spanish blood or the American birth, which shaped his personality
and his beliefs. Coll, a countryman of adequate if modest means, was
not without cultural interests, and de Valera's obvious intellectual
ability received every possible encouragement. A key to the under-
standing of de Valera, at least in the view of one of his biographers, is
to be found in his childhood impressions of:

the stormy eighties, a faint recollection of the United States, Spanish-Irish
forbears with a touch of Viking blood, the hills of east Limerick with the
crumbling coastline, patriotic legends, memories of Sarsfield and the Gaelic
heroes, in an area within twenty miles of the Shannon, an old seat of the
Gaels and Normans, warriors and monks, as nourishment for dreams and
excursions.[9]

At the age of 16 he won a scholarship which took him to Dublin,
where he subsequently settled down as a teacher of mathematics, and
married in 1910. He devoted much of his leisure time to the Gaelic
League, first as a student and later as a teacher of Irish. Like many of
the younger members of the League during that period, he developed
strong republican views, so that when the Irish Volunteers were formed
at the end of 1913 de Valera was brought into the world of revolutionary
politics. He soon came to the fore as an officer, and in the spate of
courts-martial which followed the Easter Rising in 1916 he was the
most senior commandant to escape the firing squad. The rising and its
consequent executions created a tremendous vacuum in Irish politics,
which de Valera, released from prison in 1917, was able to fill almost
without effort: he was immediately returned to Westminster as (abstentionist) MP for East Clare, and in April 1919 became President of the
revolutionary Irish Republic.[1]

Having grown up in the countryside, de Valera always projected

9. D. Ryan, *Unique Dictator: A Study of Eamon de Valera* (London, 1936), p. 7.
1. For an account of his early life, see the standard biography, by Lord Longford and T. P. O'Neill, *Eamon de Valera* (London, 1970).

himself as a 'man of the people', in close touch with the grass roots, and public opinion has by and large accepted this image. In the simplicity, even awkwardness, of his appearance, in his physical size, in the large cut of his face, and the somewhat melancholy line around the mouth, he distinctly resembled Abraham Lincoln. Indeed, he revered Lincoln, whose picture hung in his study. His background as a teacher of mathematics was clearly apparent in his political career, in his didactic style and his predilection for the manipulation of abstract concepts. Another early biographer, and one less sympathetic, described his penchant for juggling with ideas and splitting hairs as a 'theological turn of mind', and discerned a 'capacity for something perilously near sharp dealing, with a bland air of utter innocence, even self-righteousness'. Such a quality is 'rooted in the national genius, which adores reservations, loop-holes, wordy discrimination . . . anything . . . except a clear statement of simple fact or intent'.[2] A convincing case can be made in support of the view that de Valera's attitude during the years following the treaty was extraordinarily stubborn and rigid. In the eyes of a hostile critic he offered, between 1924 and 1928 'the slightly comic, slightly pathetic sight of the impractical idealist who tries to persuade himself and the world that he is a wholly practical man'.[3] But this very rigidity, this reluctance to compromise, was the key to his popularity during the Free State period. It was the quality which made the small western farmers identify de Valera as one of themselves, and which enabled him to remain for most people the personification of the republican movement long after he had broken with the IRA and Sinn Féin. In this way,

by sheer weight of persistence, by his own self-belief, by hammering day in and day out for ten years on the one idea of an independent Ireland, by refusing to admit a single error of judgment, or the slightest divergence from his ideal, de Valera was (in 1932) once more at the head of Irish affairs . . .[4]

So firmly were de Valera's republican credentials established that his support hardly diminished at all when he carried off a complete reversal of policy in 1927 by taking the oath to enter the Free State Dáil. While opponents hoped that such inconsistency would be his political undoing,[5] his supporters saw in it both a personal sacrifice and the beginning of a move towards the centre of the political spectrum. This, in the long run, was to ensure Fianna Fáil's position as the 'natural majority' party in Ireland.

In his later career de Valera became a professional politician whose

2. Sean O Faolain, *De Valera* (London, 1939), p. 68.
3. Ibid., p. 111.   4. Ibid., p. 129.
5. His action was nothing short of a tacit acceptance of the arguments put forward by Michael Collins in 1922, to the effect that the obnoxious provisions in the treaty could be eroded by peaceful methods.

primary aim was to stay in office and govern effectively within the framework of parliamentary democracy. In so far as he retained any general sense of political mission, it was to preserve and restore the Gaelic character of the country. His supporters have always referred to him as 'The Chief': a word with deep roots and special significance in Irish politics and history. It has been said that time stood still for him, that the Ireland which he loved in fact disappeared at the battle of Kinsale, in 1601, when the old Gaelic order of society was finally destroyed.[6] He had always been a fervent champion of the Irish language, and would never speak English to someone whom he knew to be an Irish-speaker. He admitted, and his political career testified to the fact, that the restoration of the language meant more to him than the restoration of the six northern counties. This determination gave his nationalism a strong romantic quality which overshadowed his cool, mathematician's mind, and contributed a good deal to the evocation of the almost mystical aura with which he was endowed in the public mind. Yet for all his nationalist zeal, which would like to refuse the term 'Irish' to everything non-Gaelic, he remained a man of considerable personal charm.

Apart from the issue of Gaelicization, the de Valera of later life in no sense became an ideologue. Basically conservative, he was above all a pious Catholic, a daily attender at Mass, and a strict observer of all church rules which called for self-discipline, although in politics he could claim to have been more independent of the church than many of his opponents. His words on St Patrick's Day 1935 accurately described the political philosophy which guided his actions:

Ireland remained a Catholic nation, and as such set the eternal destiny of man high above the '-isms' and idols of the day. Her people would accept no system that decried or imperilled that destiny. So long as that was their attitude none of the forms of state-worship now prevalent could flourish in their land; the state would be confined to its proper functions as guardian of the rights of the individual and the family, co-ordinator of the activities of its citizens. . . .[7]

His determination to restore the Gaelic order in Ireland never caused him to show impatience with the processes of parliamentary democracy: he never used his long periods in power to take revenge on his opponents of the civil war period; when the supreme court rejected as unconstitutional a clause in the School Attendance Bill, 1942 (which would have forbidden parents to send their children to foreign schools) he withdrew it;[8] and when he was rejected by the electorate in 1948 after sixteen years in power, he accepted defeat with at least as much grace as his opponents had mustered in 1932.

6. *Round Table*, xxxv (1944–5), 311.
7. Ibid. xxv (1934–5), 551.   8. *Irish Times Review*, 1943.

The response which de Valera drew from the Irish people so consistently during his long career was never the product of demagogy. He was no daemonic mob orator. His *faculté maîtresse* was rather the ability to convey a fervent sense of justice. It was in this way that his supporters interpreted his stand during the civil war, and again during the Anglo-Irish tariff war of the mid 1930s. The call found a ready echo among the depressed small farmers of the countryside, who had for generations been deprived of their rights on the land, debased, and humiliated. Such people, who had found solace in an intense piety and a highly developed moral code, saw in de Valera an uncompromising champion of their rights, far more than they ever saw in him, or he ever was, a champion of their interests. His restrained passion and convincing air of simplicity won him the unconditional trust of a majority of the Irish people, and perhaps just as important in a new state striving to establish democratic institutions, the respect of his opponents.

FIANNA FAIL

With his withdrawal from Sinn Féin and subsequent founding of the Fianna Fáil party in April 1926, de Valera moved into a position of *de facto* recognition of the Free State regime. Fianna Fáil, it was said later, was 'a *slightly* constitutional party'.[9] The programme of the new party was based on six main points:

Reunification of the country, with a republican constitution.
Cultural independence to be restored through the re-introduction of Irish as the national language and the development of a distinctly Gaelic national life.
The resources and wealth of the country to be put to the service of the whole population.
Ireland to have economic independence in order to make the country as far as possible 'self contained and self-sufficient'.
'As many families as practicable' to be established on the land.
An intensive programme of rural industrialization to be set in motion, to facilitate all this and counteract the drift to the cities.[1]

In the first of these the most important question was that of the oath of allegiance. It was to prevent the Fianna Fáil deputies from taking their seats in the Dáil for a year, and remained at the centre of political debate until abolished by de Valera as his first act of government. The abolition of the Senate, which was regarded in Fianna Fáil and Sinn

9. Seán Lemass, speaking in the Dáil, 12 March 1928. Cited in Coogan, *IRA*, p. 80.

1. The text used here is the 1934 constitution of Fianna Fáil. The original version (printed in *Fianna Fail, 1926–51*, p. 6) is less clear. It treats the first three points in more detail, and includes under the third all industrialization and protective tariffs. Point our deals with afforestation, transport, and the distribution of land, and point five with the establishment of a state bank.

Féin circles as the stronghold of conservatism and unionism, was also included in this part of the party programme. Provision was made as well for reforming the constitution so as to strengthen the government's powers. As to the demand for cultural independence, the emphasis was only slightly different from Cumann na nGaedheal policy, for the re-introduction of the Irish language was from the beginning one of the aims of the Free State. It was pursued fairly steadily, though with only limited success.[2] It is significant that these cultural aims took precedence over the attainment of new social and economic goals.

The third clause, with an eye to attracting support from the working class, hinted that Fianna Fáil intended to make radical changes in the social order, though it gave no indication of what, precisely, was to be done.

The reference to economic independence was essentially another appeal to national feeling, and the hand of de Valera is clearly apparent in the sketch of a flourishing Ireland which could surmount all problems by its own efforts, once it had escaped from its economic dependence on Great Britain. Yet Fianna Fáil's social and economic programme in its earliest years had little practical originality. Although more detail was filled in with the passage of time, the emphasis at first remained on the basic political question. Bitter memories of the 1919–23 period still dominated Republican thinking too much to enable any substantial progress to be made from the aims which Republicans had set themselves in the immediate aftermath of the civil war. A criticism made by an American writer in 1925 still held true of the early Fianna Fail: 'Dwelling inanely on what they are pleased to call the great betrayal of 1922, Republicans avoid the necessity of formulating an alternative programme.'[3] There was still the implicit assumption that complete political separation from Great Britain was the panacea by which all other problems would be solved.

In 1927 de Valera added another point to the Fianna Fáil programme by calling for an end to the payment of land annuities to the British Exchequer. Unlike Mary McSwiney and the rump of the Sinn Féin Dáil, he based his arguments not on the broad historical grounds that Britain had expropriated the land from Irishmen in the first place, but on the strictly legalistic argument that Britain's renunciation of all financial claims on the Irish Free State, under the Financial Regulation of December 1925, included her claim to the continued payment of the

2. At the 1851 census, 23 per cent of the population of Ireland described themselves as 'Irish speakers', of whom a fifth knew no English. Today not more than 35,000, 1·2 per cent of the population of the 26 counties, use Irish regularly in their daily life, although almost all Catholics who have been educated since 1923, north or south of the border, have some familiarity with the national language. See Brian O Cuiv, *Irish Dialects and Irish-speaking Districts* (Dublin, 1951).

3. J. D. Clarkson, *Labour and Nationalism in Ireland* (New York, 1925), p. 472.

land annuities.[4] The addition of such a point to the Fianna Fáil programme was bound to have strong attractions for the great mass of tenant purchasers in the Irish countryside. They were allowed to think that the ending of annuity payments to Britain would mean a complete wiping out of all individual obligations under the land purchase acts. In fact it became clear once Fianna Fail came to power that the intention was to continue collection of the annuities, at a somewhat reduced rate, and to retain them in Dublin. The rural labouring class was also won over to Fianna Fáil in large numbers by a promise to divide the great grass 'ranches' among the smallest farmers and landless men of each locality.

By 1928, details of the Fianna Fáil economic programme were also beginning to emerge: protective tariffs to stimulate the development of domestic industry; greater economy in the conduct of public administration; and the promotion of a merchant fleet, the fishing industry and afforestation, along with the exploitation of all possible raw materials in the country. In effect, a blueprint was put forward for the establishment of Irish self-sufficiency.[5]

So far as imperial relations were concerned, Fianna Fail began to develop a more soft-pedalling, cautious approach within the republican framework. De Valera did not intend to modify the treaty without a referendum. He was ready 'to face and accept existing realities: a nation cannot march on an empty stomach'.[6] The problem of the six counties was treated with even more caution: while he admitted that he could see no immediate solution, de Valera expressly excluded any possibility of the use of force.[7] Resolutions passed at the Fianna Fáil party conference in 1929 began with the question of unemployment and ended with a demand for more workers' housing. 'The Republic', for the first time, was not in the forefront.[8] Increasing emphasis was laid upon the party's proposals for the development of home industries, and it became less easy to differentiate between the programmes of Fianna Fáil and the Labour party. Indeed, the latter was to complain rather pathetically in later years that its ideas had been stolen.[9] Initially, however, the leftward move of Fianna Fáil brought the two opposition parties closer together: all the more since Fianna Fáil had little hope of winning power without the assistance of Labour votes in the Dáil. On

4. Many had believed this to be the case at the time the Agreement was signed. But it later transpired that under the terms of a secret agreement, signed by Winston Churchill and Ernest Blythe in March 1926, the land annuities debt was to be regarded as a separate account. See Round Table, xvii (1926–7), 345; xxiii (February 1933), 287.

5. See E. de Valera, Fianna Fáil and its Economic Policy (Dublin, 1928). This pamphlet is the reprint of a speech delivered in the Dáil, 13 July 1928.

6. Round Table, xviii (1927–8), 141.   7. Ibid. xxii (1932), 372.

8. Moss, Political Parties in the Irish Free State, p. 29.

9. Irish Labour party, Annual Report, 1934, p. 69.

its side, the Labour party made a friendly gesture towards Fianna Fáil by calling for negotiations with Britain to end the payment of land annuities and the oath of allegiance.

Fianna Fáil's moderate version of the Republican programme and its development of a credible economic policy attracted support on a very large scale among those who hoped to see their material circumstances improved by the achievement of full national independence. The party's advance was further accelerated by the developing world economic crisis, which put particular pressure on agriculture. By 1932 the Cosgrave administration was ten years old. Inevitably, perhaps, some old complaints remained to be dealt with, while many new grievances had arisen, so that the demand for new faces in government was increasing all the time. Fianna Fáil offered a cohesive programme of national and social advance. It was the old Sinn Féin policy in modern dress: 'ourselves alone'. De Valera and his advisers laid down a clear programme of action for those who had no faith in the ability of *laissez-faire* policies to solve the nation's problems, proclaiming an expansion of state initiative and a long-term social and economic policy clearly rooted in republicanism. The programme was well calculated to appeal to the smaller Irish farmers: a frugal, Gaelic Ireland, as little despoiled as possible by the forces of civilization, especially English civilization; a state in which there would be no rich and no poor, but rather a countryside scattered with small farmers and small industries. In order to gain real liberty, and escape from 'the kicks of the master's mansion', de Valera declared, 'we will have to be content with the plain furniture of the cottage. I have no hesitation in saying we are prepared to face the alternative and take the plain furniture of the cottage.'[1] Perhaps only the man who, despite the horrors of the civil war period, was still remembered as president of the Irish Republic of 1919–21, could have won political advantage from so stark a declaration.

The electoral progress of Fianna Fáil between 1928 and 1932 was remarkably steady. At the first Free State election, in June 1922, the anti-treaty party received only 21 per cent of the votes cast.[2] Electoral support for republicanism remained at this modest level until the second election of 1927, when Fianna Fáil announced its intention of entering the Dáil and increased its share of the vote to 35 per cent. Subsequently, in February 1932, the party came to power with 44 per cent of the vote, supported in the Dáil by the Labour party, which had received 8 per cent. Notwithstanding its temporary position of influence, Labour had in effect been crushed, along with the smaller parties, by Fianna Fáil's success: Labour, the Farmers' party, and the other small groups and independents, which had secured over 46 per cent of the poll in the

1. De Valera, *Fianna Fáil and its Economic Policy*, p. 12.
2. Excluding 16 TDs returned for uncontested constituencies.

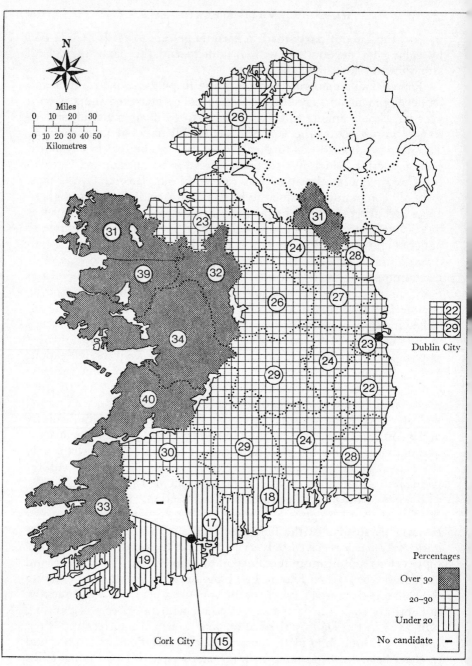

25. FIRST-PREFERENCE VOTES FOR FIANNA FAIL CANDIDATES, JUNE 1927

(104)

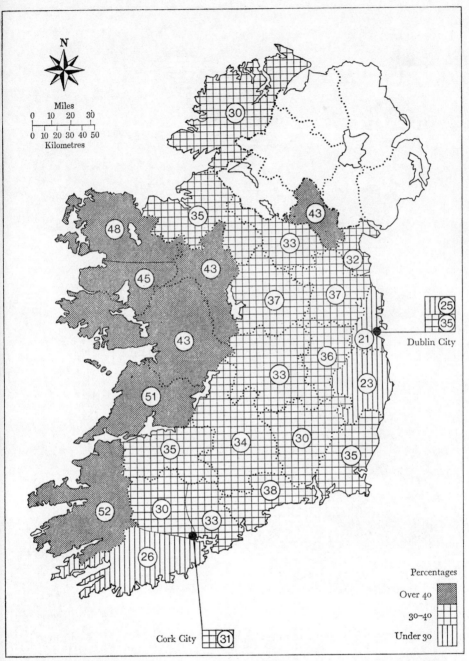

26. FIRST-PREFERENCE VOTES FOR FIANNA FAIL CANDIDATES, SEPTEMBER 1927

(105)

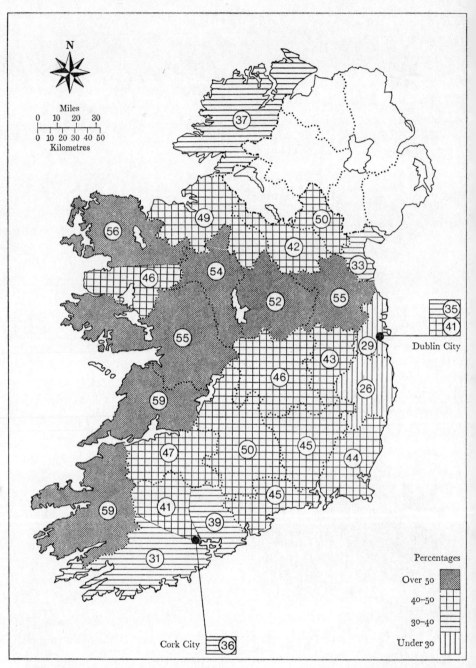

27. FIRST-PREFERENCE VOTES FOR FIANNA FAIL CANDIDATES, 1932

(106)

first election of 1927, in 1932 received a mere 20 per cent.[3] De Valera's appeal, and the social and economic programme of Fianna Fáil, had their roots in the aspirations of the workers and small western farmers who, since 1922, had been regarded as the hard-core supporters of Republicanism. In June 1927 Fianna Fáil, like the republican Sinn Féin party in 1923, drew the great weight of its support from the west of Ireland, while in Dublin it was significantly more successful in the working-class districts than in other sections of the city. In Dublin it certainly damaged Labour, whose electoral organizers reported that 'it was found difficult to arrange organising meetings. The reason appears to be that the workers expected Fianna Fáil to fulfil all their wishes.'[4] Wherever prosperous farmers or Protestants were influential, especially in the south-east and the border counties, Fianna Fáil fared less well (see map 25). But beginning with the September election of 1927 and its decision to enter the Dáil, the party seemed to do better all round (map 26). Its continued expansion in the west is less remarkable than the 50 per cent increase in support in Counties Longford, Westmeath, and Monaghan, the 90 per cent increase in Waterford, and the remarkable 100 per cent increase in East Cork. In 1932 the eastward push was even more obvious. It was clear that the more prosperous midland counties of Meath, Westmeath, and Longford were on their way to being conquered by de Valera and Fianna Fáil (map 27). The moderation and refinement of the economic programme was bearing its first fruits.

3. The figures are conveniently summarized in Basil Chubb, *The Government and Politics of Ireland* (Stanford and London, 1970), p. 334, now the standard work on Irish politics.
4. Irish Labour party, *Annual Report, 1932*, p. 7.

CHAPTER FOUR

The Republican Epoch

OUT OF THE COMMONWEALTH

The first action of de Valera in office was the abolition of the oath of allegiance as 'an intolerable burden, a relic of medievalism'. The necessary legislation was passed by the Dáil on 19 May 1932.[1] At the same time the judicial precedence of the treaty over the Free State constitution was declared to be at an end. The office of Governor-General was deprived as far as possible of all representative significance and dignity, and was subsequently filled by a defeated Fianna Fail parliamentary candidate who performed rubber-stamp duties only from a house in suburban Dublin.[2] Later the government took advantage of the constitutional difficulties created by the abdication of Edward VIII to abolish the office altogether. Relations with the British Commonwealth were redefined by the External Relations Act of 1936, under which the king continued to be recognized as a 'symbol of co-operation' for as long as the Irish Free State remained associated with the Commonwealth, but was deprived of all but one of his remaining functions. He retained only formal power concerning the accreditation of diplomats.[3] De Valera's concept of 'external association' had at last been realized.

In 1938 good relations between Ireland and Britain were fully restored. The trade war between the two countries, which had broken out in 1933 after de Valera's government ceased to hand over the land annuity payments to London, was finally brought to an end. At the same time the British government, under its new Prime Minister

1. *Fianna Fáil, 1926–51: The Story of Twenty-five Years of National Endeavour and Achievement*, p. 8; *Round Table*, xxii (1932), 489.
2. He was Domhnall Ua Buachalla (Daniel Buckley), a Maynooth merchant and veteran of the 1916 rising. See Coogan, *Ireland since the Rising* (London, 1966), p. 75; *Round Table*, xxiii (1933), 291.
3. *Irish Times Review, 1936*, p. 5.

Neville Chamberlain, recognized the new Irish constitution of 1937 and, most important of all, agreed to evacuate the Irish naval bases which it held under the 1921 treaty.[4] Chamberlain was motivated, no doubt, by the desire to ensure that Ireland would be a friendly neighbour and perhaps a willing ally for Britain in the European crises which loomed on the horizon. In the second of these hopes he was to be disappointed. As early as 1927 it was clear that most Irish politicians of all parties regarded neutrality as the best policy for Ireland in the event of Britain becoming involved in a war.[5] It might have been anticipated that de Valera, of all people, would be supremely conscious of the capital which the IRA might have made out of Fianna Fáil's involvement in a 'British war'. Thus he declared in the Dáil on 13 July 1938 that while two obstacles to good Anglo-Irish relations, the oath and the treaty ports, had been removed, the question of partition and the exclusion of the six northern counties from the Irish state remained.[6] Very probably he may have felt at the time that his good relations with Chamberlain brought the ending of partition into the arena of practical politics.[7]

This proved not to be the case, but the association of the partition issue with neutrality was none the less of vital importance in Irish politics. Abroad it ensured that Irish neutrality remained acceptable to Irish-Americans, for instance, even after the United States entered the war, while at home it gave neutrality a bi-partisan respectability which grew deeper roots as the success of the policy became apparent. De Valera steered this course with patience and astuteness throughout the war, protesting vehemently against every violation of Irish territory, north and south of the border, whether it was German bombs in Belfast and spies in Dublin, or the British threat of conscription for Northern Ireland.[8] To the very end he maintained scrupulous diplomatic respect for the Axis powers. His reward was continued political stability at home and the stifling of the IRA; the price was a renewed bitterness towards

4. For a full account of these negotiations see Lord Longford and T. P. O'Neill, *Eamon de Valera* (London, 1970), pp. 313–26.

5. C. C. O'Brien, 'Ireland in international affairs', O. Dudley Edwards (ed.), *Conor Cruise O'Brien Introduces Ireland* (London, 1969), p. 119.

6. Ibid.

7. At the time of Pearl Harbour and America's entry into the war, in December 1941, Churchill did offer to reopen the partition question in exchange for Irish participation in the war against Germany. But de Valera, whose political memories of course went back to the treaty and the Boundary Commission, showed no enthusiasm for a proposal which called for Irish commitment at once in exchange for vague promises of British action at some future date. See Longford and O'Neill, *Eamon de Valera*, pp. 392–5.

8. *Irish Times Review*, *1941*, p. 5; ibid., *1942*, p. 16. Against the advice of the Northern Ireland government, the British government decided that the advantages of introducing conscription for Northern Ireland were outweighed by the danger of provoking large-scale disaffection among Ulster Catholics.

him in the post-war years on the part not only of Ulster Protestants but also of politicians of both major parties in Great Britain. The presence of an estimated 150,000 Irish volunteers in the British forces during the war had no political impact. [9]

The over-all trend of Anglo-Irish relations in the immediate post-war years was by no means clear. A new trade agreement and an official visit to Ireland by a British fleet in the autumn of 1946 pointed to an extension of the harmony that had been established in 1938. But the war had ended with a violent public controversy between de Valera and Churchill,[1] while the renewed vigour of anti-partitionist (Catholic) political organization in the north soon made an impact on southern politics. A new party, Clann na Poblachta, was able to win ten seats, mainly from Fianna Fáil, at the 1948 election by combining social radicalism with a militant expression of opposition to partition.[2] The change was sufficient to tip the balance of parliamentary forces, and Fianna Fáil was replaced in office by a five-party coalition. One result of this was to drive de Valera, whose attention to the partition issue ever since 1938 had been at least partly motivated by his concern to maintain neutrality, into devoting the first months of his period in opposition to a world-wide publicity campaign against partition. In the opinion of at least one historian this development was responsible for the inter-party government's decision to maintain neutrality and steer completely clear of the newly formed NATO alliance.[3] Under the new circumstances, J. A. Costello of Fine Gael, head of the new and rather precarious coalition, found himself placed in a difficult position by conflicting pressures and rumours over the future of the somewhat ambiguous External Relations Act of 1936. Suddenly he took the world, and apparently his own ministerial colleagues, by surprise with an announcement (made in the course of a state visit to Canada) that Ireland was to become a republic and leave the Commonwealth forthwith.[4] Another irony was thus added to the course of Irish history: just

9. *Round Table*, xxxv (1944–5), 310.
1. Churchill, in his victory speech of 12 May 1945, referred to 'the great generosity of the British people in respecting Eire's neutrality', even though de Valera had 'frolicked with [the Axis powers] to his heart's content', *The Times*, 14 May 1945. On 16 May de Valera responded with a denunciation of 'the continued occupation of Irish soil by British troops' in the six counties. *Irish Press*, 17 May 1945.
2. See below, pp. 144–7.
3. O'Brien, 'Ireland in international affairs', pp. 124–5.
4. This episode is discussed more fully in F. S. L. Lyons, *Ireland since the Famine* (London, 1971), pp. 556–61. It seems that Costello and his cabinet colleagues had already agreed that Ireland's existing constitutional status, under the External Relations Act, was equivocal and ought to be changed. What provoked Costello's hasty announcement however was not (as was once thought) an insult he had received from the Governor-General of Canada, who was an Ulster Protestant, but an inspired leak in the *Sunday Independent* newspaper, which panicked him into adopting the view that the only course open to him at his prearranged press conference was to make a full and frank statement of his government's intentions.

as de Valera, the avowed republican, had in the late 1930s and early 1940s taken the strongest steps since the civil war to stifle the IRA, so in 1948 a government led by the supposedly 'pro-British' Fine Gael party finally brought into formal existence the Irish Republic. De Valera, meanwhile, was still maintaining in 1947, as in 1939, that 'under the External Relations Act . . . we have a republic in effect'.[5]

There is little doubt that the inter-party government's decision was tactlessly conceived and executed. In return for a formal ending of the links between Ireland and the United Kingdom (which admittedly removed a tiresome issue from Irish politics) it had dealt a fatal blow at its own anti-partitionist campaign. The Unionist party in the Northern Ireland parliament was able to take advantage of the issue at a subsequent general election to rally Protestant feelings and regain all the votes it had lost to Labour in 1945. The British government was stung by the unilateral declaration, and included in its own Ireland Act of 1949 a new pledge that the constitutional position of Northern Ireland within the United Kingdom would not be altered without the consent of the Northern Ireland parliament. Remarkably, however, this exchange of diplomatic hostilities did not presage an era of worsening general relations between Ireland and the United Kingdom. The special status of Irish citizens living and working in Great Britain, made secure by the British Nationality Act of 1948, was in no way diminished,[6] neither were the close trade links which had been progressively restored since 1938.

THE ATTACK ON THE CONSERVATIVES

A central feature of Fianna Fáil policy had always been the weakening of the remaining political links which bound Ireland to Great Britain. So far as the constitutional relationship was concerned, the final honours were shared between de Valera, with his External Relations Act of 1936, and Costello, with his Republic of Ireland Act of 1948. But when it came to breaking down the power and influence which the 'pro-British' classes retained in Ireland after independence, Fianna Fáil took by far the more active role. As we have seen, the party in its early years combined a substantial element of social radicalism with its republicanism. Both these facets of the party programme could be brought into action together by a move against the ex-Unionist population, which was also the traditional upper-class section of the community.

The most obvious bastion of this class in the Free State was the

5. Cited in *Round Table*, xxix (1938–9), 800; see also *Dail Debates*, cvii, cols 86–87, cited in Lyons, *Ireland since the Famine*, p. 557.

6. It continued to be the case, however, that legislation of the Northern Ireland parliament imposed stringent restrictions on the right of people not born in Northern Ireland to work there.

Senate, the upper house which had been established under the 1922 constitution. A certain stigma had always been attached to it, for it had not been part of the revolutionary governmental structure of 1919–21. Its origins lay rather in the obsolete British schemes of 1914 and 1920, which had aspired to dilute the full force of nationalist democracy. Its final appearance in the Free State constitution was in large part the result of talks between Arthur Griffith and the leaders of southern Unionism to see how the interests of that class might best be safeguarded. But 'in thus attempting to reconcile the minority to the new order, the architects of the treaty exposed the Senate to the hostility of the extreme section of their party'.[7] Furthermore, the composition of the first Senate, in particular, underlined its association with the ascendancy class: its 60 members included 13 who had been educated at public schools or universities in England, or at Trinity College, Dublin; 11 who had served as officers in the British army; 8 peers, 4 baronets, and 1 knight. Twenty-six out of 60 were non-Catholic.[8] After 1925, when it was provided that the Senate would be elected by members of the two houses voting together, membership began to reflect the political climate in the country more closely but, since only one-quarter of its membership was replaced every three years, it reflected change very much more slowly than did the Dáil.

When Fianna Fáil came to power for the first time in 1932, it was confronted with a Senate which, in so far as it had lost its ascendancy domination, had been moulded during the years of Cumann na nGaedheal leadership. The powers which the Senate possessed were not considerable, compared to most second chambers: it could not initiate money bills, but merely delay them for twenty-one days, while it could only delay other bills which the Dáil had passed for 270 days (after 1928, eighteen months). Its power under the 1922 constitution to require a referendum was never used, and was abolished in 1928.[9] Under Cumann na nGaedheal, the Senate had played a useful, if minor, role in the legislative process.[1] But it was objectionable to de Valera on two counts: as an apparent bastion of privilege it ran counter to the radical streak which characterized Fianna Fáil during this period, described recently as 'a Catholic version of Jacobinism';[2] secondly, though its

7. J. L. McCracken, *Representative Government in Ireland: A Study of Dáil Eireann, 1919–48* (London, 1958), p. 138.
8. Ibid.   9. Ibid., p. 139.
1. For a powerful defence of the Free State Senate, see the famous speech, *Pro Doma Sua*, made and later published by its chariman, T. W. Westropp-Bennett (Dublin, 1934).
2. D. R. O'Connor Lysaght, *The Republic of Ireland* (Cork, 1970), p. 102. One Fianna Fail leader branded the Senate as an institution designed 'to give political power to a certain class that could not get that power if they had to go before the people at a free election' (*Dáil Debates*, xxii, col. 598, cited in McCracken, *Representative Government in Ireland*, p. 142).

constitutional powers were by no means absolute in any field, it was in a position to make itself a considerable nuisance when de Valera came to implement the wide-ranging constitutional changes which he had in mind. What he wanted to present as a great constitutional reform programme might be turned by a hostile Senate into a first-rate constitutional crisis instead. Furthermore, de Valera's personal feeling was that the ideal second chamber had not yet been devised, and that on the whole such bodies were more trouble than they were worth.[3]

No one was very surprised therefore, when the inevitable clash came over Senate resistance to Fianna Fáil's policies towards Great Britain abroad and the developing Blueshirt movement at home, to find that de Valera's response was a bill to abolish the Senate altogether. It ceased to exist on 29 May 1936.[4] The new constitution of 1937 was brought into being by a uni-cameral legislature, and although de Valera subsequently made a gesture to the advocates of a second chamber by bringing a new Senate into being, it was, and is, a modest institution, very much on the fringe of the political process. Its powers, which could be abridged in an emergency by the government, were limited to a ninety-day suspension of ordinary bills and a twenty-one-day suspension of money bills. Devised in the shadow of fashionable 1930s ideas about the corporative state, the basis for membership was intended to be vocational. In practice, however, it has been thoroughly party-political.[5]

In other fields the Fianna Fáil assault upon privilege was less contentious. The Cosgrave administration's Local Government Act of 1925 had done nothing to remove the bias in the franchise in favour of the propertied classes, which operated to the disadvantage of Fianna Fáil in local politics. Accordingly, in the spring of 1933, the new government introduced two measures: the separate commercial franchise for Dublin corporation elections was abolished and the general franchise in local elections throughout the country was extended from ratepayers only to all persons over 21 years of age. The old system, declared the Minister for Local Government, Sean T. O'Kelly, had been 'class legislation of the worst kind'.[6] Both bills were rejected by the Senate, but ultimately passed into law early in 1935. It was a step forward for the 'little man', championed by Fianna Fáil, at the expense of the business classes. The same trend was also reflected in the decreasing part which the non-Catholic population came to play in public administration. In 1926 non-Catholics, who constituted 7·4 per cent of the population,

3. McCracken, *Representative Government in Ireland*, p. 146.

4. D. O'Sullivan, *The Irish Free State and its Senate* (London, 1940), is a very full and well-documented, though strongly partisan, defence of the institution.

5. Lyons, *Ireland since the Famine*, p. 537; see also B. Chubb, 'Vocational representation and the Irish Senate', *Political Studies*, ii (1954), 97–111.

6. O'Sullivan, *Irish Free State*, pp. 349–50.

made up 8·4 per cent of the public service, whereas in 1946, when the proportion of non-Catholics in the population had dropped to 5·7 per cent, the proportion in the public service was only 3·8 per cent.[7] There is no doubt that this was the result, in part at least, not of discrimination against Protestants but of greater egalitarianism and a general rise in the social and educational circumstances of the mass of the Catholic population.

THE STRUGGLE FOR ECONOMIC INDEPENDENCE

Fianna Fáil's policy of political and social dissociation from British influence was perhaps less pronounced than the party's efforts to sever economic links between the two countries. In 1931 Ireland depended on Britain for 81 per cent of her imports and 96 per cent of her exports.[8] That such intense economic dependence must inevitably make a deep impact on the political and cultural life of the country would have been obvious to a leader with far less nationalist awareness than de Valera. If a drastic change of economic direction were possible at all, it would involve losses as well as gains: it called for an over-all change in the organization of the economy.[9] Thus economic dependence could only be broken by a party which looked for its support to those classes with no apparent feeling of economic interest in the British connection, ie small farmers and workers. In addition to these classes de Valera had with him those for whom the preservation and restoration of a truly national way of life was worth some economic loss. The national pride of such people suffered considerably from the fact that Ireland, notwithstanding her political independence, was to all intents and purposes England's back-garden, providing her larger neighbour with cheap food. They feared that with the continued influx of English goods and money, English language, customs, and culture would continue to stifle the remaining elements of Gaelic civilization.

To attain what they believed to be the vital goal of economic autarchy, Fianna Fáil and its supporters were therefore prepared to take on England in a bitter and destructive trade war. The origin of the conflict, in 1932, was the new government's decision to keep in Dublin the annual payments which Irish tenant purchasers were still obliged to make to the British Treasury in accordance with the Land Purchase Acts of 1885–1909. De Valera contested the validity of the agreement by which the money, amounting to some £5 million annually, was handed over to Britain, and began to withhold payments

---

7. *Census of Ireland, 1946,* ii. 197 ff.
8. *Statistical Abstracts for the British Empire, 1931.*
9. For a detailed discussion of this topic, see the standard work by J. Meenan, *The Irish Economy since 1922* (Liverpool, 1970).

shortly after coming to power. Great Britain replied by imposing punitive tariffs on the major Irish exports, especially cattle and butter, in order to recoup her losses. The Irish government was not slow to impose reciprocal tariffs, but of course the impact on Irish producers and consumers was very much greater than it was on anyone in Britain.[1] The Irish market was scarcely a crucial field for British exporters, and if British consumers could no longer afford to buy Irish beef, then a number of other countries were more than willing to supply a cheaper alternative. It was not difficult for Irish consumers to find substitutes for British imports (non-British imports increased in 1934 by £2·2 million), but to find new export markets was a problem which proved insurmountable. After a great effort, exports to countries other than Great Britain were increased only by £22,000.[2] Soon the cost of living in Ireland stood at a ratio of 10:7 to that obtaining in Britain. The domestic market for goods previously exported was certainly expanded, but in the case of cattle this was achieved only by means of a drop in price from £16 11s per head in 1931 to £8 per head in 1935.[3] In 1937 the adverse trade balance reached its highest point at £20,700,000.[4] Economic war, as one of de Valera's old adversaries remarked, was proving more expensive than civil war.[5]

It was not in fact economic progress that was at stake, however much the protagonists may have deceived themselves into believing that the policy would eventually lead to Irish prosperity.[6] The fundamental aim was to redirect the economy of the country to accord with nationalist political aspirations. Feeling was widespread within Fianna Fáil that 'it was a damn good job that the English cattle market had gone, as it would make the farmers realise that they should take off their coats and till the land for the production of food'. It was hoped that by artificially impeding the export of cattle, the growing of wheat would be encouraged. Reference was made to the late eighteenth- and early nineteenth-century period when grain production had been a central part of Irish agriculture, and the growing of crops was declared to be a national duty. An Ireland 'Gaelic and free', cultivated by a nation of small farmers, was of course a central idea of romantic nationalism. Such ideas were very attractive to the west of the country, which was dominated by small farms: there Fianna Fail secured over 60 per cent of first preference votes in the general election of 1933 (map

1. For a discussion of these issues see P. G. Harkort, 'Der Irisch-Englische Handelskrieg' (trade war), Berlin Univerity PhD thesis, 1938.
2. *Round Table*, xxv (1934–5), 348.   3. Ibid. xxvi (1935–6), 575.
4. Ibid. xxviii (1937–8), 75.   5. Ibid. xxiv (1933–4), 587.
6. De Valera once declared that 'if there is to be any hope of prosperity for this country it is by reversing that policy which made us simply the kitchen-garden for supplying the British with cheap food'. Cited in P. N. S. Mansergh, *Britain and Ireland* (London, 1942), p. 84.

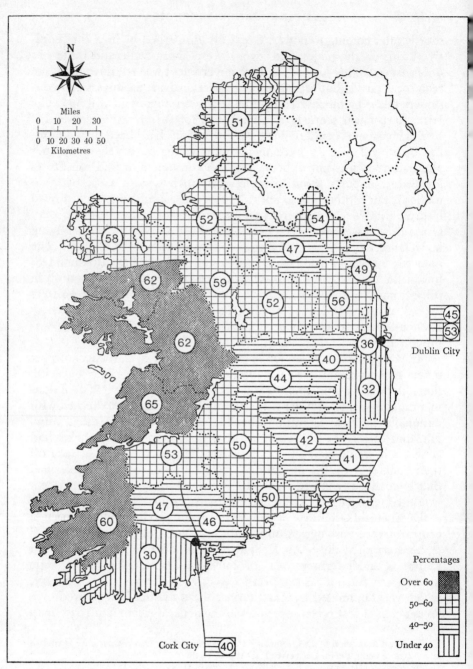

28. FIRST-PREFERENCE VOTES FOR FIANNA FAIL CANDIDATES,
1933

(116)

28). The government sought to present the economic war to the electorate as a new phase in the Irish struggle for liberation, as a battle against British encroachment, a battle in which the opposition parties had taken the side of the national enemy.[7] In this it was largely successful, for the party won not only the west, but many other areas of the country also, in the general election of 1937.

A balance sheet for six years of 'national' economic policy was drawn up by the Commission of Inquiry into Banking, Currency, and Credit, in 1938.[8] The value of cattle and cattle products had declined from £54·6 million in 1929–30 to £31·1 million in 1935–6, while crop production (excluding potatoes) had only risen from £4·1 million to £5 million during the same period. Great Britain remained the chief customer for Irish products. After five years of trade war and the accompanying economic sacrifices there had been some progress in reducing the proportion of Irish imports which came from Great Britain (81 per cent in 1931, 50 per cent in 1937), but no parallel success in developing other export markets. Britain, taking 96 per cent of Irish exports in 1931, still took almost 91 per cent in 1937.[9] Thus, although the agreement of 1938 was favourable to Ireland to the extent that Great Britain gave up all claim to further annuity payments under the Land Acts in exchange for a single payment of £10 million,[1] the trade war had not achieved its main objective in that there had been no appreciable weakening of the economic links which bound Ireland to Britain.[2] The underlying structure of Irish agriculture had not been altered. Irish farmers had not gone over to tillage on a large scale, but had instead chosen to sweat it out, living off capital and hoping for a change in government policy. The changing balance of Irish savings account deposits illustrates this clearly:

Fluctuation of savings account deposits (in £ millions)	1931	1932	1933	1934	1935
	+1·2	+1·4	−5·7	−3·8	−0·5

It was estimated that during these years Irish farmers were living on capital and credit up to a total of £15 million per year.[3]

The Anglo-Irish trade agreement of 1938 implied a return to normal conditions, so far as Irish agriculture was concerned, but this was greatly delayed by the outbreak of the Second World War in 1939.

7. O'Sullivan, *Irish Free State*, p. 321.

8. *Commission of Inquiry into Banking, Currency and Credit* (Dublin, Stationery Office, 1938).

9. *Statistical Abstracts for the British Empire, 1937*.

1. *Irish Times Review, 1938*, p. 11.

2. The Coal–Cattle Pact of 1936 between the two countries had been an earlier indication of a desire to return to economic normality and, in particular, to save the Irish cattle trade.

3. Labour party, *Annual Report, 1939*, p. 21.

War, even though it was for Ireland merely an 'emergency', made an increase in crop production quite vital, and the government took emergency powers to compel farmers to till a minimum of 12·5 per cent of their land. The result was that the attempt to prevent the decline of livestock production was postponed until the end of the war, while tillage expanded from 1·5 million acres in 1939 to 2·5 million in 1945.[4] After this date, however, farmers reverted as quickly as possible to their former balance of activities, just as they had done after the tillage boom of the First World War. But the debate continued over the direction which the economy in general, and agriculture in particular, should take, and at least until the 1950s Fianna Fáil remained in theory strong advocates of economic autarchy.

In practice, however, there has developed a broad, if tacit, consensus in Irish politics that Ireland's future prosperity cannot be considered apart from that of the United Kingdom. The wide range of support for entry into the European Economic Community which emerged in 1971–2 is evidence of this.[5] Among the major parties, only the Irish Labour party has opposed Ireland's Common Market entry. Only on the Sinn Féin/IRA fringes of Irish politics is it still argued that Ireland remains the victim of British economic imperialism. Ireland's geographical position has proved to be more powerful than any nationalist economic theory. As early as 1939 the Fianna Fáil minister for agriculture had to admit that the country had no choice when it came to the disposal of its agricultural surplus: 'No market offered an opportunity for that increase . . . except the British market. Anything, therefore, that would tend to impede the fair course of trade between the two countries . . . was a matter of the gravest concern.'[6] The findings of the official Committee of Inquiry on Post-Emergency Policy (the Smiddy Commission) of 1945 represented another step in the direction of a sober compromise on this issue,[7] and the trend continued through the Anglo-Irish trade agreements of 1946 and 1953, which added new safeguards designed to increase the export of Irish beef to Great Britain.[8] The latter agreement even stipulated that Britain would purchase 90 per cent of the cattle on the hoof.[9] Simultaneous German efforts to secure a larger proportion of Irish meat exports were in fact discouraged at this time, on the grounds that Britain was likely to prove a steadier and more convenient trading partner. Thus, twenty years after de Valera first assumed the direction of the country's affairs, economic ties between the two old enemies were so strong that a firm of American

4. Meenan, *Irish Economy*, p. 103.
5. The original decision to join the EEC was taken by Seán Lemass's Fianna Fáil government in 1961, but was rendered nugatory by the French veto on British entry in January 1963.
6. *Round Table*, xxix (1938–9), 377.   7. Meenan, *Irish Economy*, pp. 103–4.
8. *Round Table*, xxxvii (1946–7), 82.   9. *Daily Mail*, 18 July 1953.

experts, called in to analyse the Irish economy, came to the conclusion that the country's dependence on Britain was so strong as to be incompatible with the status of political sovereignty.[1]

Another basic problem, with which successive governments have had only very limited success, has been the inefficiency of Irish agriculture relative to other countries, notably Denmark.[2] The Cumann na nGaedheal regime in the 1920s made numerous efforts to stimulate the quality and the quantity of agricultural output, but neither these nor de Valera's later appeals to national pride made much impact on the farmers' way of life. In the early 1950s the average annual yield of an Irish milch-cow was only 400 gallons, compared with 750 gallons in Denmark.[3] Similarly, the output per landworker was valued at £198 per annum, compared with a figure of £558 for England.[4] Many experts still hold the view that, while Irish agriculture and the Irish economy as a whole cannot be categorized as inefficient, there are large sections of it which are so, and that Ireland as a whole is 'an economy in which inefficiency carries very light penalties'.[5] Whether the reasons for this are to be found in the constraints exercised on itself by a traditional society, in the country's enervating climate, or even in the fundamental character of the people, are questions beyond the scope of this study.

INDUSTRIALIZATION

From the beginning, one of the most important planks in the Fianna Fáil platform was the need to industrialize the country. Why, the party asked, was it necessary to depend on Great Britain for almost all industrial products? Couldn't a large proportion of the imported goods be made in Ireland, thereby improving the balance of trade, bringing new employment, and encouraging general economic independence? De Valera and his ministers, particularly Seán Lemass, who served as Minister for Industry and Commerce for nineteen of the years between 1932 and 1959, devoted considerable energy to attempts to realize such plans. The net output of transportable goods rose from £18·2 million in 1931 to £28·2 million in 1940.[6] In some areas there was remarkable

1. *The Industrial Potentials of Ireland: An Appraisal*, by IBEC Technical Services Corporation (New York, 1952), p. 27.
2. It should be noted, however, that while over-all statistics suggest that Denmark's climate is not very different from that of Ireland, in fact it gets very much more of its sunshine during the vital spring and summer months than does Ireland. The harvesting of cereals is therefore a relatively hazardous business in Ireland. Meenan, *Irish Economy*, p. 89.
3. *Round Table*, xlii (1951–2), 254.
4. *Abstracts of Report of United Nations Commission on the Agricultural Economy of Western Europe*, cited in *Irish Times*, 5 March 1953.
5. Meenan, *Irish Economy*, p. 390.   6. Ibid., p. 132.

success. Shoe imports, for instance, dropped from five million pairs in 1931 to little over a quarter of a million pairs in 1938.[7] Expenditure on the import of clothing dropped during the same period from £5·3 million per year to less than £1 million.[8] Progress in other areas was more disappointing, but on the whole the achievement was considerable: many categories of goods which had previously been imported were now produced at home. By and large the change was achieved through the imposition of protective tariffs and the subsidizing of new domestic industries. As soon as an article was being produced in sufficient quantities in Ireland, the government throttled imports by the imposition of a tariff.

There is no doubt that, politically, the industrialization policy was a tremendous success for Fianna Fáil. It has always been popular, and the businessmen whose prosperity stemmed from it have been good friends of the party. Judged from a strictly economic point of view, however, the achievement seems a more modest one. Many of the industries would have been unable to withstand the force of unimpeded British and other foreign competition. The new industries were for the most part enterprises subsidized by the state, and therefore developed at the expense of the taxpayer, and of the consumer. Since most consumers still earned their living either directly or indirectly from agriculture, it follows that agriculture was in fact subsidizing industrialization.[9] Might it not have been possible to achieve a larger profit by encouraging agriculture as an export industry with this money, and buying industrial goods more cheaply abroad? This argument has been put forward repeatedly by economic experts, and the IBEC study criticized investment in agriculture at the beginning of the 1950s as 'shockingly low'.[1]

Linked with the creation of new industries, however, has been the effort to reduce the level of unemployment, which remained consistently high, though disguised to some extent by emigration. It is pointed out by defenders of the industrialization policy that in the twenty-five years from 1927 to 1952 the number employed in industry rose from 102,000 to 200,000. On the other hand, however, the number engaged in agriculture dropped during the same period by 140,000. The total number of employed persons in fact remained unchanged, while a persistent trickle of emigration continued.[2] Whether the 98,000 people who found work in industry during this period would have emigrated had industry received less government encouragement and agriculture more it is impossible to say. Attempts to answer such questions are,

---

7. *Fianna Fail, 1926–51*, p. 12.   8. *Irish Times Review, 1938.*
9. For a development of this argument, see *Irish Times*, editorial, 21 May 1953.
1. IBEC report, p. 24.
2. *Irish Times*, 18 March 1953; *Round Table*, lxii (1951–2), 254.

almost inevitably, partisan. From the standpoint of the early 1950s, all that could be said with any certainty was that the elimination of visible and invisible unemployment by industrialization had not yet been achieved. Furthermore, Ireland's experience in the Second World War had shown that the lack of coal and other vital raw materials could effectively paralyse her industrial production. Such economic independence as the country possessed was clearly very fragile.

The drawbacks of industrialization have been stressed here because this aspect of economic policy seems to be an especially good example of the primacy of national motives over questions of practical economics. There is no doubt that a nation's feelings of security and self-confidence are bolstered up by the knowledge that it can produce many of its own goods: an important symbol of power and status in the modern world. Industrialization, judged by this criterion alone, and regardless of economic issues, was a necessary aspect of de Valera's policy.

LAISSEZ-FAIRE OR STATE INTERVENTION?

One of the reasons for the success of the Sinn Féin party between 1919 and the treaty in leading a united Irish people through the revolution was that its response to any potentially fissiparous social and economic questions was either to avoid them or to answer them in terms so broad and bland as to be no guide to the real intentions of the politicians. It is probably true that most of the revolutionary leaders were not very interested in such questions, so that when the time came to formulate policies on these issues in the post-independence period, there were very few ideological constraints, save those of the nationalist-democratic framework and the strong position in the community of the Catholic church. There were, on the other hand, examples and constraints of another kind. The intractability of Irish social and economic problems had established a tradition of state intervention and assistance in, especially, the rural economy, during the time of the British administration. Furthermore, there was an entrenched tradition of investing Ireland's meagre capital deposits in Britain, and little industrial or managerial tradition in the country at all, outside small-scale commercial enterprises. For these reasons, the development of collectivist economic organization, or public ownership, 'was never a matter of doctrine or even conscious deliberation in Ireland. It was largely a matter of necessity'.[3]

Even during the economically cautious and conservative years of the Cosgrave administration, the state was obliged to pay more attention to the economy than accorded with traditional *laissez-faire* theory. In 1927 an Electricity Supply Board (ESB) was set up, along with a

3. O. MacDonagh, *Ireland* (Englewood Cliffs, NJ, 1968), p. 123.

large state-sponsored hydro-electric scheme for the Shannon. Soon afterwards a second public board was set up to develop and operate the sugar beet industry.[4] When Fianna Fáil came to power this type of state intervention was expanded more rapidly: the exigencies of the economic war, and the party's greater commitment to the most backward western areas, called for an increase in activity. Between 1932 and 1945 eighteen new bodies were added to the five established under Cumann na nGaedheal.[5]

But public enterprise remained none the less a pragmatic and piecemeal affair, undertaken essentially in response to particular needs. The Labour party, although of course it might hope for electoral benefits from an industrialization policy in the long run, complained bitterly that 'the "public ownership" policy of the Fianna Fáil party in opposition has become the "private enterprise" fetish of the same party in office'.[6] Despite Labour's continual urging, it was not until 1944 that the transport industries were nationalized, and then, as in Britain, the stimulus was the impending bankruptcy of the organizations concerned.[7] The gas industry, curiously enough, remains under private ownership. Fianna Fáil's pragmatic, almost haphazard approach to state-sponsored bodies—the more contentious term 'nationalization' was generally avoided—kept it clear of ideological conflict. Seldom, if ever, did its activities clash with the interests of private enterprise in the way that the British Labour party's did over steel nationalization, for instance. Although state intervention reached a new peak during the Second World War, and was, by and large, maintained and expanded afterwards, Fianna Fáil did not become more radical on social and economic matters during these years, but if anything less so. As Minister for Finance, Seán MacEntee, once regarded as being on the left wing of the party, declared in June 1953 that a reservoir of unemployed was necessary for the smooth running of the national economy.[8] Seán Lemass at the same time made an unequivocal declaration in favour of private enterprise.[9]

Thus although both major Irish parties, especially Fianna Fáil, had moved a long way from the *laissez-faire* approach to social and economic matters, it would be misleading to portray their commitment to state intervention as being in any way indicative of a move towards socialism. Fianna Fáil's conception of the state in the post-war years is better described as paternalistic. Indeed Erskine Childers, as a junior minister,

4. MacDonagh, *Ireland*, p. 123; for a discussion of the establishment of the ESB and of the Shannon scheme, see Meenan, *Irish Economy*, pp. 169–75.

5. Lyons, *Ireland since the Famine*, p. 607.

6. Labour party, *Annual Report, 1932*, p. 51.

7. For the establishment of the Irish transport board, Coras Iompair Éireann (CIE), see *Irish Times Review, 1944*, p. 7.

8. *Irish Times*, 20 June 1953.   9. Ibid., 24 June 1953.

said in 1946 that 'paternalistic care of a community by a civil service acting on instructions from a government elected by the people could alone preserve the fundamental freedom and sanctity of human existence'.[1] The state's function, according to this view, was to exercise a controlling supervision of the economy, to ensure the operation of the free play of forces. It was a view exemplified by the Restrictive Practices Act of 1952, which established a Fair Trade Commission and set out to investigate the operation of such matters as resale price maintenance.

LAND POLICY

One particular aspect of the early Fianna Fáil programme which attracted small farmers had been the pledge to withhold payment of the land annuities from the British government. It was clear that the majority of farmers interpreted this as meaning that they would not have to make any more payments. Such payments indeed weighed increasingly heavily on the smaller farmers when Irish agriculture began to feel the impact of the world economic crisis. As the ownership of the land came to be taken increasingly for granted, so there was an increasing reluctance to make the annual payments, which in most cases still had another thirty to fifty years to run. Arrears became larger and larger.[2] De Valera's intention, however, was not to erase land annuity payments altogether, but simply to retain them in Dublin instead of passing them on to Great Britain. His original idea was to use them for various Irish governmental purposes, especially the reduction of ground rents. In the general election of January 1933 he was forced into a more radical position by the pledge of the main opposition party, Cumann na nGaedheal, that if elected it would stop annuity payments for two years and then restore them at half the original level.[3] In order to prevent this attempt to steal its clothes Fianna Fáil felt obliged, in addition to withholding the payments from London, to reduce by half the amount purchasers would have to pay (without lengthening the repayment period), and to cancel all arrears of more than three years' standing.[4]

The second point in the Fianna Fáil programme which appealed to the poorer sections of rural society was the pledge to speed up land redistribution. The Cosgrave administration had not been idle in the field of land reform, for the 1923 Land Act had continued and com-

1. *Irish Independent*, 2 December 1946.
2. In 1921, arrears were reckoned at less than 0·5 per cent of the annual contribution, whereas in 1933 they stood at over 100 per cent. E. R. Hooker, *Re-adjustments of Agricultural Tenure in Ireland* (Chapel Hill, NC, 1938), p. 210.
3. *Round Table*, xxiii (1933), 297.
4. Hooker, *Agricultural Tenure in Ireland*, p. 112.

pleted the process of land purchase initiated under the British administration, and the sale of tenanted land was now almost completed
throughout the country.[5] But the Land Commission had continued to
demand punctual annuity payments, and had shown itself to be an
active creditor, not hesitating to sue indolent or incompetent purchasers
and dispose of their farms.[6] The Cosgrave administration was thus not
altogether popular in country districts. In addition, landless men in the
countryside were very disappointed that the distribution of the large
grass ranches had been undertaken so cautiously, in accordance with
the principle of voluntary sale through the owner. With the onset of
world economic depression and the ending of open immigration into
the USA in 1928, there was a great intensification of the demand from
unemployed and underemployed farmers' sons for prompt expropriation and distribution of the large ranches.

De Valera had promised that Fianna Fáil would end the clamour
for land. The Land Act of 1933 was to provide the means to do this.
Under it the Land Commission was empowered to expropriate, with
compensation, any property which seemed suitable and to distribute it
among very small farmers and landless men. In future, however, once
these reforms were in operation, annuity payments could be enforced
without the need to resort to legal proceedings. During the period of
Cumann na nGaedheal government, 1923–32, 452,000 acres were dis-
tributed to 24,000 families; under Fianna Fail and subsequent inter-
party rule, 1933–51, 744,000 acres were divided among 57,700 families.[7]
Since the second period was almost twice as long as the first, it does not
appear that Fianna Fáil was noticeably more active in the distribution
of land than its predecessors had been. But the process of land redistribution was not endless, and as it progressed it was naturally the more
difficult cases which remained to be dealt with. If we take another
yardstick, we find that, in its early years at least, the Fianna Fáil
government spent very much more money on land distribution than
had its predecessor: £7·6 million in 1936, compared with £2·7 million
in 1931.[8] In later years there was a predictable falling-off in activity,
and the Land Commission made only cautious use of its increased
powers, preferring instead to work by co-operation and goodwill.

The persistence of 'land hunger' into the post-independence period
was of course symptomatic of rural Ireland's chronic unemployment
problem as much as it was a grievance in itself. It could only be solved
by a general uplifting of the economy and the diversification of employment. Assuaging land hunger with land could be effective in dealing

5. Hooker, *Agricultural Tenure in Ireland*, p. 120.   6. Ibid., p. 107.
7. Information provided privately by the Irish Government Information
Bureau [E.R.].
8. *Commission of Inquiry in Banking, Currency and Credit* (Dublin, Stationery Office,
1938,), p. 102.

with the worst cases of hardship and of exploitation, could provide a limited short-term remedy, and could take the sting out of the agitation. But on its own it could not suceed, simply because a finite amount of land could not support an infinite number of people.

Agricultural production, in fact, did not show any over-all increase during the long period of Fianna Fáil government after 1932, notwithstanding the great increase in the amount spent on farm improvements.[9] The explanation is that, as had been the case in other sectors of the economy, reforming measures were often undertaken with social and political, rather than economic goals in mind. Thus money was invested heavily in the improvement of small farms, even in areas where the poor quality of the soil meant that small increases in yield could be achieved only at great cost. The larger units, with greater potential for expansion, were given little help, and were in fact damaged considerably by the trade war of the 1930s. The division of grass farms into smaller units did not always produce an increase in yield. In the conditions of the 1930s many new men came to grief and sold off their land again, so that as early as 1937 there were fears that a new class of large farmers would come into existence as a result of speculative buying. One American expert formed the impression that a cyclical process was under way, and that land agitation and distribution would inevitably become a major issue again within fifty years.[1] It was even feared that the powers of expropriation given to the Land Commission, in the interests of efficiency, struck directly at the roots of the principle of security of possession, the issue which had originally ignited the land agitation back in the 1880s. But the trend towards conservatism, to be seen in other aspects of Fianna Fáil policy from about 1938 onwards, also came to influence the party's position on the land question. In 1947 the minister for lands admitted that the redistribution policy had gone far enough, if not too far already.[2] After his return to power in the 1950s de Valera announced that future public assistance with the improvement of land would be in strict accordance with economic criteria. Only worthwhile land would be improved, so that the emphasis would shift to different areas and different types of farmers.[3]

SOCIAL POLICY

We have already seen that support for de Valera and his party during the early years of Fianna Fáil spread out from a secure base among the poorer, western section of the population. The party was pledged to

9. Between 1923 and 1932 £1·7 million was spent in this way; for the period 1933–51 the figure was £6·8 million.
1. Hooker, *Agricultural Tenure in Ireland*, p. 117.
2. *Round Table*, xxxvii (1946–7), 162.   3. *Irish Times*, 5 May 1953.

wage an energetic fight against unemployment and increase the involvement of the state in matters of social welfare. Cumann na nGaedheal had never adopted anything other than a conservative attitude on
matters of employment. 'It is no function of government to provide
work for anybody', its Minister for Industry and Commerce had once
declared in the Dáil.[4] Fianna Fáil, especially when it was in opposition,
willingly assumed such responsibilities, and lost no opportunity to
showing its concern for the poor.[5] It was frequently asserted, especially
by its own supporters, that Fianna Fáil was 'Ireland's labour party'.

When the party came to power in 1932 extensive relief measures
were put into operation, and house building in particular was given
priority. Between 1932 and 1942, 132,000 houses were built or restored
in Ireland, probably the greatest achievement of de Valera's early
ministries.[6] The new government introduced cuts in the salaries of civil
servants ranging from 2·5 per cent to 20 per cent.[7] Unemployment
insurance was extended to include a wider section of the population,
and in 1933 a system of supplementary support was introduced for
those groups, including small western farmers, which were still excluded from the insurance scheme. At the same time provision for the
aged, blind, infirm, widows, and orphans was increased.[8] In 1936 a
number of state regulations regarding working conditions were introduced, giving workers legal security on matters which the trade unions
had previously fought case by case.[9] A welfare benefit of a rather
special kind came in with the decision to grant pensions to IRA veterans
who had fought on the Republican side in the civil war, pro-treaty
veterans having been catered for by the Cosgrave administration. As
well as restoring what many argued was simply a just balance to the
question of military pensions, this move had, and was intended to have,
a soothing effect on the militancy of those who retained their old
allegiance to extra-parliamentary politics.

It is somewhat ironic that the development of social services in Ireland has remained consistently one or two steps behind developments
in Britain. Nearly all Irish socialists believed in the early part of the
century that Ireland could only hope to achieve a major social advance
by separating herself completely from Britain. As it has turned out she
would have obtained a large measure of moderate socialist and welfare
legislation much more quickly by remaining within the United Kingdom. The models for most social advances made under de Valera's

4. *Dáil Debates*, ix, col. 585.
5. See, for example, the party's newspaper, *Irish Press*, 18 January 1933.
6. *Fianna Fáil, 1926–51*, p. 18; the amount spent on relief works rose from £156,000
in 1932 to £1 million in 1933.
7. *Round Table*, xxii (1932), 764.
8. *Department of Social Welfare, 1st report, 1947–9*, pp. 9, 16, and 24.
9. *Irish Times Review*, 1935, p. 19.

leadership were changes already under way in Britain: the Social Welfare Act of 1948 and the Health Act of 1953 were as much British-inspired as the reforms of the 1930s had been. Where Ireland did *not* change during this period, she retained such institutions, traditions, and practices as she had inherited from the British regime in 1922: Irish legal practice in the 1950s was closer to that of Britain in 1920 than Britain in 1950, while many people even today would still describe the Irish civil service as 'Victorian'.

The industrial strike was a weapon well established in Ireland during the last years of British rule. Although its use for political purposes withered away after 1922, it remained a popular method of wage-bargaining. The aim of Fianna Fáil in this field, under de Valera's leadership, was to extend the machinery of arbitration as far as possible. During the period of war emergency this policy was developed in such a way as to aggravate industrial relations. Under the Wages Standstill Order of 1941 the government effectively prohibited wage increases and the right to strike for the duration of the emergency. After April 1942, some wage increases were permitted, but they were strictly limited in scope and related only to future increases in the cost of living. It was estimated that during the entire period of war emergency the cost-of-living index rose by two-thirds while the wages of industrial workers rose by one-third.[1] From this unpopular work of the Wages Advisory Tribunal there developed the Industrial Relations Act of 1946 and a permanent Labour Court which soon established a more favourable public image. It was an independent body, made up equally of representatives of employers' associations and trade unions, and could make only non-binding recommendations for the settlement of disputes. But it won the confidence of both sides of industry, and stood to the credit of Fianna Fáil as a constructive contribution to the settlement of social conflicts.[2] The Act gave at least some substance to the claim of Fianna Fáil to be a party which catered for the interests of the urban workers as well as those of the commercial and rural classes.

There was criticism of Fianna Fail's social policy, however, and it came from two sides, just as criticism of its national policy had done. The Labour party and the TUC could not be expected, of course, to acquiesce in Fianna Fáil's over-all policy, but there was more than party politics in their complaints that the cost of living was rising faster even than in the United Kingdom. This was the outcome, not only of

1. D. Nevin, 'Industry and labour', in Nowlan and Williams (eds), *Ireland in the War Years and After*, pp. 96–97; *Statistical Abstract, 1947–8*, tables 241 and 258.
2. For a discussion of the act, see an article by the first chairman of the court, R. J. P. Mortished, in F. C. King (ed.), *Public Administration in Ireland*, vol. ii (Dublin, 1949); between 1949 and 1959, 81 per cent of the court's recommendations, covering 85 per cent of the workers involved, were accepted. See O'Connor Lysaght, *The Republic of Ireland*, p. 160.

wartime emergency conditions, but also of a problem which had remained chronic throughout the 1930s, and was badly aggravated by
the trade war with Britain. The relationship between wages and production had grown worse, and average earnings in 1937 were approximately 9 per cent below the 1931 level.[3] Against this it might be maintained that there were compensating advantages in the form of extended
and improved social services, although the unemployment problem
was by no means solved during the long period of de Valera's premier-
ship, swinging between 50,000 and 100,000. Even in 1953 it stood for a
while at 90,000.[4]

Fianna Fáil's long-term record was attacked with equal vigour from
the standpoint of *laissez-faire* economics. The expansion of social services
of course necessitated a sharply progressive scale of direct taxation,
which was far more selective in its application than in the United
Kingdom. Because of the relative poverty of the country only one wage-
earner in seven was subject to income tax.[5] A number of public inquiries over the years expressed doubts as to whether such social services
could be justified in a country at Ireland's stage of development. The
Banking Commission of 1938 for instance was greatly alarmed at the
violent rise in the national debt, from £20·9 million in 1926 to £71·1
million in 1936, while the government-commissioned IBEC report of
1952 argued that the amount of investment in public housing was too
great in relation to over-all national production.[6] It is difficult to
evaluate such matters with the impartiality claimed by the economist,
for political questions are inextricably linked with economics. What is
clear is that throughout the decades of Fianna Fáil dominance under
the leadership of de Valera, Ireland found it far more difficult than any
of her neighbours to maintain the high level of social services which the
inhabitants of the countries of northern Europe had come to expect.

OPPOSITION: THE BLUESHIRT PHASE

Cumann na nGaedheal's programme of January 1933, pledging the
party to break off the tariff war at once, win back the British market,
and negotiate a new deal over land annuities, made little impact on the
position of the new government, which returned to the Dáil fully independent of other parties for the first time, with an over-all majority of
one seat. The tariff war went almost unnoticed by many people, who
were more aware of the increased provision for the old, free milk for
children, and, ironically, lower food prices, as the interruption of ex-

3. Labour party, *Annual Report, 1937*, p. 39.   4. *Irish Times*, 3 May 1953.
   5. In Great Britain the figure was three in every five; in Northern Ireland, one
in three. *Irish Times*, 29 July 1953.
   6. *Commission of Inquiry into Banking, Currency and Credit, 1938*, p. 104; IBEC report,
1952, p. 24.

ports produced a surplus on the home market.[7] De Valera's appeal at this election was essentially to the masses and against the classes. His utopia, a frugal Christian Ireland in which there would be neither great wealth nor poverty, which would be economically independent and genuinely Gaelic in its culture, came nearer to credibility during these early years of power than at any other time during his career. It won the adherence of almost 50 per cent of the electorate, compared to the 30 per cent who voted for Cumann na nGaedheal.

The Cumann na nGaedheal image, judged by the standards of a party which had never previously been out of power, seemed irretrievably tarnished. The development of a new 'farmers and ratepayers' Centre party was eating into its support in the eastern and midland districts, and the party leadership in general was aware of a need for new ideas and improved organization. At the same time Fianna Fáil's two victories had induced in the IRA a sort of euphoric militancy, which showed itself primarily in determined and highly effective efforts to deny free speech to Cumann na nGaedheal politicians. Just as in 1932 the new Fianna Fáil government had feared that the old regime would not give up power merely at the request of the electorate, so the new opposition feared that its rights would receive scant respect now that its old enemies were in power.

It is against this background of political bankruptcy, coupled with a fear of reprisals from the new regime, that the emergency of the Blueshirt movement must be seen. There is no doubt that some leading members of what must still be called, revealingly, the pro-treaty side, believed that they had found the necessary new ideas, and more important an effective political *style*, in the continental fascist movements. One such movement had cemented cordial church–state relationships for the first time in the history of modern Italy, while another was at that very moment sweeping dramatically to power in Germany. The new swagger of the old anti-treaty IRA, reinforced by the leadership of Marxists who were reputedly skilled in more sophisticated revolutionary theory, was for many Cumann na nGaedheal supporters ample justification for the street violence which seemed inseparable from fascist movements everywhere.

The Blueshirt movement had its origins in the Army Comrades Association (ACA), founded in 1931.[8] The association also claimed as a further goal the reunification of Ireland—but what national organization did not give lip-service to this aim? Following the first Fianna Fáil victory of 1932 the ACA opened its membership list to the general public; almost immediately its numbers rose to 30,000, and at its height

7. *Round Table*, xxiii (1933), 302.
8. For a full and dispassionate account of the Blueshirt phenomenon, see M. Manning, *The Blueshirts* (Dublin, 1971).

in 1933 it claimed a membership of 100,000. When de Valera relieved the Cumann na nGaedheal appointee, General Eoin O'Duffy, of his post as Commissioner of Police early in 1933, the new movement received both a martyr and a leader. It was O'Duffy who added an anti-communist flavour to the original anti-Republican character of the ACA, and soon he carried the continental style further by changing its name to the National Guard, and instituting the fascist salute and the wearing of a blue shirt as a uniform.

When the Cumann na nGaedheal newspaper, the *United Irishman*, began to publish a series of anonymous articles in support of Mussolini's policies and O'Duffy's activities, it became clear that opposition politicians had recognized the potential of the new movement.[9] O'Duffy at first would have none of it. 'Party politics has served its period of usefulness', he declared, emulating his continental models.[1] Thus, when he decided to inaugurate his new organization with a massive demonstration in Dublin in honour of the dead pro-treaty heroes, Collins, Griffith, and O'Higgins, he found that the government and public opinion were inclined to take his fascist leanings seriously. Whether or not he intended any analogy with Mussolini's 'March on Rome', it was assumed that he did. The 'march' was banned, and O'Duffy lamely backed down. It has been suggested that this set-back caused him to take a more lenient view of the old-style politicians of the parliamentary right.[2] At all events he seems to have rapidly revised his opinion of Cosgrave and his colleagues, and in September 1933 a new political party, subsuming the Blueshirts, was announced.[3] Fine Gael, or the United Ireland party, as it was known at first, had O'Duffy as its leader in the country, and the Blueshirts behind it on the platforms, but at the parliamentary level it was essentially a union between the old Cumann na nGaedheal and the small Centre party. Cosgrave remained parliamentary leader, and continued very much as before, showing little enthusiasm either for Blueshirt 'vigour' or the theories of the corporative state. It was easier for the Centre party group to merge with him in this way, under the cloak of O'Duffy's charisma, rather than have to accept openly the leadership of a somewhat discredited politician.[4]

In the long run it became clear that the headstrong and politically inept O'Duffy had been used, albeit ineffectually, by the party politicians he affected to despise. But for a while in the autumn of 1933 it

9. Manning, *Blueshirts*, p. 57.
1. D. Thornley, 'The Blueshirts', in F. MacManus (ed.), *The Years of the Great Test, 1926–39* (Cork, 1967) p. 46.
2. Ibid., p. 47.
3. Meanwhile, to avoid government proscription, the National Guard had been renamed the League of Youth, although the blue shirts were retained.
4. Thornley, 'The Blueshirts', p. 48.

had seemed possible that the opposite was happening, that Fine Gael was about to become a vehicle for fascist doctrines. The cultivation of the League of Youth as the battle squad of Fine Gael was very much in the fascist tradition. Although many opposition politicians stood quite aloof from the new rhetoric, there was an influential body of opinion which held that the Dáil was not suitable for modern government. 'Looking at Italy, they saw that there was much good in the fascist system as against the present rotten system in this country', declared Ernest Blythe, the former Cosgrave minister who, more than any other, embraced Blueshirtism with enthusiasm.[5] It was 'rotten', one suspects, only to the extent that a rival party had gained political power.

There was, too, a body of opinion, influenced as much by Pius XI as by Mussolini, and including O'Duffy himself, which seriously advocated the development of the state along 'corporative' lines, with political representation according to and within occupational groups, instead of geographical parliamentary representation.[6] In such a system every worker would belong to a state trade union and there would be no strikes or lock-outs.[7] 'Voluntary disciplined public service on the part of all our citizens', declared O'Duffy, 'must be made a permanent feature of our public life.'[8] But he was a volatile public figure, and could easily be diverted from corporative theorizing into the kind of violent outbursts which had not been heard in Irish politics since the civil war. 'We must make life intolerable for those who will not yield to our demands', he declared.[9] Such language, while it may have been responsible for attracting many of the activists to the Blueshirt banner, made things difficult for Fine Gael politicians who were trying to construct a more respectable image, with a sharp eye on the attitude of the Catholic church, and it helped to build up their feeling of exasperation with him.

It is difficult to assess the seriousness of Fine Gael's new ideological front. It was a political fashion adopted from Europe which rapidly proved ineffectual, on account of O'Duffy's personal shortcomings as a political figure. Accordingly it withered away, leaving little permanent impression on the political system. Had O'Duffy been more able, it is possible that the roots would have sunk deeper. There was certainly a strong element of class antagonism in the Blueshirt clashes with Fianna Fáil and the IRA.

In part a revival of the bitterness of the civil war period, Blueshirtism was also an attempt on the part of those who had previously

5. Speech on 6 May 1934, cited in Labour party, *Annual Report, 1934*, p. 9.
6. Manning, *Blueshirts*, pp. 214–16.
7. E. O'Duffy, *The Labour Policy of Fine Gael* (Dublin, 1934), p. 7.
8. E. O'Duffy, *An Outline of the Political Policy of Fine Gael* (Dublin, 1934), p. 16.
9. Speech on 11 April 1934, cited in Labour party, *Annual Report, 1934*, p. 10.

supported the state to resist the social revolution thought to be at hand after de Valera's election. The Blueshirt ranks were full of larger farmers and their sons, who had to bear the full burden of the tariff war, and as early as 1932 the movement had condemned 'the chauvinistic policy of the government'.[1] Blueshirt agitation was especially strong in the south, where annuity payments were withheld from Dublin on a large scale, and there was particularly intense feeling in Co. Cork, which had so strikingly turned away from de Valera and the republican movement in 1922–3. The Catholic Bishop of Cork, who had opposed the IRA even in 1920, lamented that the methods of the land war had re-appeared.[2] This time, ironically, it was a republican government which used force to collect its dues, while resistance came mainly from the larger farmers. Supporters of the Labour party alleged that the great weight of the business class was also solidly behind the Blueshirt movement, though there seems to be little evidence for this.[3] Probably, in places like Cork city at least, there was as much Blueshirtism among workers as among employers. But it was the farming class which provided the real spearhead of the movement.

The government was not slow to counter the attack from the right with legislation banning all party uniforms and the carrying of weapons, and specifically banning the National Guard altogether. At the time it seemed that the government had treated the Blueshirts far more harshly than the IRA, which to many appeared equally guilty of violence and disorder.[4] In the long run, however, the special legislation (which included the re-establishment of the old Military Tribunal, abolished in 1932) brought in to deal with the challenge from the right was brought forcefully into play against the Republican left also. The Labour party, of course, was also more sensitive towards fascist tendencies than towards communist ones. The 'fascist danger' formed the central topic at the party conference for three years running, from 1933 to 1935. But a considerable section of the Catholic church sympathized with Fine Gael, even during its Blueshirt period, regarding it as a bastion against the twin dangers to the faith of radical nationalism and socialism. Had the Blueshirt phenomenon continued for a few more years, it might have been interesting to note whether the anti-Christian features of German National Socialism would have been of more concern to the clergy than the apparently friendly relations with the Pope enjoyed by Mussolini.

Blueshirtism was in fact a very brief interlude in Irish history, and left surprisingly little mark. It petered out gradually in 1936, as O'Duffy

1. *Round Table*, xxiii (1933), 122.
2. Statement of 5 June 1935, cited in *Round Table*, xxv (1934–5), 780.
3. Labour party, *Annual Report, 1934*, p. 66.
4. In 1934, by far the most disturbed year, the Military Tribunal convicted 349 Blueshirts and 102 IRA men. T. P. Coogan, *The IRA* (London, 1970), p. 104.

led about 2,000 followers to Spain to fight for Franco, while the IRA provided some 700 volunteers for the other side.[5] There is a danger in analysing Blueshirtism in terms of its own rhetoric, for the upheavals of 1933–4 represented not 'the death-agonies of a Gaelic Weimar', but rather 'the nemesis of civil war'.[6] The emotions and the bitterness were not really those of Europe in the 1930s but of Ireland in 1922. De Valera was hated in Blueshirt circles not as the Irish Kerensky so much as the old villain of the civil war. The style and ideology of Blueshirtism were, however, unmistakably continental. There was nothing originally Irish about them, except very indirectly in so far as the corporative theories had some papal sanction. This was the reason why the movement left so slight a mark. Strong national feeling, which provided most of the dynamism in German and Italian fascism, was in Ireland the preserve of the other side, of Fianna Fáil and the IRA. Conservative elements, which on the continent seemed mesmerized by the spell of the dictators, in Ireland soon grew tired of the 'generally destructive and hysterical leadership' of General O'Duffy, who was forced out of Fine Gael after a bare year as party leader.[7] Within a year Fine Gael was much the same party, with much the same leaders —reinforced by James Dillon and Frank MacDermott from the Centre party—as Cumann na nGaedheal had been.[8]

It is worth dwelling for a moment on the parallels and differences between developments in Ireland and Germany during this period. In both countries political conflict between 1921 and 1932 centred on a treaty which appeared to many to stand in the way of a full and just realization of national aspirations. In both countries the moderate parties had signed the treaty and later tried to alter it by mutual agreement, while a national opposition, more or less extra-parliamentary, steadily won the support of the electorate for a programme of unilateral renunciation. The coupling of this nationalistic pressure with a radical social programme proved in both instances to be a stronger force than either pure socialism or old-style liberalism. The ultimate victory of the nationalist opposition was, in Ireland as in Germany, accelerated by the consequences of the world economic depression after 1929. The decisive difference between Hitler's NSDAP and de Valera's Fianna Fáil was the absence of any strong Nazi ideology in the character of Fianna Fáil, though it was not entirely lacking in either the Marxist or non-Marxist wings of the IRA. Fianna Fail, after 1927, adhered

5. These are the figures given in *Round Table*, xxvii (1936–7), 365. Manning (*Blueshirts*, p. 205), probably a more reliable source, suggests that only 700 Blueshirts actually reached Spain.

6. Lyons, *Ireland since the Famine*, p. 531.

7. The most forceful condemnation of O'Duffy from within the party came from Professor James Hogan. See *Cork Examiner*, 22 September 1934.

8. Thornley, 'The Blueshirts', p. 42.

faithfully to the institutions of parliamentary democracy, and any hint of fascism came from the other side.

There are several reasons for the remarkably sturdy growth of democracy in Ireland, in face of what, in the early 1920s, appeared very unpromising conditions. In the first place, despite the intensity of feeling with which the Irish revolutionary generation disliked Britain, British parliamentary and civil service traditions were very deeply implanted in Ireland's experience. This democratic tradition was reinforced by the influence of Irish-America. Second, and more important, the establishment of Dáil Eireann in Dublin was the fruit and symbol of a glorious struggle for liberty. It was not a parliament imposed by the treaty, an instrument of national subjection, as many Germans held Weimar to be. Finally, because of its small size and isolated situation, the Irish nation was not susceptible to the urge to dominate international politics, which would have necessitated the establishment of an authoritarian regime. In Ireland it was possible for de Valera, notwithstanding his long background as a revolutionary leader, and even though he remained an object of suspicion and hatred to many of his countrymen, to play a central role in the development of the country as a democratic state.

FIANNA FAIL MOVES TO THE RIGHT

During the first generation after independence and even later, the majority of Irish people cast their votes in general elections for or against the treaty of 1921. The belief continued that the most important thing worth knowing about a politician was which side his family took in the civil war. Others have argued that this continuing bitterness about the past was not only pointless but seriously damaging so far as Ireland's present and future were concerned. As late as October 1952 the President of the Republic, Seán T. O'Kelly, appealed to both Fine Gael and Fianna Fáil to forget old hatreds and re-establish the Sinn Féin unity of 1919. Then, he maintained, the spirit and determination of pre-treaty days would be revived, and the lasting problems of partition and continuing emigration would easily be solved.[9]

Irish party politics are certainly incomprehensible without a knowledge of the events of 1916–23: in political speeches the conjuring up of the 'four glorious years' and the 'tragic era' have performed an important function, and friendships and enmities of those days have without doubt influenced political allegiances and opinions. Most important, it is by no means clear that Ireland would have been able to construct a viable party system without the civil war split to serve as a basis, and it is no clearer how the ending of that ongoing conflict could have made any

9. *Cork Examiner*, 13 October 1952.

impact on the problems of partition and emigration in the way that O'Kelly suggested. Furthermore, although the civil war issue may have remained the factor conditioning political allegiance, so many new issues have inevitably arisen which could not be decided by reference to such allegiances that we must look beyond them to the important changes that have taken place in Irish politics since independence.

The greatest of these changes is the shift which has taken place in the character of support for Fianna Fáil since the early days. In 1938 the trade war with Britain ended by agreement. Britain recognized Ireland's new status, as laid down in the Constitution of 1937 and the External Relations Act, and evacuated her naval bases in Free State territory. In the same year the Commission for the examination of Banking, Currency, and Credit strongly criticized the economic policy of the government from the point of view of traditional economics. The government did not reject the report.[1] All these things were indications that de Valera's period of *sturm und drang* was coming to an end, and that henceforward he and his party would adopt more cautious policies in the hope of establishing a secure hold on the middle ground in politics. Opposition parties did their best to keep his controversial past in the public mind, alleging in 1938 that during his period in office annual exports had dropped by over £13 million, the income of farmers by a total of £134 million, and the wages of farm labourers by £9 million, at a time when taxes had been increased by £21 million.[2] Nevertheless, de Valera's 1938 agreement with Britain appeared to the electorate to be a more likely way of reversing this trend than did the mere election of an alternative government.

On the national question also, de Valera began to assume a more moderate stance, declaring himself to be satisfied with Ireland's national status under the External Relations Act, with the exception of the Ulster irredenta—for the sake of which, he made quite clear, he was not prepared to precipitate another crisis in Anglo-Irish relations. He had proved himself in six years of office a strong leader, who had not only kept the IRA in check as firmly as the Cosgrave administration had ever done, but who had also brought credit to Ireland abroad by his work at the League of Nations, and managed to maintain and develop the framework of constitutional politics at home. His administration had belied the fears which once underpinned the Blueshirt movement, and had proved to be an eminently 'responsible' government. He had restored good Anglo-Irish relations, more or less on his own terms, and shown himself to be more independent of the Catholic church than Cumann na nGaedheal had been, while avoiding any possible suggestion of anti-clericalism. Furthermore, the success of the Fianna Fáil social programme had, by 1938, obliged the Labour party to raise its demands

1. *Round Table*, xxix (1938–9), 372.   2. Ibid. xxviii (1937–8), 739.

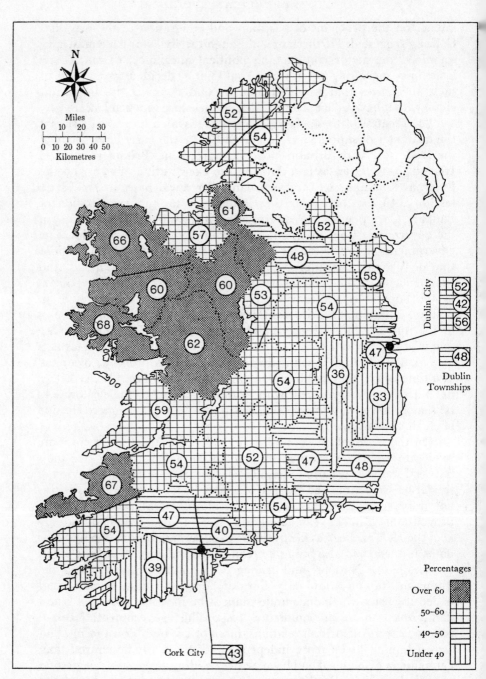

29. FIRST-PREFERENCE VOTES FOR FIANNA FAIL CANDIDATES, 1938

(136)

for social change to the extent that many of the more conservative elements in Irish society which might more naturally have remained attached to Fine Gael, came to feel that only de Valera had sufficient popular appeal to resist Labour's electoral challenge.

De Valera's overwhelming electoral victory in 1938—the only time since the foundation of the state that any party has won an over-all majority of votes cast—was almost certainly produced by an increase in the conservative vote.[3] A comparison of the general elections of 1933 and 1938 (maps 28 and 29) shows that the expansion of support in Fianna Fáil's western strongholds had come to a halt, and indeed in Clare and Kerry that there had been something of a falling-off. In 1937 the party had lost some support to Labour and independents. The increase in the proportion of Fianna Fáil's support in 1938 which came from counties east of the Shannon (Dublin, Louth, Leix, Offaly, Wexford) must be evaluated in conjunction with the social and economic data discussed earlier in Chapter Two (pp. 38–62). It indicates a movement away from dependence on radical nationalism towards the conservative centre of Irish politics, and it was reflected in the balance of parties in the Dáil. With its outright majority, Fianna Fáil was able to throw off the last shreds of the tacit alliance with the Labour party which had begun when the two parties were in opposition together in the late 1920s.

By 1943 Labour felt so confident that Fianna Fáil was no longer a party chasing the radical vote that it made its long-delayed bid to re-enter parliamentary politics on a major scale by running seventy-one candidates, forty more than it had ever run since the entry of Fianna Fáil into constitutional politics in 1927, and increasing its number of seats from nine to seventeen. When, in future, Fianna Fáil required the support of other deputies to pass its measures this came not from Labour but from independent candidates, some of whom owed their election to the vestigial unionist vote in the border counties.[4]

On the radical flank, de Valera's relationship with his former comrades-in-arms in the IRA grew steadily more strained after Fianna Fáil assumed office, until in 1936 the IRA was declared an illegal organization in the Free State. It continued to exist, of course, and in January 1939 its leaders, after calling vainly on the British government to withdraw all troops from Northern Ireland, began a widespread bombing campaign in England and in Ulster.[5] After the outbreak of war the IRA leadership inevitably began to work for a rising in the north, in accordance with the traditional Fenian doctrine that 'England's

3. There is a useful summary of Irish electoral statistics in B. Chubb, *The Government and Politics of Ireland* (London, 1970), pp. 331–6.
4. For example, William Sheldon, a Protestant who sat as an independent deputy for Donegal, and voted with the Fianna Fáil government during the winter of 1952–3.
5. For the text of the ultimatum see Coogan, *IRA*, pp. 164–5.

difficulty is Ireland's opportunity', and de Valera was obliged to produce energetic counter-measures in order to avoid endangering Ireland's neutral status. An internment camp was set up at the Curragh, Co. Kildare, which housed several hundred men for the period of the war emergency.[6] Old enemies in Fianna Fáil and Fine Gael now pulled together, and when the government admitted in the Dáil that measures were necessary similar to the controversial special legislation brought in by the Cosgrave administration in 1931, a leading member of the opposition, James Dillon, shouted out 'we have now arrived on common ground'.[7] On 6 September 1940 the first IRA men convicted of murder since Fianna Fáil had come to power were executed. [8]

Where Fianna Fail's electoral support has declined from its 1938 peak, the loss has occurred among those sections of the population from which it drew its original impetus. A comparison of the elections of 1932 and 1951 (maps 30, 31) shows that the decline occurred predominantly in the west of Ireland, in Counties Kerry, Galway, Mayo, Roscommon, Leitrim, and Sligo. The gains which more or less exactly compensated for these losses came without exception in those areas which during the 1920s had shown most resistance to de Valera's electoral appeal: Cork city and county, Dublin and the 'Pale', and Donegal. The 1957 general election (map 32) showed that Fianna Fáil's following in the east was relatively even greater, County Dublin for instance giving 62 per cent of its votes to the party, compared to a mere 29 per cent in 1932. A final comparison of the results of June 1927 (map 25) with those of 1957 demonstrates the almost complete reversal in the geographical distribution of Fianna Fáil votes.

These changes were closely related to the political achievements and failures of the party during its long periods of office. Fianna Fáil under de Valera was a party of considerable achievement, but the relationship between those achievements and its original aims is not particularly close. We have seen again and again how the attempt to 'undo the conquest', as set out in the Fianna Fáil programme of 1926, was set back by harsh realities. The unity of Ireland was not achieved, and indeed the two parts of the country moved, if anything, further apart. In spite of all the efforts and expense, the Irish language, the restoration of which had been the second point in the programme, was revived to so small an extent that the proceedings at Fianna Fail conferences, not to mention those of the Dáil, had for the most part to take place in English. The number of people for whom Irish remained the language of everyday life decreased by 10 per cent between 1936 and 1946.[9] Ireland's

6. The highest total of internees, in 1943, was 653. *Irish Times Review, 1943*, p. 20.
7. Ibid., *1940*, p. 37.
8. Coogan, *IRA*, p. 194. The two men had been convicted by a military court of shooting a Dublin police detective.
9. *Sunday Press*, 26 April 1953.

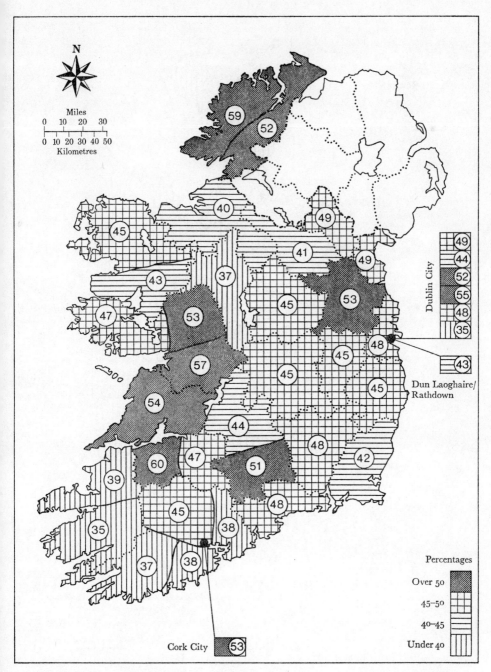

30. FIRST-PREFERENCE VOTES FOR FIANNA FAIL CANDIDATES,
1951

(139)

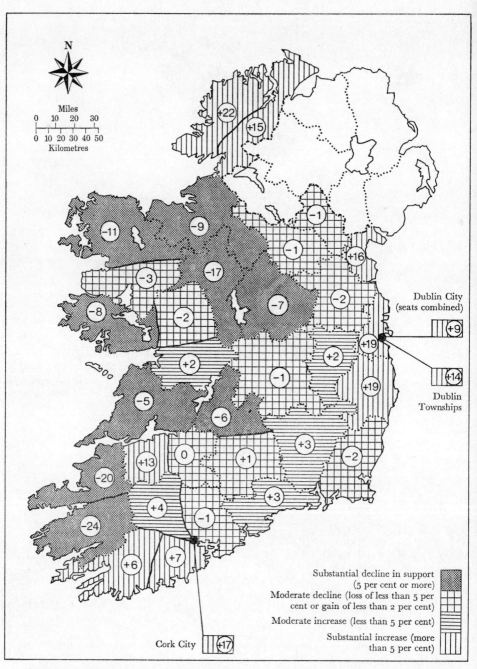

31. A COMPARISON OF FIANNA FAIL SUPPORT IN 1932 AND 1951

The figures indicate the percentage increase or decrease in first-preference votes in the 1951 General Election compared with that of 1932. As the party's over-all share of the vote was 1·9 per cent higher in the later election, increases of less than 2 per cent are shaded as a moderate decline.

(140)

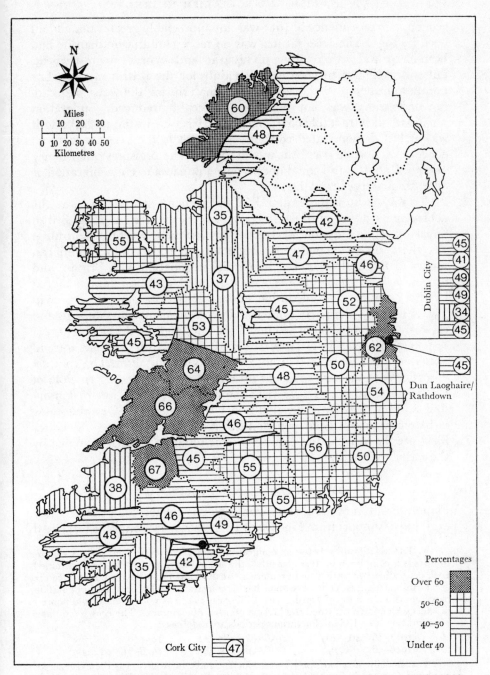

32. FIRST-PREFERENCE VOTES FOR FIANNA FAIL CANDIDATES, 1957

economic independence in 1951 was not appreciably greater than it had been in 1931. The Irish farmer was no more enthusiastic than he had been in 1914 about ploughing up his grasslands in order to grow wheat, but still preferred to keep cattle, mainly for the British market. The number of unemployed, though lower than during the worst period of the depression, was not otherwise noticeably reduced. Emigration remained an intractable characteristic of Irish life in the 1950s,[1] and it was at last demonstrated conclusively, if not to the satisfaction of all concerned, that land reform was limited by the pressures of efficiency and profitability, and could not become a panacea to end emigration or even to preserve rural life.

To the credit of the Fianna Fáil governments of 1932–48 stand the achievement of practical sovereignty, and the evacuation of the British naval bases, so essential for Ireland's subsequent wartime neutrality. Yet these achievements were won not by the intractable republican tactics of the trade war, but by cordial negotiation with Britain, and indeed were a logical outcome of the expanded dominion status achieved by the Cosgrave administration under the Statute of Westminster in 1931.[2] Equally, the party's other main achievements—the difficult and expensive encouragement of home industries and the development of a system of social services—were very much in line with the general trend of materialist western society towards welfare capitalism. The contrast with de Valera's early concept of a state guided by the principle of Gaelic frugality is clear. By 1948 the once semi-revolutionary Fianna Fáil could appeal for re-election under the slogan 'The Dev you know is better than the devil you don't'.[3] No short formula could better illustrate the conservative character which Fianna Fáil had assumed by the end of the 1940s.

OPPOSITION AND COALITION

Fianna Fáil's new appeal to conservative electors caused a steady draining of support from Fine Gael. In the 1937 election, Fine Gael used

1. The relationship between emigration and poverty or lack of job opportunities is a complex one. It is clear that the boom conditions of the 1960s stemmed Irish peacetime emigration to a greater extent than any other development since the great famine. Yet, as T. W. Freeman has demonstrated in his studies of population movement in the west of Ireland (see Bibliography), it is not generally the poorest districts which have provided the highest number of emigrants. The census estimates of emigration from Ireland for various periods are as follows:

1911–26	404,029	1936–46	187,111	1951–6	196,763
1926–36	166,751	1946–51	119,568	1956–61	212,003

2. Ironically, a second prerequisite for Ireland's neutrality was the existence of partition. Great Britain could only afford to respect the neutrality of the twenty-six counties because she had sufficient bases in the six counties to satisfy her most urgent needs. See T. D. Williams, 'Neutrality', *Irish Press*, 17 July 1953.

3. *Round Table*, xxxviii (1947–8), 700.

the capital it had made out of its opposition to the trade war, and the partisan enthusiasms developed during its Blueshirt phase, to increase its share of the poll from 30 to 35 per cent. It probably also gained some advantage from its opposition to the new constitution, which was submitted to a referendum on the same day as the election. But after this the party went into a steep decline, from which it did not begin to emerge until the mid 1950s. Ironically, its electoral support reached an all-time low of 19·8 per cent of the total poll in the 1948 election, when it returned to power as the leading member of the inter-party government which at last put Fianna Fáil out of office. During this same period also, the number of electors voting for neither of the old civil war factions increased from 14·8 per cent in 1938 to 38·3 per cent in 1948.

After the establishment of the new constitution in 1937, republican in all but name, the old issue of the treaty versus the republic no longer merited much serious discussion, and as Fianna Fáil moved into the centre at the same time, the vital differences between the programmes of the two main parties became less obvious. Certain basic features still remained, however. Fine Gael continued to lay more stress on the requirements of agriculture, by which it tended to mean the requirements of the medium and larger farmers. It was this class which stood to benefit most from maintaining strong economic links with Britain, which Fine Gael advocated. The party was unenthusiastic about extending the welfare services, and in favour of strict limitations on state intervention, in opposition to the more paternalistic style cultivated by Fianna Fáil. Fine Gael's over-all image was that of a party of modified classical liberalism pillorying the swollen bureaucracy which it portrayed as the product of Fianna Fáil's over-disciplined and stupid parliamentary majority.[4]

This was Fine Gael's policy during its years of opposition, down to 1948. But the policies it developed during the period of inter-party government, 1948–51, were completely at variance with earlier ideas on a number of major issues. In particular, of course, the party had always stressed the connection with the British Commonwealth, and had not modified that position even during the 1948 election campaign.[5] It came as all the more of a surprise, therefore, when the new Taoiseach,[6] John A. Costello, announced that his government intended to repeal the External Relations Act and take Ireland out of the Commonwealth.[7] In its social and agricultural policies also, the new government proved

4. For an exposition of this point of view see *Irish Independent*, 2 December 1946.
5. The then party leader, General Richard Mulcahy, had said in January 1944 that Fine Gael 'stood unequivocally for membership of the British Commonwealth', *Round Table*, xxxix (1948–9), 151.
6. 'Taoiseach' has since 1937 been the formal title of the Irish prime minister.
7. See above, p. 110.

to be more adventurous than Fianna Fáil had been during its last administration. The Social Welfare Act of 1948 was a consolidation and extension of all earlier social legislation, while under the dynamic direction of Dr Noel Browne a vigorous campaign was started which at last got the better of the great Irish scourge of tuberculosis. In agriculture, a new trade agreement with Britain obtained more favourable terms for Irish farm produce, while a land rehabilitation project was set underway which, in the view of at least one economist, was the best news 'for people emotionally involved in the west of Ireland . . . since the activities of the Congested Districts Board'. [8]

Since its embarrassment over the Blueshirt episode, Fine Gael had fought very shy of innovation. These sudden changes with which it celebrated its first period in office took the wind out of Fianna Fáil and ended the allegations that Fine Gael was insufficiently aware of national and social needs. The new policies were not simply manufactured out of thin air or the minds of civil servants, however, but were to a considerable extent concessions on the part of Fine Gael to the more radical junior partners in the inter-party coalition: the Labour party, National Labour, Clann na Talmhan, and Clann na Poblachta. When Fine Gael returned to opposition in 1951, it became apparent that its new image had been largely transitory, and could not be maintained independently by its own leaders. At the party conference of 1953 it was declared that the Fine Gael party stood emphatically for keeping political influence and government interference out of industrial work. It stood for the profit motive in agriculture and industry for those who invested their savings therein as well as for those who were personally employed. [9] But throughout these changes of policy the party's share of the vote steadily increased from its rock-bottom 19·8 per cent in 1948 to 26 per cent in 1951 and 32 per cent in 1954, indicating the extent to which the electorate was coming to recognize the party once more as the alternative government to Fianna Fáil. It showed also that voting habits were less affected by the declared policies of the party in opposition than by the extent of the electors' displeasure with the party which happened to be in office, groping inadequately with the problems of a stagnant economy in the grip of rising prices.

Clann na Poblachta (The Family of the Republic) is the most remarkable of the small parties, now approaching a dozen in number, which have appeared fleetingly on the Irish hustings since independence. It existed effectively for less than ten years, and never held more than ten seats in the Dáil, but during the period of the first inter-party government, and immediately beforehand, it was in the very forefront of

8. P. Lynch, 'The Irish economy in the post-war era', Nowlan and Williams (eds), *Ireland in the War Years and After*, p. 198.
9. Cited in *Irish Times*, 18 February 1953.

politics. Founded in 1946 by Seán MacBride,[1] once an IRA man, it expressed the dissatisfaction of the more constructive members of the younger generation of Republicans, both with the growing conservatism and machine politics of Fianna Fáil and with the arid brutality which had characterized the IRA since the departure of most of its left-wingers in 1934. It was also an attempt to develop progressive social policies in a more dynamic atmosphere than the Irish Labour party had ever been able to generate since the days of James Connolly, and as such it attracted into its ranks Dr Noel Browne, a man with radical views on health and welfare matters.[2] MacBride became Minister for External Relations in the new government, and it was primarily his influence, notwithstanding Costello's hasty, unilateral action in Canada, which led to the severing of Ireland's links with the Commonwealth.

Just as the new party cut through the ambiguity of de Valera's old External Relations Act, it also tried to breathe new life into other ideas which had grown old and lifeless at the back of the Fianna Fáil platform. A serious attempt to end partition, a more active policy in support of the Irish language, the creation of financial independence from Great Britain, government stimulation of the national economy on a large scale, and assistance for the small farmer and businessman, were all points of the Clann na Poblachta programme which resembled in many respects the early aspirations of Fianna Fáil.[3] Thirteen per cent of the national poll in its first general election in 1948, followed by two seats (MacBride and Browne) in the inter-party cabinet, seemed a promising beginning for the new party (map 33). Yet within three years it became clear that the party had been only a flash in the pan. MacBride and Browne certainly established personal reputations in Irish politics, but two events underlined the weakness of the party's position.

First, the anti-climax of the declaration of a Republic brought in its wake a firm and final 'no' to the anti-partition movement from London and Belfast. It was followed by the fiasco of Browne's 'mother and child scheme' for a thoroughgoing public health service, which was vetoed by his colleagues following adverse criticism from Catholic church leaders.[4] Once the postwar phase of anti-partition feeling had died away, a vote for Clann na Poblachta was seen to be no more in practice than a vote

1. MacBride is the son of John MacBride, executed for his part in the 1916 Rising, and Maude Gonne, the actress and republican sympathizer. As as teenager MacBride fought on the anti-treaty side in the civil war of 1922–3. His career in Irish politics ended with his electoral defeat in 1957, since when he has served as secretary-general of the International Commission of Jurists, and as chairman of Amnesty International.

2. Browne later became a prominent member of the Irish Labour party after a brief flirtation with Fianna Fáil and several periods as an independent.

3. Seán MacBride, *Our People—Our Money* (three lectures, Dublin, 1943).

4. For a full discussion of this episode, see J. H. Whyte, *Church and State in Modern Ireland* (Dublin, 1971), pp. 196–272.

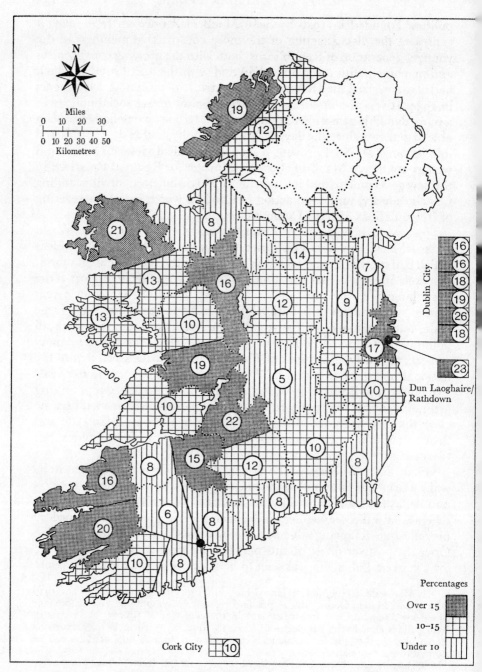

33. FIRST-PREFERENCE VOTES FOR CLANN NA POBLACHTA CANDIDATES, 1948

for an anti-Fianna Fáil coalition. The party received only 4 per cent of
the vote in 1951, and by 1957 was down to 1·7 per cent, since when it
has survived only in Cavan, which is more than anything else a measure
of the petrification of political activity in that remote county. The party
was formally dissolved in 1965.

The smallest[5] formal party in both the interparty governments,
of 1948–51 and 1954–7, was Clann na Talmhan (The Family of the
Land). One might have expected that, in a country so heavily agricultural as Ireland, endowed with an electoral system favourable to smaller
parties, a farmers' party would have found itself a permanent niche in
the system. The snag has been that, because of the diverse nature of
Irish land and Irish farming, farmers in different areas do not have
very many interests in common. Their parties have thus had a narrow
social and regional base only. The original Farmers' party of 1922–32
had been the political arm of the Farmers' Union, virtually an employers'
federation of larger farmers, mainly in the south and east, while Clann
na Talmhan—founded in 1938 at Athenry, Co. Galway—spoke always
for the smaller, predominantly western, farmers.[6] Its programme
included demands for national afforestation, more land drainage and
reclamation schemes, and complete derating of smaller agricultural
holdings. Giving cohesion to these practical demands was a more general
call for increased rural amenities, and for government intervention to
help preserve the quality of rural life.[7] The programme was an implicit
attack on Fianna Fáil's record, and differed from that of Clann na
Poblachta only in the absence of a militant nationalist tone. Again like
Clann na Poblachta, Clann na Talmhan was very much a flash in the
pan, running 44 candidates to win 14 seats in its first campaign in 1943,
but thereafter declining steadily (map 34). Its ultimate departure from
the political scene in 1965 was more protracted than that of Clann na
Poblachta, probably because it relied heavily on the personal popularity
of a few local figures,[8] rather than the heady but more brittle appeal of
MacBride's new republicanism.

THE LABOUR MOVEMENT: A LATE SPLIT

The old Irish problem, of conflict between intense national consciousness
and physical proximity to Britain, reappeared during the 1940s. There
was a sharp split in the ranks of Irish labour, the more serious because

5. From 1948 to 1950, National Labour was technically the smallest coalition
party. But once it had joined the inter-Party government alongside Labour, reunion
of the bodies was not far off.
6. Chubb, *Government and Politics of Ireland*, p. 83.
7. McCracken, *Representative Government in Ireland*, p. 109.
8. J. A. Murphy, 'The Irish party system, 1938–51', Nowlan and Williams (eds),
Ireland in the War Years and After, p. 156.

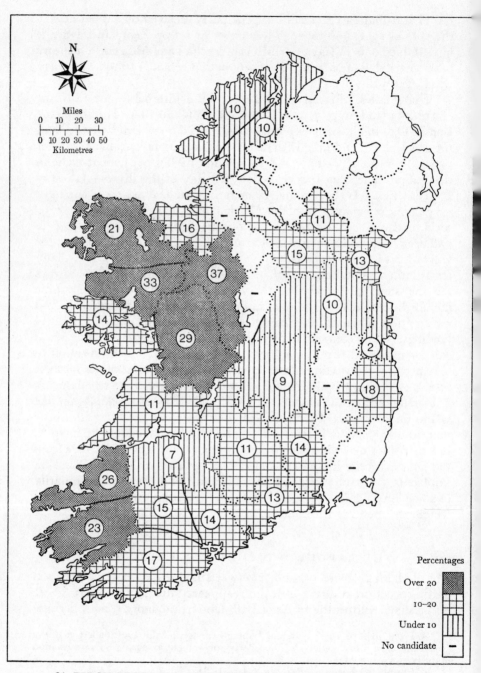

34. FIRST-PREFERENCE VOTES FOR CLANN NA TALMHAN CANDIDATES, 1943

The party ran no candidates in the cities of Dublin and Cork.

it had been delayed for so long and came at such a crucial time for the future of the movement.

The Irish Trades Union Congress had been founded in 1894, when Ireland was still a part of the United Kingdom, and included the Irish sections of trade unions with headquarters in Britain, together with Irish-based unions. This arrangement continued even after 1921, and the ITUC did not change to take account either of Ireland's separation from Britain, or of the new frontier established within Ireland itself. So far as the unions were concerned, a powerful argument in favour of continuing this situation was the fact that thousands of Irishmen found temporary or permanent work in Great Britain every year, and therefore had a strong interest in maintaining unimpeded movement of labour between the two countries. Not since the defeat, by the Belfast delegates, of a separatist motion at the 1906 ITUC conference had there been a serious attempt to cut the cross-channel ties.

It seemed in the early stages of the Second World War that the stage was set for the re-emergence of a strong Labour party in Irish politics, operating from a steady trade union base. The pre-war depression, which was ended in Britain and elsewhere by strenuous efforts to prepare the country for war, drifted in neutral Ireland into war-time depression, as unemployment and prices rose. Wages remained static. Fianna Fáil, in power for almost a decade, could no longer make a convincing appeal as a radical party. Labour at first seemed likely to benefit from the situation. In 1943 it increased its share of the national poll from 10 per cent to 15 per cent, and its tally of seats from 9 to 17, the best result since the short-lived Dáil of 1927. But in less than two years this gain had been almost entirely lost, and both the political party and the trade union movement were divided into two rival organizations. The explanation for such a dispiriting course of events is complex and confusing, and no detailed historical analysis of the episode has yet appeared. It seems clear, however, that there were three main factors: the position of the Irish Transport and General Workers' Union, and its aspirations within the structure of Irish trade unionism; the bitter feelings which had existed between Jim Larkin and William O'Brien, general secretary of the ITGWU, since Larkin's expulsion from that union in 1923-4; and the inherent contradictions in the cross-border and cross-channel links of the ITUC after 1922.

The ITGWU had been Ireland's biggest union ever since the herculean efforts of O'Brien and his colleagues in 1916-18. At that time nationalistic appeal, together with a pledge to force up wages in a period of full employment, had enabled it to recruit throughout the country on a large scale. It became, and essentially remained, an organization whose primary goal was increased membership. In the early years it adduced the arguments of syndicalism in support of its drive to become the 'one big union', but its success was by no means complete. By the end of the 1930s there still remained too many ineffectual small unions, as well as two major rivals, the British-based Amalgamated TGWU, and Larkin's Workers' Union of Ireland. For a Fianna Fáil government the proliferation of small unions, and the influence of large unions with headquarters outside the state, was an unsatisfactory state of affairs, especially in wartime. To this extent the government and the largest trade union had an important interest in common, and the new ITGWU catchword for expansion became 'rationalization'.

In 1941 the government put through its Trades Union Act. It obliged unions to obtain licences and deposit substantial sums of money in the High Court, and established a tribunal with power to determine that a union which organized the majority of any class of workers might be allowed a monopoly of that class; but only if it were an Irish-based union.[9] Under the circumstances, it was not surprising that the ITGWU failed to show the same vigour as other unions in opposing the measure. The ITUC, declared O'Brien bluntly, had only itself to blame.[1]

There was thus, by the end of 1941, considerable suspicion of the ITGWU within the Irish labour movement, and it is against this background that subsequent developments must be judged. In 1943 the Dublin Labour party nominated Jim Larkin as an official Labour candidate, and he was elected to the Dáil.[2] O'Brien, however, still felt as he had done since 1914, that Larkin was an irresponsible demagogue who would wreck any movement in which he was involved.[3] The ITGWU element in the Labour party therefore tried to exclude Larkin, as they had done consistently for twenty years, but failed to do so. All members of the party's administrative council, other than the ITGWU representatives, voted in support of Larkin's admittance.[4] Its loss of influence now apparent, the ITGWU announced its disaffiliation from the party which, it alleged, had been captured by Communists.[5] Five of

9. The last provision (part III of the act) was in fact thrown out by the Supreme Court in 1946 as repugnant to the constitution.

1. Nevin, 'Industry and Labour', Nowlan and Williams (eds), *Ireland in the War Years and After*, p. 98.

2. Larkin had previously been returned to the Dáil in September 1927 for the Irish Workers' League (though described in the press as a 'Communist' candidate), but was disqualified as an undischarged bankrupt. In 1937–8 he sat in the Dáil as an independent.

3. This personal bitterness also reflected a very basic conflict within the socialist movement, hammered out in most European countries before 1914, between revolution and reformism. Lyons, *Ireland since the Famine*, p. 664.

4. This episode, and the subsequent split in the ITUC, is described in more detail in Nevin, 'Industry and Labour', pp. 94–108.

5. It seems quite clear that this allegation was empty rhetoric, put out to disguise the true nature of the split. Larkin himself had been a Communist, and in fact received some modest financial assistance from the Comintern prior to 1928. His

its eight deputies reformed themselves into a National Labour party, which in the 1944 Dáil acted in informal concert with Fianna Fáil.[6]

Worse was to come. Another row sprang up in 1943–4, this time within the national executive of the ITUC. It was over the question of Irish attendance at the British-sponsored World Trades Union Conference to be held in London in 1945, and revealed a similar balance of forces as had been apparent during the Labour party debate over Larkin. Once again the ITGWU, leading a group of Irish-based unions which objected to the proposal on the grounds that it would constitute a breach of neutrality, progressively lost its grip on the situation. By 1944 there was a determined majority opposed to its influence on the national executive of the ITUC, just as there was on the advisory council of the Labour party.

Early in 1945 the ITGWU accordingly announced its withdrawal from Congress, shortly afterwards forming a new group, the Congress of Irish Unions (CIU), along with some, though not all, of the other Irish-based unions.[7] The issue was a real one, involving both questions of personal ambition and deep-seated differences of opinion about the future of Irish trade unionism,[8] just as the ITGWU's opposition to the admission of Larkin had been. But any coherent explanation of the double crisis must have as its focus the removal of the ITGWU in 1943–4 from its powerful position at the centre of the Labour party and the ITUC. This was mainly the outcome of widespread distrust of that union's attitude towards the Trades Union Act, and its general relationship with the Fianna Fáil government.[9]

With the ending of the war, the retirement of O'Brien from the ITGWU in 1946 and the death of Larkin in 1947, the tension began to ease. The Supreme Court's invalidation of part III of the Trades Union Act dashed CIU hopes of displacing the ITUC.[1] In spite of the ITGWU's personal, and to some extent ideological, involvement with Fianna Fáil

---

biographer is in no doubt, however, that he had quietly but conclusively dissociated himself from the international communist movement by 1934. E. Larkin, *James Larkin* (London, 1965), pp. 268–9.

6. *Irish Times Review, 1944*, p. 7.

7. One outcome of the ITGWU's secession, for instance, was a decision of the ITUC to admit Larkin's Workers' Union of Ireland, founded in 1924, to membership for the first time. Membership of the two bodies, following the split, was as follows: ITUC, 145,000; CIU, 77,500. The balance remained about the same until the reunion. See Lyons, *Ireland since the Famine*, p. 668.

8. Nevin, 'Industry and Labour', p. 102.

9. The ITGWU was believed to be 'mildly sympathetic' to the new transport bill, which might increase its own influence, as well as the government's control, over Irish railways. The union also showed a readiness to co-operate with the government's plans for a central bank, which would bind the Irish economy more closely to sterling. William O'Brien of the ITGWU was subsequently appointed a director of the bank. O'Connor Lysaght, *The Republic of Ireland*, p. 158.

1. Ibid., p. 159.

—the desirability of having Irish-based trade unions was as evident to de Valera and his followers as the need for a separate Irish Red Cross, a separate language, or an independent economy—the primacy of party politics soon reasserted itself. The National Labour deputies lost no time in entering the all-party coalition alongside rival Labour men in 1948, when the chance came to turn Fianna Fáil out of office at last. From then on, the reunion of the Labour party in 1950 was a matter of course.

The division within the industrial side of the movement proved more intractable. The material interests of large numbers of people were involved, and the practical administrative problems considerable. Furthermore, the broad national question of how far an independent Ireland ought to have large numbers of trade unionists controlled from outside the state posed problems greater in scope than either the Larkin issue or the relationship of the ITGWU with its fellow-unions. Not until 1959 were final arrangements made for the reunification of the ITUC and the CIU in a new body, the Irish Congress of Trade Unions, which was open not only to unions with headquarters in any part of Ireland, but to unions based outside Ireland, provided there were proper safeguards to ensure the autonomy of their Irish members.[2]

IRELAND SINCE DE VALERA

The second inter-party government of 1954–7 was dominated by Fine Gael, with fifty seats. It never seemed anything more than a rather pedestrian alternative to Fianna Fáil, and even in its early stages was unable to arouse public enthusiasm in the way that the first had done. Clann na Poblachta, which had generated so much public interest in 1948, was now a declining force with only three seats, and supported the new government only from the back-benches of the Dáil. The government made little impact on the country's main economic difficulties: intractable inflation, a balance-of-payments deficit, and accompanying unemployment and emigration. On another front the IRA, which had quietly regrouped during the easy-going regime of the 'anti-partition' years, began guerrilla activities along the border late in 1956. The campaign was ultimately thwarted by hostile and apathetic public opinion on both sides of the border, but during its early stages the country seemed for a while to be hovering 'on the brink of a deep emotional commitment to a desperate crusade'.[3] In this case the government acted promptly, imprisoning as many known IRA leaders as the police were able to round up.

Both these issues were sensitive ones for Clann na Poblachta. In February 1957, MacBride proposed a motion of no confidence in the

2. Lyons, *Ireland since the Famine*, p. 668.
3. J. B. Bell, *The Secret Army* (London, 1970), pp. 354–5.

government on the grounds of its failure either to deal with the economic crisis or make progress towards the unification of Ireland.[4] The Fianna Fáil opposition took up the question, and Costello, faced with a defeat in the Dáil, called a general election. Fine Gael tried to fight on the question of its brisk treatment of the IRA, but no-one really doubted that de Valera was equally capable of sternness in that quarter. The main issues of the election proved to be the government's failure to arrest the economic decline and, associated with that, the question of whether a heterogeneous coalition of parties could ever hope to cope with such difficulties.[5] Fianna Fáil returned to office with an impressive seventy-eight seats, but little enthusiasm was generated during the campaign—perhaps because even those with short memories could cast their minds back to the party's own failure to shake off the economic malaise between 1951 and 1954. The main interest of the election was the appearance of nineteen Sinn Féin candidates, mostly imprisoned IRA men, all pledged not to take their seats if elected. Sinn Féin, with very little organization, and fighting almost exclusively on the border issue, obtained 65,640 first preference votes (just over 5 per cent) and had four of its candidates elected (map 35).[6] It was an unexpected result, though a limited and ultimately insignificant one. Analysis suggests that Sinn Féin votes were taken mainly from Fianna Fáil.[7] The outcome, however, was not that Fianna Fáil adopted a militant posture against partition but, on the contrary, that it endeavoured to stifle the re-emergence of extremism as quickly as possible.[8]

The new government looked for all the world like a return to Fianna Fáil normalcy. De Valera was back at the head of his eighth administration, flanked by an old guard of four ministers who had sat in his first 1932 cabinet, along with three more who had been founder members of

4. Ibid., p. 358, maintains that MacBride took this action in response to pressure from his rank and file, realizing himself that the outcome could only be a Fianna Fáil victory and the further weakening of his own party. This, however, is dubious. There was no advantage to Clann na Poblachta in keeping in office a government committed to stern measures against the IRA.

5. For a detailed analysis of this election, see F. B. Chubb, 'Ireland 1957', D. E. Butler (ed.), Elections Abroad (London, 1959), pp. 183–226.

6. In the border constituencies of Monaghan and Sligo–Leitrim, in adjacent Longford–Westmeath, and in the traditional republican stronghold of South Kerry.

7. Chubb, 'Ireland 1957', p. 215.

8. Some representatives of IRA opinion had called on de Valera in 1956 to seek his co-operation, or at least connivance, in their proposed border campaign. He told them that in his view partition could not be ended by force (Longford and O'Neill, Eamon de Valera, p. 444). On the contrary, indeed, he extracted from the Fianna Fáil shadow cabinet before it took office an agreement that, in the event of IRA activities claiming innocent lives, internment would be implemented in the south (Bell, Secret Army, p. 358). Documents recently made available indicate that even in August 1921, in a private session of the Dáil, de Valera had opposed the use of force as an effective means of bringing Ulster into the Irish state (Private Sessions of the Second Dáil, cited in C. Cruise O'Brien, States of Ireland (London, 1972), p. 295).

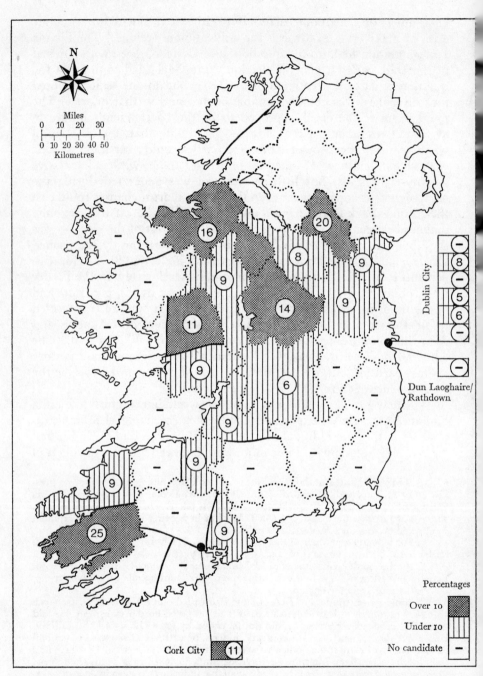

35. FIRST-PREFERENCE VOTES FOR SINN FEIN CANDIDATES, 1957

the party.[9] But appearances in this case were deceptive. Four new men, much younger than the revolutionary generation, found places in the government.[1] More important, a new economic departure was imminent. The take-off is most commonly associated with the name of the senior civil servant in the Ministry of Finance, T. K. Whitaker. His report became the basis for the new government's first programme for economic expansion, which appeared towards the end of 1958. Nothing was heard of the old pre-war Fianna Fáil slogans of self-sufficiency and Gaelic frugality. In their place came a new businesslike image, exemplified in the election slogan, 'Beat the crisis, let's get cracking'.[2] In accordance with Whitaker's proposals there was a new emphasis on attracting capital from abroad by means of tax concessions, on expanding and widening the country's exports, and on modernizing agriculture.[3] The programme was a remarkable success. Over the following five-year period, the gross national product rose by over 4 per cent per annum (in contrast to the anticipated 2 per cent), the volume of capital investment almost doubled, and emigration, which in the 1956–61 period was running at 14·8 per thousand, was in 1961–6 reduced to 5·7 per thousand.[4] How much this was the outcome of Whitaker's proposals, and how far it was simply a reflection of the general upswing in the western economies, is still uncertain.[5] It is clear, however, that Whitaker's ideas, and their enactment by his government, ensured that the country was able to take advantage of changed international circumstances.

Early in 1959 de Valera, at the age of 77, retired from the position of Taoiseach. His decision coincided with the expiry of Seán T. O'Kelly's term of office as President, and in June of the same year he transferred to the ceremonial position of head of state.[6] Seán Lemass, deputy leader for fourteen years, replaced him as head of government. Lemass, the youngest political member of the revolutionary generation, was well equipped by his long experience as Minister for Industry and Commerce to foster the party's new businesslike image. He led the party successfully through two general elections, before retiring in 1966. Contrary to the fears of party pessimists, de Valera's departure did not herald the termination of Fianna Fáil's easy ascendancy over its rivals. In the absence of the Chief's charisma, the relative professionalism of Fianna Fáil's constituency organization became its electoral trump-card. As a result, 'the party's need for more money to finance its operations was

9. Manning, *Irish Political Parties* (Dublin, 1972), p. 51.
1. The four new ministers were Neil Blaney (Posts and Telegraphs), Kevin Boland (Defence), Jack Lynch (Lands), and Michael Moran (Gaeltacht).
2. Cited in Chubb, 'Ireland 1957', p. 199.
3. Lyons, *Ireland since the Famine*, p. 474.   4. Ibid., pp. 619–20.
5. For a detailed discussion see Meenan, *Irish Economy, passim*.
6. De Valera won the presidential election comfortably against a Fine Gael opponent. But his proposal to abolish proportional representation was defeated in a referendum held on the same day.

driving it into closer and closer alliance with major business interests'.[7] The infant business concerns which had associated with Fianna Fáil during the first generation of national independence had grown in stature alongside the party, and helped contribute to Fianna Fáil's latter-day image as the party of the new establishment.

Fianna Fáil has not become a 'conservative party', however, although it has long since lost its particular western orientation. A survey undertaken in 1969 indicated that its continued success has been achieved on a very broad social base. The party appears to have had (in 1969) more middle-class support than the predominantly middle-class Fine Gael; as much support among farmers as Fine Gael; and more support among the working class than the Labour party.[8] Only among the younger members of the working class did its support seem to be relatively weak, though whether this indicates simply that working-class voters turn to Fianna Fáil as they get older, or whether on the other hand it should give the party's long-term planners cause for alarm, is hard to say.

Fine Gael, by contrast, was revealed in the same survey as a predominantly middle-aged and middle-class party, with strong support among the larger farmers, though whether it is in fact 'an ageing party'[9] as opposed to a party attracting ageing people, is again not entirely clear. At all events the party, which had been given a much-needed injection of credibility by the formation of the 1948 inter-party government, was thrown back into the doldrums by its defeat in 1957. The economic problems which had beset it disappeared after 1957, and Fianna Fáil was able to reap the benefit of the boom of the early 1960s. The second inter-party government had not been a happy one, and it was clear after its defeat that Fine Gael and Labour would keep their options open so far as future co-operation was concerned.[1]

Fine Gael subsequently went through a long period of identity crisis. At the best of times it was difficult to differentiate the party from Fianna Fáil, and if it was no longer to be the obvious lynch-pin of any alternative government, then the outlook was bleak.[2] In the mid 1960s Declan Costello, son of the former taoiseach, sought to inject into the party something of the currently fashionable style of liberal idealism known after its main American proponent as 'the Kennedy touch'. His pro-

7. Manning, *Irish Political Parties*, p. 54.
8. Ibid., p. 60. For further details of the survey, conducted by Gallup (Ireland), see pp. 114–18.
9. Ibid., p. 31.
1. The attitude of Labour towards joining another coalition, even during the 1957 election campaign, was an equivocal one. (See Chubb, 'Ireland 1957', p. 190.) After the election, Labour's annual conference committed the party against coalition —a decision that was not rescinded until 1970. See J. H. Whyte, 'Ireland' in R. Rose (ed.), *Electoral Behaviour: A Comparative Handbook* (New York, 1974), p. 643.
2. Manning, *Irish Political Parties*, p. 28.

gramme, *The Just Society*, was accepted with apparent reluctance by the Fine Gael leadership shortly before the 1965 election, but failed to bring about success, resulting instead in its promoter's withdrawal from public life for some years. Whether the electorate rejected Fine Gael because it disliked the programme, or because it did not believe the party leaders were in earnest about the programme, is hard to say.

The Labour party contributed to Fine Gael's difficulties. Under the new leadership of Brendan Corish, it entered the 1961, 1965, and 1969 elections on an independent platform, pledged not to enter a coalition. The 1960s was a decade of growth for Labour, and there was plainly some hope that a few years of consolidation and self-denial by a younger generation of leaders might enable the party to outgrow its fifty-year-old third-party status. Relations with the trade unions grew closer during the decade, so that in 1965 the two old rivals, the ITGWU and the Workers' Union of Ireland both affiliated. In 1966 the party allowed the word 'socialism', which has the same kind of emotive significance for the Irish left as 'nationalization' has had for the British Labour party, to reappear in its programme for the first time in over a quarter of a century. Since 1969 the party's old image of drabness and parochialism has been left further behind by the accretion to the Dáil party of three distinguished Dublin academics, one of whom (Dr Conor Cruise O'Brien) had also served as an Irish and a UN diplomat and as vice-chancellor of the University of Ghana.[3] Somewhat remarkably, all three were candidates sponsored by the ITGWU.[4] The importance of this new strength was not just that it improved the quality of the party's personnel—though it did that as well, even if it ruffled the feathers of some older trade unionists—but that it also helped to give the party an appeal to radically minded members of the younger generation which had eluded Irish Labour since the days of Larkin and Connolly.[5]

Yet in electoral terms the party's success has been a limited one. It increased its number of Dáil seats from 12 in 1957 (110,000 first preference votes) to 21 in 1965 (192,740 votes). But in the year of its greatest effort, 1969, when it mounted almost 100 candidates in an attempt to appear as a credible alternative government, it increased its total vote to 223,280, but its number of seats fell to 18. It was still no more than a successful *third* party in the state. As we have seen, the indications of a 1969 Gallup survey are that Labour has the allegiance

3. For Dr O'Brien's views on the contemporary Irish situation, see his *States of Ireland*.

4. Dr O'Brien's fund-raisers, at least, spread their net in other directions also. While working in Tennessee in 1969, I received a circular which invited all those on the mailing list of the American Committee for Irish Studies to contribute to the advance of socialism in Dublin North-east [A. C. H.].

5. For an analysis of the personnel of the party, see M. A. Busteed and H. Mason, 'Irish Labour in the 1969 election', *Political Studies*, xviii. 3 (September 1970).

of the younger members of the working class, but we have no way of knowing whether this may not also have been the case forty years ago, or whether the party is likely to retain its young supporters of this generation.

Irish Labour's persistent weakness has attracted the attention of historians and political scientists for some time. The country's lack of a broad industrial and urban base, and the associated absence of any widespread degree of class consciousness (as opposed to small-town social distinctions and snobbery) are often put forward as explanations. While there is clearly some truth in such arguments, they do not account for Labour's frequent failure to win any seats in Cork city or even (until 1969) to hold its own with the two larger parties in the Dublin constituencies. During most of its existence Labour's centres of strength have been in farming districts of mid and south Leinster.[6] While this may be a very pale reflection in Ireland of what has been demonstrated in China, Cuba, and Africa—that, notwithstanding Marx, left-wing parties can thrive in a non-industrial environment—it is to a much greater extent a tribute to the popularity and organization of a few individual politicians. Labour's real problem has been breaking into a pattern of voting along 'national' lines which was established in the early years of the state. A recent article, taking this view to its logical extreme, arrives at the conclusion that Labour's failure lies in its decision not to contest the 1918 election.[7] Such a view offers little hope for the future, outside the present politics of coalition.

But if Labour's recent expansion has been a limited one, its new style can, almost certainly, take some of the credit for the relative absence of student intellectuals and the like from the contemporary IRA; remarkable, in an age of general student militancy. The latter organization, however, along with its political arm, Sinn Féin, has not been without a new style itself. It seemed for a while in the middle and later 1960s to be capable of attracting just that support which Labour has in fact gained. The guerrilla campaign against the border, which won the IRA international publicity and four seats in the Dáil in 1957, petered out in a squalid and wasteful fashion over the next four years. The leaders paid little heed to the political impact of the sporadic border ambushes and barracks raids which they were able to mount, seeming to assume that their modest election successes provided them with sufficient moral momentum to overcome any resistance. They were thus harassed mercilessly by the governments on both sides of the border.[8] Their military strategy was such as to subject their men to sporadic action

6. Manning, *Irish Political Parties*, p. 80.

7. B. Farrell, 'Labour and the Irish political party system: a suggested approach to analysis', *Economic and Social Review*, i. 4 (July 1970), 477–502.

8. Bell, *Secret Army*, p. 362.

followed by enervating months on the run, living frequently in dugouts in the mountains of Tyrone or the border districts. Since the IRA's political propaganda was negligible,[9] its failure to achieve significant military successes meant the end of any popular support. In the 1961 election Sinn Féin won no seats, and with twenty-one candidates in the field, only 3 per cent of the total first preference vote. An indication of how little impact their campaign had made on Irish life is the fact that in the Northern Ireland elections of 1958 and 1962 even the Unionist party, so skilled at marshalling Protestant support on the border issue, was unable to make enough capital out of the crisis to resist inroads on its vote by the Northern Ireland Labour party.

Mainly because of its poor showing in the Dáil election of 1961, the IRA formally ended its campaign early in the following year.[1] From this time on there was a growing feeling within the leadership that any future the movement might have in the short term must lie in some sort of involvement in everyday issues. Few, however, could find much enthusiasm for orthodox political work on behalf of a party which was pledged not to take its seats. On the other hand there was, especially outside Dublin, a dominant old guard of 'pure Republicans' who saw nothing in any non-military, leftward departures except gestures of censure and ingratitude towards themselves. It thus proved impossible to build up a united body of opinion within either Sinn Féin or the IRA's Army Council in favour of terminating the principle of abstention from parliamentary attendance. What was achieved, however, was the reintroduction of radical socialist republicanism into the movement, and its subsequent association with practical courses of action, in both the north and the south of Ireland.

Many of the new Marxist doctrines—though in fact they were very like the ideas publicized by O'Donnell, Gilmore, and Ryan thirty years earlier—were produced by Dr Roy Johnston, formerly a London member of the Connolly Association, and disseminated by the party's revamped newspaper, the *United Irishman*. Attention was drawn to issues such as poor housing conditions and the ownership of ground rents in Dublin, strike-breakers, and the operation of certain foreign-owned business concerns to the detriment of local interests. All these issues provided opportunities for direct action, violent or otherwise. By 1967–8 such activities were beginning to attract interest and support

9. Most of the IRA leaders of the 'campaign' generation were strongly military in their emphasis. A splinter group, Saor Uladh (Free Ulster), whose members had fallen from grace over the recognition of the Dublin government, did harbour some radical political thinkers. The group assisted in the return of an independent 'unemployed workers' candidate' for a Dublin constituency in 1957, and some of its members were subsequently associated with an Irish Trotskyite faction in London, but it was otherwise ineffectual. Bell, *Secret Army*, p. 396.

1. Ibid., pp. 394–5. The following account of the IRA in the 1960s is based largely on Bell, *Secret Army*, chs xvii and xviii.

from people of radical views who had never previously had any time for
the IRA. In the north at the same time there was developing a civil
rights campaign among younger Catholics, focusing on religious
discrimination in employment and the allocation of public housing, and
gerrymandering and franchise restrictions in the field of local government. In origin this movement was independent both of the Catholic
political groupings at Stormont and of the IRA. But the IRA chief of
staff was consulted, and apparently expressed grave doubts as to
whether the intended programme of non-violent demonstrations
(modelled on those of Martin Luther King in the USA) would be
effective in Northern Ireland. He agreed to co-operate none the less.[2]
The proposed tactics, though on a much larger scale, were similar to
those being developed by the IRA/Sinn Féin in Dublin and elsewhere.
But in the north they were self-generating: 'it would be fair to say that
the civil rights movement had far more influence on the IRA than the
reverse'.[3]

There was, however, a strong body of opinion in the south which
remained sceptical about the social radicalism of the new approach, and
suspected that it was the prelude to a renewed effort to turn the IRA
into 'Free State party number four'. In the invasion of the Catholic
ghettos of Belfast in August 1969, with the IRA virtually nowhere to be
seen, the fundamentalists found a stick with which to beat the radicals.
While Marxists theorized in Dublin, they argued, northern Catholics
went undefended against Orange mobs. It was an issue on which the
fundamentalists could forge an alliance with northern republicans who
had previously been diverted into the new approach of the civil rights
movement. At meetings of the IRA Army Council in December 1969
and at the Sinn Féin Ard Fheis a few weeks later the fundamentalists,
finding themselves in a minority amongst the heavily organized Dublin
contingent, staged a walk-out and established two parallel bodies, the
Provisional Army Council of the IRA, and a Caretaker Executive of
Sinn Féin. The remaining 'Officials' took a sanguine view. The fundamentalists were an apparent minority, mainly names from the past who
had done little since the end of the border campaign. They were dismissed as 'custodians of an irrelevant past'.[4] The Officials had already
embarked on a reorganization of the movement in Ulster with a view
to military defence. It was not at all clear how the Provisionals could
'improve' on such a policy.[5]

The new body soon revealed unexpected vigour and support,

    2. Coogan, *IRA*, p. 421.   3. Bell, *Secret Army*, p. 421.   4. Ibid., p. 433.
    5. In June 1970 Conor Cruise O'Brien, more recently the most vigorous critic of
the IRA in southern politics, found Ruairi O Bradaigh, ex-chief of staff of the IRA,
1960–2 and from 1970 the head of Provisional Sinn Féin, to be 'a very gentle, quiet,
good-humoured man, who seemed more interested in preventing violence than in
starting it'. O'Brien, *States of Ireland*, p. 222.

however, when it manifested its intention to take the offensive in the north, in effect taking up the traditional IRA military policy which the Official movement had endeavoured to set aside. Unlike the campaign of 1956–62, the new IRA strategy in the north was urban (and therefore avoided sentencing volunteers to long winters in mountain dug-outs) and apparently well supported in the Catholic districts of Belfast and Derry. During the later months of 1970 the two wings of the IRA fought out a private battle for territory, and in 1971 there began a serious and sustained Provisional campaign of bombing property and shooting soldiers in the towns and cities of Northern Ireland. The Officials attempted to maintain a 'defensive' and 'retaliatory' position, distinct from the 'sectarian' and 'anti-working class' bombing campaign of the Provisionals, though it was on occasion difficult to discern the difference in practice. Early in 1972 the Officials attempted to make the best of a weakening position by announcing a cease-fire, but the Provisionals' campaign continued in face of increasing harassment and hostile public opinion on both sides of the border.

In 1970 there was considerable speculation about the possibility of Fianna Fáil complicity in the IRA split. It seemed to many observers that the emergence of a 'green', northern-oriented Provisional force in opposition to the 'red' Officials, with their emphasis on bringing about radical social change in the south, was a convenient diversion for the southern government. It subsequently became clear that some members of the cabinet who had concurred in the compromise appointment of Jack Lynch as Taoiseach in 1966 now saw in the crisis a chance of displacing him on a platform of 'Irish unity now'. But there were also some strong feelings involved, over and above party politics. During 1970, a number of ministers were dismissed from the cabinet and charged with importing arms, with a view to their use in the north.[6] For a while, however, Mr Lynch's position seemed a weak one as, without much apparent conviction, he moved Irish army units up to the border as 'field stations', and called for United Nations intervention, in an effort to appear tough and conciliatory at the same time. But as the level of IRA violence in the north came to exceed that of Protestant mobs or British soldiers, so public opinion in the south quietened, and by 1972 Mr Lynch was able to take his first tentative steps towards effective action against the IRA, arguing that the alternative was not an early reunification of the country but the spread of Ulster's violence to the south.

The northern situation continued to play an important role in southern politics, but not a dominant one. Mr Lynch's decision to call

6. For an account of these developments see the *Sunday Times* Insight team, *Ulster* (London, 1972), ch. 11. All the defendants in the arms trial were in due course acquitted.

a snap election early in 1973 was certainly occasioned by his wish to clear the decks before the British government introduced its new and possibly controversial constitutional proposals for the north. But once the election was called, the campaign was fought out on very different questions of domestic social policy. Fine Gael and Labour who, according to Fianna Fáil strategy, should have been caught on the hop by the election, very quickly put together a 'National Coalition' to fight the campaign on a fifteen-point programme of social reform. These, it transpired, were the issues the electorate wanted to hear about. Fianna Fáil's plans to hold a 'national interest' election based around the personal popularity of Mr Lynch fell through, as did their secondary strategy of questioning the integrity of the hurriedly formed coalition and its programme. A week before the poll, the party leadership more or less admitted its failure by coming out with a whole new series of concessions, including a sensational proposal to abolish rates.[7] This proved too much for public opinion to take, and the party found itself out of office for the first time in sixteen years.[8]

Fianna Fáil's campaign misfired, therefore, and the quality of its personnel was generally not such as could argue persuasively to regain the ground lost. In spite of, or perhaps because of, their very long period in opposition, Fine Gael and Labour seemed to have an easy ascendancy of talent over Fianna Fáil. Along with the leading Labour figures already mentioned was a group within Fine Gael, based around the old 'just society' programme of 1965. Despite what the polls said about the party's conservative electoral profile, it was the progressive social thinkers in Fine Gael who made the running in policy formation, and enabled so rapid an agreement to be reached with Labour.[9]

The 1973 election results confirmed what the campaign had suggested —that however angrily Irish people might respond to individual events in the north, the electorate was simply not interested in political leaders who advocated a militant policy. 'United Ireland' politics cut no ice in the southern election of 1973. Sinn Féin, which contested ten constituencies, received only 15,366 first preference votes, little more than 1 per cent of the total poll. It was challenged for this slender body of opinion by a new party, Aontacht Eireann (United Ireland), formed in 1971 by Kevin Boland, a former minister. Mr Boland had resigned from the Fianna Fáil cabinet in protest at the prosecution of two of his colleagues on arms smuggling charges, calling for a determined effort by southern politicians to end partition. His new party differed from Sinn Féin

7. The effect of the announcement was somewhat spoilt by the appearance on the same day of a campaign newspaper advertisement issued on behalf of a member of the outgoing cabinet which poured scorn on the practicability of such proposals.

8. For an analysis of the campaign, see D. Kennedy, 'Fail or Gael', *Fortnight*, 57 (March 1973).

9. M. McInerney, 'A just society?', *Fortnight*, 58 (March 1973).

mainly in that it operated within the constitution, recognizing the Dáil, and having no known links with the IRA. It failed to catch the public imagination, however, and fared even worse at the hands of the electors than Sinn Féin, gaining only 12,321 votes in twelve contests, less than 1 per cent of the national poll. The lesson for southern Irish politicians seems to be that there is no mileage at all for them in a traditional manipulation of the national question. The only men to advance their status through contact with it during the present crisis have been Jack Lynch, who resisted the temptation to play the national card when pressed to do so, and Conor Cruise O'Brien, who dismissed hopes of attaining a united Ireland in the foreseeable future as an impractical dream.

CHAPTER FIVE

Northern Ireland: The Politics of a Divided State

PARTITION AND DEVOLUTION

At the end of the nineteenth century Unionists in all parts of Ireland shared a common political outlook: maintenance of the legislative union with Great Britain, and general opposition to the nationalist movement. Their representatives at Westminster acted as a group within the Conservative party, and in the Dublin-based Irish Unionist Alliance they possessed a nationwide central organization and propaganda body. But this formal cohesion concealed a vital difference between Unionists in the north-east of Ireland and those of the rest of the country. In the provinces of Leinster, Munster, and Connaught the Unionists or Protestants (the labels were virtually interchangeable) were a tiny ascendancy class, declining in influence and prosperity on the land, though still flourishing in the professional and business life in Dublin. In the province of Ulster, on the other hand, they constituted a majority of the total population, as Table 5.1 shows.

TABLE 5.1

Percentage of Protestants in the Ulster Population, 1911

Belfast	75·9	Fermanagh	44·3
Antrim	79·8	Tyrone	44·4
Down	68·6	Donegal	20·8
Armagh	55·0	Cavan	18·7
Londonderry: city	43·9	Monaghan	25·4
county	58·6	TOTAL	56·4

Source: R. Rose, *Governing without Consensus* (London, 1971), p. 90.

Unionism in Ulster, therefore, was not merely the political creed of a small social and economic élite, but a mass movement with an extremely broad social base. The Protestants in Ulster could not be termed an élite except in the very special sense that they constituted (and still do) a disproportionately large element of professional, managerial, and skilled manual workers, and a correspondingly smaller proportion of the unskilled and semi-skilled groups.[1] The relationship between Protestants and Catholics in the north was thus not, as it was in the rest of the country, simply a more than usually virulent form of class antagonism, but an extremely complex structure of sectarian suspicion, animosity, and segregation. In rural areas there had been two separate communities since the plantation of the seventeenth century, when Catholics had been obliged to surrender all but the worst quality land. Even today, the predominantly Catholic areas in rural Ulster are the rough, upland districts (see maps 36 and 37).[2] In many Ulster towns the existence of old names such as English Street, Scotch Street, and Irish Street suggests a long-established segregation. But the pattern of segregation has been sharpest and the hostility most overt in the two largest towns, Belfast and Londonderry, both essentially products of the mid-nineteenth-century Industrial Revolution. In Belfast especially, the relatively larger increase in the Catholic population during the third quarter of the nineteenth century was the basic stimulus for a whole series of riots, which encouraged the development of strict segregation between Catholics and Protestants in working-class districts (see maps 38 and 39). When Gladstone introduced his first Home Rule Bill, in 1886, rioting in the city came to assume a political as well as a community significance.[3] Protestant Belfast had emerged as the most powerful weapon in the Irish Unionists' arsenal.

It was not very surprising, therefore, when a separate Ulster Unionist Council came into being in 1905 and the parting of the ways with the

1. There are no official statistics to illustrate this. D. P. Barritt and C. F. Carter (*The Northern Ireland Problem* [2nd edn, London, 1972], p. 54) carried out a survey in Portadown, Co. Armagh, in 1960, which indicated that 51 per cent of the Catholics surveyed were in the semi-skilled and unskilled categories, as against 26 per cent of Presbyterians, 33 per cent of Church of Ireland members, and 21 per cent of Methodists. In Lurgan, Co. Armagh, in 1961, 48 per cent of Catholics were in these categories, as against 27 per cent of Presbyterians, 40 per cent of Church of Ireland members and, 36 per cent of Methodists. See T. Kirk, 'The religious distribution of Lurgan, with special reference to segregational ecology' (Queen's University of Belfast, MA thesis, 1967), p. 57.

2. There are some exceptions to this rule, notably the barony of Lecale, around Downpatrick, Co. Down, where Catholics remained in control of rich valley land. The explanation seems to be that the inhabitants were 'old English', ie descendants of Anglo-Norman settlers who remained Catholic and were left undisturbed by the seventeenth-century plantations. See M. W. Heslinga, *The Irish Border as a Cultural Divide* (2nd edn, Assen, Netherlands, 1971), p. 73.

3. A. Boyd, *Holy War in Belfast* (Tralee, 1969), is a carefully detailed narrative of the main nineteenth-century riots, although its emphasis on Orange malevolence to the virtual exclusion of all other causes of disorder is probably an oversimplification. A more dispassionate study is S. E. Baker, 'Orange and Green', in H. J. Dyos and M. Wolff (eds), *The Victorian City: Images and Reality* (London, 1973).

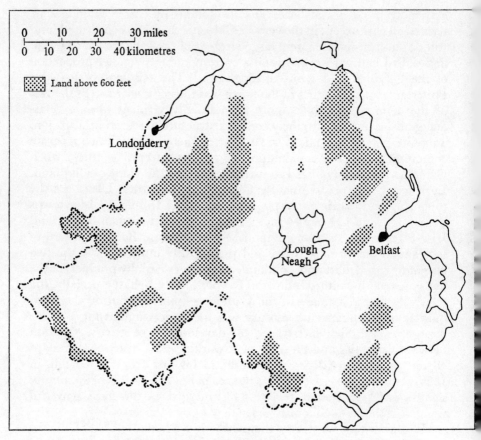

36. NORTHERN IRELAND, SHOWING LAND ABOVE 600 FEET

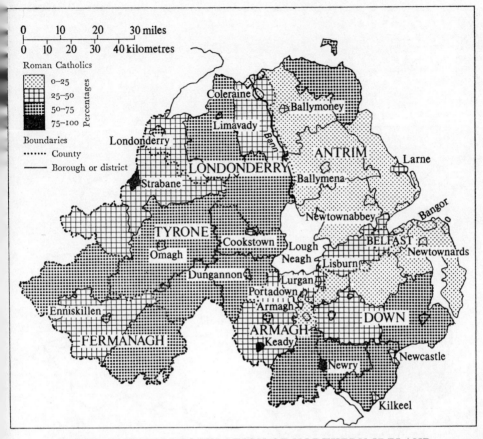

37. THE CATHOLIC POPULATION OF NORTHERN IRELAND

By local government districts, the map indicates Catholics as a percentage of the total population.
The central and western areas of the province are more thinly populated than the eastern districts.
Source: Annual Register, 1969, p. 52.

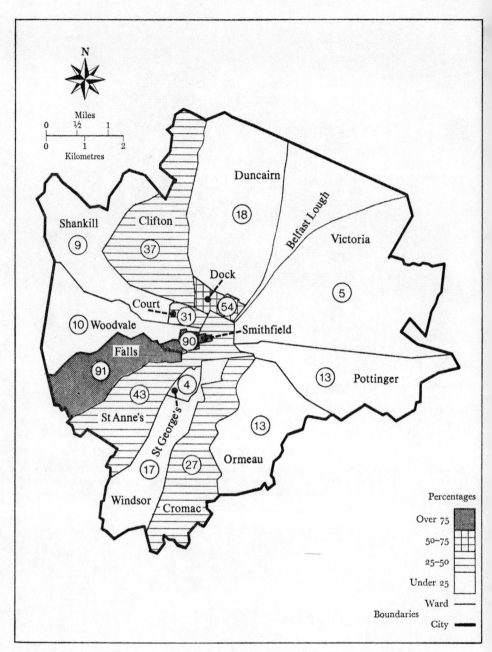

38. THE CATHOLIC POPULATION OF BELFAST, 1961

The map shows the number of Catholics as a percentage of the population, by ward divisions. In the city as a whole, Catholics constituted 27 per cent of the total population of 415,856. The map does not reveal the intensive segregation that exists within each ward. *Source: Census of Northern Ireland, 1961.*

(168)

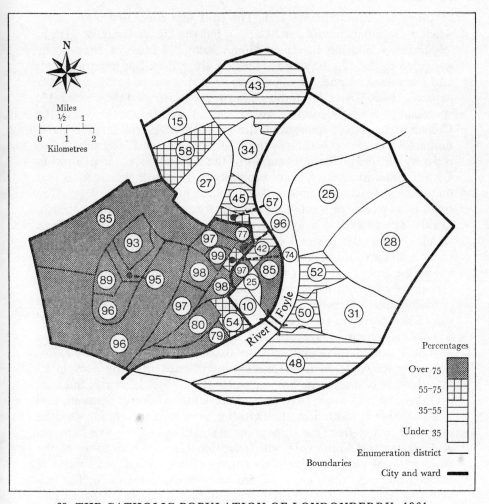

39. THE CATHOLIC POPULATION OF LONDONDERRY, 1961

This map shows the number of Catholics as a percentage of the population, by census enumeration districts. In the city as a whole, Catholics constituted 67 per cent of the total population of 53,762. The use of enumeration districts, rather than the much larger wards, gives a more precise indication of the real intensity of segregation than the Belfast map opposite. *Source:* We are grateful to Alan Robinson, of the New University of Ulster Institute of Continuing Education, Londonderry, for providing this data, which arises from his own research into the social geography of the city.

southern Unionists commenced. The split was concealed for a while when a Dubliner, Sir Edward Carson, led the Ulster Unionist MPs at Westminster. During the third Home Rule Bill crisis of 1912–14 he struggled to resist home rule for Ireland altogether. But the arguments and the means of resistance, perhaps even the will to resist, no longer existed outside Ulster. Thus the years 1912–14 witnessed the remarkable spectacle of a king's counsel, aided and abetted by the leader of the Conservative party, sponsoring the creation and arming of a para-military force of 100,000 men, the Ulster Volunteer Force, pledged to resist by all means the application of the Liberal government's bill to Ulster. Unionist apologists are probably correct in their assertion that only the existence of such a well-disciplined force under the leadership of an officer class prevented serious sectarian rioting during the crisis. On the other hand, it is not easy to see how the crisis could have been terminated, or the Ulster Volunteer Force peacefully disbanded, had it not been for the intervention of the First World War.[4]

By the end of the war it was clear that, while twenty-six counties of Ireland would fight for as much independence as they could win, the predominantly Conservative coalition government at Westminster would not permit the coercion of the Protestants of north-east Ulster. The Government of Ireland Act of 1920 introduced the expected partition—along a six-county, rather than a four- or nine-county line—but otherwise differed from pre-war partitionist thinking only in its introduction of a separate home rule legislature for the north. Such an arrangement had never been part of the Ulster Unionist demand, and was probably instituted by the British government mainly for the sake of appearances—from the standpoint of world opinion, it was better to give all Ireland home rule with partition than to give some of the country home rule and retain six counties under the direct control of Westminster. A six-county subordinate parliament in Belfast was accepted by the Unionist leaders, grudgingly, 'as a final settlement and supreme sacrifice in the interests of peace . . . although not asked for'.[5] In fact, however, these leaders soon came to appreciate the positive advantages of the scheme. The new border could be far more effectively defended politically (and, if necessary, militarily) by Unionists in charge of their own administration in Belfast than ever it could be by a small group of Unionist backbenchers at Westminster. It was felt, correctly as

4. The story of the Ulster Volunteer Force is told in A. T. Q. Stewart, *The Ulster Crisis* (London, 1967). The high politics can be followed in R. Blake, *The Unknown Prime Minister* (London, 1955); R. Jenkins, *Asquith* (London, 1964); F. S. L. Lyons, *John Dillon* (London, 1968); and D. R. Gwynn, *The History of Partition* (Dublin, 1950). See also P. J. Buckland, *Irish Unionism: Ulster Unionism and the Origins of Northern Ireland, 1886–1922* (Dublin, 1973).

5. Letter from Sir James Craig to Lloyd George, cited in F. S. L. Lyons, *Ireland Since the Famine* (London, 1971), p. 683.

it turned out, that the provision made in the articles relating to the Council of Ireland for an ultimate federal settlement could be treated as a dead letter. Elections were therefore held in May 1921 under the single transferable vote system of proportional representation, in Belfast and Counties Antrim, Armagh, Down, Londonderry, Tyrone, and Fermanagh, to return fifty-two members to the 'parliament of Northern Ireland'. The constitution of the new state also provided for the establishment of a senate, and a governor representing the Crown.[6] The latter's powers were to be mostly formal, though he was to retain certain discretionary powers, such as the right to withhold the royal assent to proposed legislation, or refer it to the Judicial Committee of the Privy Council (each of which was exercised on one occasion)[7] and residual powers similar to those exercised in Britain by the monarch, so far as the choice of a prime minister was concerned.[8]

Apart from the replacement of proportional representation by single-member constituencies of the British type in 1929, this constitution remained fundamentally unchanged until its suspension and subsequent repeal in 1972–3. Nor did the powers granted to the new parliament undergo any substantial change during the half-century of its existence. Subject only to a general provision against religious discrimination in legislation, it took over full control of the police and courts (except the supreme court), education, agriculture, health and social services, commerce and development, along with a wide variety of minor matters. Topics remaining the responsibility of the Westminster parliament included all foreign, military, and fiscal affairs, together with posts and customs duties. The mother parliament indeed retained the ultimate authority to override any decision taken by Stormont,[9] but made no direct political intervention before the disturbances which started in 1969. Under a quickly established 'convention', Northern

6. The senate consisted of twenty-six members: twenty-four elected by the MPs, with the lord mayors of Belfast and Derry, *ex officio*. For an exposition of the 1920 constitution see N. Mansergh, *The Government of Northern Ireland: A Study in Devolution* (London, 1936) and R. J. Lawrence, *The Government of Northern Ireland: Public Finance and Public Services, 1921–64* (Oxford, 1965).

7. In 1922 the Governor withheld assent from the bill to abolish proportional representation in local government elections from July until September (see Lawrence, *Government of Northern Ireland*, p. 28); in 1935, at the instance of the Belfast Corporation, he referred the new Finance (NI) Act to the Judicial Committee on the grounds that it was *ultra vires*, but the decision was unfavourable. See I. Budge and C. O'Leary, *Belfast: Approach to Crisis* (London, 1973), pp. 152–3.

8. Apparently, the governor of Northern Ireland was solely responsible for the selection of Terence O'Neill in 1963 (see *The Autobiography of Terence O'Neill* [London, 1972], p. 42). When the Unionist party formally decided in the mid 1960s to choose future party leaders by election within the parliamentary party, this residual power disappeared.

9. 'Stormont' became the customary way of referring to the Northern Ireland government or parliament after the opening of the permanent parliamentary buildings there in 1932.

Ireland's domestic affairs were to all intents and purposes excluded from debate. In one typical year, 1934–5, a total of one hour and fifty minutes was spent in discussion of the province's affairs.[1]

But if the constitutional separation of Northern Ireland's devolved powers proved to be a straightforward exercise, the consequent adjustment of the financial position was very much less so. The bulk of Northern Ireland's revenue was to be allocated from imperial revenue by a joint exchequer board: an arrangement which had two major drawbacks. A substantial deduction had to be made from the agreed sum in the form of an 'imperial contribution' and, of more fundamental importance, the arrangement meant that the provincial government was obliged to plan its whole social and economic strategy with practically no power to regulate the size of its annual revenue. The former difficulty was resolved in 1925, when an arbitration committee under Lord Colwyn recommended that the imperial contribution be reduced from a first charge on the provincial exchequer to being whatever was left over at the end of the financial year. The second problem remained, however, until the main social and economic policies of the sovereign parliament were simply copied at local level, as must probably happen with any devolved legislature lacking fiscal autonomy. The Colwyn Committee had agreed that since Northern Ireland paid taxes at the same rate as the rest of the United Kingdom, her *per capita* expenditure should increase in future at the same rate: that is, 'step by step'. But it also asserted that in view of the province's general social and economic disparity with Great Britain it could not expect to be able to finance services to the same standard as Britain. Not until 1946, when the British Labour government began to implement its welfare state legislation, was parity of social services at last underwritten by the British Treasury. The *quid pro quo* was a substantial increase in Treasury control over any proposed future change in the pattern of Northern Ireland expenditure.[2]

During the inter-war period social and economic development was seriously aggravated by the financial relations which existed between the province and the mother parliament. The heavy burden of unemployment in particular put such a strain on provincial finances that no money was available for anything but the most short-term projects. This remained true even after the Unemployment Insurance Agreement of 1926 committed the UK government to meeting three-quarters of the cost of expenditure on unemployment benefit in Northern Ireland to the extent that it exceeded *per capita* expenditure in Britain. Thus until after the Second World War little was done in Northern Ireland towards modernizing the province's outdated schools, urban and rural housing,

1. Lyons, *Ireland Since the Famine*, p. 688.
2. The financial problems of devolution are summarized in Lyons, *Ireland Since the Famine*, pp. 687–93 and 729–31.

and road system, or tackling the widespread ill-health, especially tuberculosis, which was primarily the product of these bad conditions. Since 1946, however, Northern Ireland and its Unionist government have derived considerable benefit from the revised financial links. The government was able to deflate its left-wing critics by the painless importation of expensive British social reforms which, at the same time, gave the province a far more progressive appearance in terms of social welfare provisions than the neighbouring republic in the south. Although Northern Ireland continues to suffer from serious economic difficulties, they have been the more general and deep-rooted ones of declining industries, remote location, lack of raw materials, and chronic un-employment.

More fundamental than the financial difficulties of the province, or even its endemic economic handicaps, however, have been the sectarian animosities arising out of the long-standing segregation and mutual suspicion of the Protestant and Catholic communities. In education, a thoroughgoing segregation has persisted everywhere except in the technical colleges and universities. Although the financing of state schools (in effect Protestant) and Catholic schools was worked out more or less amicably by 1930, Catholic determination to maintain separate schooling, and Protestant pressure for the provision of acceptable religious teaching in the state schools, has ensured a hardening of the edges of segregation and the elimination—apart from a small number of independent, mainly middle-class, schools—of the non-denominational atmosphere necessary for any degree of integration.[3]

These basic divisions in the community have been the background to more bitter disputes over the state's methods of maintaining law and order, and its conduct of public administration. The Catholic minority in the six counties never accepted partition, and was therefore fundamentally 'disloyal', according to the wide interpretation of the term applied by many Ulster Protestants. In the early years, the mass of Catholics, like their parliamentary representatives, abstained from participation in the public life of a state which they did not believe would ever establish itself. There were thus few Catholics in the Royal Ulster Constabulary, and little Protestant encouragement for them to join it. In the Ulster Special Constabulary, a force recruited specifically for security duties, there were practically none, certainly not among the part-time 'B' Specials, who survived as a militia of Protestant activists until their disbandment in 1969.[4] From the earliest

3. For a full study of the education question see D. H. Akenson, *Education and Enmity: The Control of Schooling in Northern Ireland, 1920-50* (Newton Abbot, 1973).

4. Sir A. Hezlet, *The B Specials* (London, 1972), though scrupulous in its approach to established facts, admits to being a case for the defence. Given the lack of reliable documentary evidence, an impartial history of such a controversial force is unlikely to be forthcoming.

years of the State there existed a strong animosity between the mass of the Catholic population and the police. It was paralleled by opposition to the basis on which the law was enforced, for the Special Powers Act of 1922, brought in as an emergency measure to combat the widespread IRA activity of the time, continued on the statute book after that emergency was over, being reviewed annually until 1933, when it was made permanent. While it has been possible to make out some sort of case for the measure's existence during the 1922–3 troubles, the period of the Second World War, or the more recent post-1969 disturbances, its perpetuation during the long intervening periods of calm has seemed to many Catholics simply a device to permit an Orange Minister of Home Affairs, or an Orange policeman, to harass anyone expressing republican sentiments.

Catholic bitterness found an even broader base in the belief that the state sought to discriminate against Catholics on general social and economic grounds, with the attributed motive of keeping down the Catholic proportion of the population by encouraging emigration. It was easy, for instance, to produce figures in support of the argument that Unionist-controlled local councils gave preference to Protestants in the fields of public employment and housing (although a similar process of discrimination seems to have operated in the few councils where Catholics were in the majority).[5] It was equally clear that in some areas, notably the city of Londonderry, the effect of the new local government ward boundaries introduced in 1923 and after was to produce councils with Protestant–Unionist majorities in areas where Catholic–Nationalists constituted a clear majority of the voting population.[6] The local government franchise, furthermore, with its exclusion of non-ratepayers, also tended to debar disproportionately more Catholics than Protestants.[7]

At the parliamentary level there is less evidence of large-scale gerrymandering.[8] The most obvious attempt by the Unionists to

5. The best attempt at a dispassionate survey of this issue is Barritt and Carter, *Northern Ireland Problem*.

6. The ward divisions established in Derry in 1936 made possible 'a continuous Unionist majority in the corporation of twelve to eight, despite the fact that Unionists can claim the allegiance of only about 41 per cent of the population of voting age in the city, and Protestants constitute only about 37 per cent of the total population', Barritt and Carter, *Northern Ireland Problem*, p. 120.

7. There are no figures available to indicate the relative degree of enfranchisement among different denominations. The proportion of adults enfranchised in Belfast in 1966, however, was 79 per cent at a time when between 95 and 100 per cent of adults in the major British cities had the vote. This disparity developed only after the Second World War, when the local government franchise in Britain was recognized as a right inhering in the individual, and not in property. See I. Budge and C. O'Leary, *Belfast: Approach to Crisis* (London, 1973), p. 175. The principle of 'one man, one vote' was implemented in Northern Ireland local government elections in 1972.

8. For a complete electoral record see S. Elliott (ed.), *Northern Ireland Parliamentary Election Results, 1921–72* (Chichester, 1973). The calculations which follow are all based on this source.

manipulate the electoral system in their favour was the abolition of proportional representation in 1929. This was frankly intended to operate to the disadvantage of third parties in the system, but it also resulted in a slight decrease in the number of Catholic–Nationalist seats. The Catholic population of Co. Antrim, which was large enough to return one member under proportional representation, was too diffused within the county to have influence in any seat after 1929. Similarly, the division of Co. Armagh into four single-member seats reduced the number of Catholic representatives from two to one. But the most often quoted cases of gerrymandering at the parliamentary level, Co. Fermanagh and Derry city, do not stand up to cross-examination.[9] It is true that the Catholic South Fermanagh constituency was a very peculiar shape (partly explained by the long barrier of Lough Erne), and that the county as a whole, with a majority of Nationalist voters, returned two Unionists to one Nationalist after 1929. But viewed in a wider perspective, the eight single-member seats in Counties Fermanagh and Tyrone returned four Unionists and four Nationalists after 1929, just as the large two-county proportional representation constituency had done in 1921 and 1925. In Co. Londonderry, Nationalists held two of the five seats after 1929, as they had done beforehand. The gerry-mander there was symbolic only. So that the constituency which bore the name Londonderry City should have a Unionist representative, the boundary was drawn around the walled city centre in such a way that the city's Catholic majority was included in another, more exclusively urban seat with the name Foyle.

The underlying force of the discrimination argument, however, has been derived not from any direct evidence of institutional discrimination but from wide and obvious differences in the relative prosperity of the two communities. The Protestants very plainly control the economic life of the province, with the Catholic middle class, until recently, consisting only of a narrow group of professional men, teachers, shopkeepers, and publicans. Lower down the social scale Protestants have dominated the skilled and best-paid manual jobs in the Belfast shipyards and elsewhere, while Catholics have tended to predominate only among the unskilled and the unemployed. The explanation lies partly in the attitude of employers, many of whom apparently find that to employ only members of their own community makes for more harmonious office, factory, and customer relationships,[1] and partly in the development of the two communities since the industrial revolution. When Catholics flocked into Belfast and other Ulster towns in the aftermath of the great famine

9. For a statement of the nationalist position on these cases, see L. de Paor, *Divided Ulster* (London, 1970), pp. 148–9.

1. For an analysis of religious discrimination in the field of private employment see Barritt and Carter, *Northern Ireland Problem*, pp. 100–5.

they entered at the bottom of the social scale. In the increasingly stagnant economic climate of the province, faced with organized opposition from the Orange Order, physically repressed and morally cocooned by the ghetto, they have to a considerable extent remained there. The community conflict this engendered had its roots in and was reinforced by a real conflict over the national status of the province. This conflict is consequently as alive in the 1970s as it was a century ago. It remains the only realistic framework within which to study the politics of the province.

PROTESTANT POLITICS

The Unionist party enjoyed a near monopoly of Protestant representation throughout the existence of the Stormont parliament. It won all twelve general elections held between 1921 and 1969, never holding less than thirty-three out of the fifty-two seats, and sometimes winning as many as forty.[2] Its control over the twelve Ulster seats at Westminster has been even more pronounced. Until 1970 it always held at least nine seats, and was sometimes able to win some or all of the three 'Catholic' seats as well.[3] The party, consequently, has retained exclusive control of the government of Northern Ireland. Continuity of personnel, in both government and parliament, has been pronounced. There were only six prime ministers during the fifty years of the system's existence, and only three in the first forty years.[4] Of the six members of the original 1921 cabinet, four were still in office in 1936. Of the thirty-six sitting Unionist MPs in 1936, twenty-one had been members since the state's inception.[5] The turn-over of personnel seems to have been slightly more rapid in the post-war period, since the average length of service for a Unionist MP over the entire period 1921–69 was 9·7 years. In fact, however, an important proportion of the turn-over has been the transfer of lawyer MPs to appointments in the judiciary. If lawyers are excluded from the calculations, then the average length of service over the entire period has been 13·5 years.[6]

The corollary to this in electoral terms was lack of competition. Between 1929, when single-member constituencies replaced the PR

2. The number was reduced for a while to twenty-eight in 1970–1 as a result of by-election losses, defections, and temporary withdrawals of the party whip.

3. In 1970 it lost a seat to a Protestant Unionist. In 1973 its total was reduced to seven by a defection to the Alliance party.

4. Sir James Craig (cr. Viscount Craigavon, 1927), 1921–40; J. M. Andrews, 1940–3; Sir Basil Brooke (cr. Viscount Brookeborough, 1952), 1943–63; Captain T. O'Neill, 1963–9; Major J. D. Chichester-Clark, 1969–71; and A. B. D. Faulkner, 1971–2.

5. J. L. McCracken, 'The political scene in Northern Ireland, 1926–37', in F. MacManus (ed.), *The Years of the Great Test* (Cork, 1967), p. 155.

6. J. F. Harbinson, *The Ulster Unionist Party, 1882–1973: its Development and Organisation* (Belfast, 1973), p. 112.

system, and 1969, 47 per cent of Unionist electoral victories were unopposed. Like the Nationalist party, the Unionists' surest strength has been outside Belfast. Outside the city, it lost control of a seat with a Protestant majority only once, at a by-election, for a period of four years.[7] Unlike the Nationalists, however, the Unionists also remained their community's most powerful party in the city of Belfast: six of the sixteen seats remained exclusively theirs, and a further six were in their hands for twenty years or more.

The Unionist party, through its Ulster Unionist members at Westminster, always had formal links with the British Conservative party (until the new developments of 1974). Its members are consistently referred to as 'Tories' by the Northern Ireland Labour party and the anti-partitionist groups in the province. There is clearly considerable justification for such a view: the 1927 Trades Disputes Act, which impeded the political activities of trade unions, was repealed in Great Britain in 1946, but in Northern Ireland not until 1959; plural voting in parliamentary and local elections was retained until 1969, long after it had been done away with in Britain. The political representatives of the party have been drawn mainly from the social and economic élite of the province. The social base of the party's representation has broadened slightly since 1921, as Table 5.2 indicates, but by and large the Unionist party remains a party 'dominated by business and professional men'.[8] The artisan element, social group C2, which was quite substantially represented in the first parliament, actually fell away to almost nothing after 1925.

But if the Unionist party is essentially Tory at the parliamentary

TABLE 5.2

Social class of Unionist MPs, 1921–69 (percentage)

Social class	1921	1949	1969	1921–69
A. Higher administrative, managerial, professional, large farmers	75·0	89·2	63·9	85·5
B. Intermediate administrative, managerial, professional	10·0	10·8	19·4	6·9
C1. Supervisory, clerical, lower professional	—	—	13·9	3·8
C2. Skilled manual	10·0	—	—	2·5
D. Unskilled manual	—	—	—	1·3
E. Casual, pensioners	—	—	—	—

Source: J. F. Harbinson, 'The Ulster Unionist Party, 1882–1970: its development and organisation' (Queen's University of Belfast, PhD thesis, 1972), p. 169.

7. North Down, 1941–5. The intruder was an Independent Unionist, disgruntled at being denied the official nomination. In 1945 he was returned as the official party nominee.

8. Harbinson, *Ulster Unionist Party*, p. 109.

level, the nature of its grass-roots support has made it something more than that, and explains how, in Belfast and other towns, the party has been able to retain the regular support of thousands of active trade unionists and how, in country districts, small farmers have consistently given support to candidates in whose selection the larger landowners have had the most prominent voice. One reason for the party's success in this respect has been its close association with the Orange Order, a social and benevolent organization which combines the paranoid Protestantism of the counter-reformation era with a Tammany Hall approach to local affairs. Its total membership in Northern Ireland was estimated in 1969 as 125,000.[9] Founded in Co. Armagh in 1795, the Order was increasingly taken up by influential society during the following generation, and boasted two royal dukes as successive grand masters. Protests in Britain against its alleged secret influence led to its formal dissolution by the Grand Lodge in 1836. The grass roots refused to die however, although for the next fifty years the Order remained distinctly plebeian in character. But after the first home rule crisis of 1886, it began once more to attract politically active middle- and upper-class Unionists on a large scale.[1] The extent of its political influence in the twentieth century is amply illustrated by the fact that of the 149 Unionist MPs elected to Stormont between 1921 and 1969, 135 were Orangemen. Of the fourteen non-subscribers, four were women, three had ceased to be members of the Order for various reasons, and one was a former member of the Northern Ireland Labour party.[2] The Orange Order has perhaps been the strongest influence in the province against the development of class-based party politics.

Some observers have characterized the Unionist party as populist, or compared it to the American Democratic party. The structure of its leadership, however, has been too traditionally Tory to permit the application of such labels. Part of the explanation is that, as we have seen, Unionist strength has been in the rural areas and the suburban districts of Belfast. Quite often the party has been obliged to surrender the support of working-class Protestants to Labour or to proponents of a blatantly sectarian (and perhaps also socially radical) policy. The latter were the true populists. Recurrent crises, real or imagined, over the maintenance of partition enabled the Unionists to regain a footing in such areas from time to time, and so prevent the permanent erosion of their support.

9. Harbinson, *Ulster Unionist Party*, p. 93.
1. J. C. Beckett, *The Making of Modern Ireland, 1603–1923* (London, 1966), pp. 316, 399.
2. Harbinson, *Ulster Unionist Party*, p. 91. Two other non-Orange Unionists were the Hall-Thompsons, father and son. The father, none the less, habitually conducted his election campaigns in Belfast mounted on a white horse, symbol of William of Orange himself.

In 1917–19 there had been concern among Westminster and Belfast politicians that the red revolutions sweeping the capitals of central Europe might be imitated in the industrial cities of the United Kingdom. The local response of Sir Edward Carson had been to stir certain trade unionists in Belfast who had been active in the resistance to home rule a few years earlier, into forming an Ulster Unionist Labour Association, within the Unionist party, but with access to trade union voters which the party as a whole did not have. Three nominees of this body sat as 'Labour Unionists' at Westminster from 1918 to 1922, while no less than five of them were returned for the Northern Ireland parliament in 1921. They account for the artisan element in the parliamentary party. Most of them had disappeared from the political scene by 1929, however, and only one, William Grant, made a place for himself in the inner councils of the party. The association seems to have been created by Carson in a moment of inspired panic, and many middle-class Unionists soon came to regard it as a tiresome and unnecessary expedient.[3] Such objections were based solely on the grounds that the Labour men took up places which more orthodox Unionists also sought after, for, so far as party policy was concerned, the interlopers had neither the inclination nor the ability to urge the party along more radical lines. The character of the Unionist Labour Association is illustrated by the fact that its president for very many years was J. M. Andrews, MP, who was deemed a suitable figure to hold the office on the grounds that he was a very large *employer* of labour. The association continues to exist, though it has sent forward only one new candidate to the commons, and a handful to the senate, since 1921. In the opinion of the party's historian, the association is now practically moribund.[4]

But perhaps the main reason for the Unionists' effortless maintenance of power lies in the ultimate insignificance of the local parliament. Once a working agreement was reached between Westminster and Stormont on the financial aspects of devolution (as it had been by the end of the inter-war period) social progress could be maintained, with no additional effort or expense, simply by reproducing Westminster legislation. Stormont's powers to modify British levels of taxation were so slight that there was no inducement to conservative social forces to resist the duplication in Ulster of the British government's 'socialistic' innovations. The choice was not open to Ulstermen in the post-war period of avoiding sharp increases in taxation by rejecting the improved welfare and education services that accompanied them. A section of Unionist party opinion accordingly drew the conclusion that Northern Ireland would

3. Recollections of Sir Wilson Hungerford, first secretary of the Unionist party, in an interview with members of the PRONI staff in November 1965. Cited in P. J. Buckland (ed.), *Irish Unionism, 1885–1923* (Belfast, 1973), pp. 441–2.
4. Harbinson, *Ulster Unionist Party*, pp. 66–68.

be better off outside a socialist Britain, and pressed the Prime Minister, Sir Basil Brooke, to move towards a greater degree of provincial autonomy, or perhaps even dominion status. He was able to stave off any major crisis, however, and the demand disappeared with the return of the Conservatives to office in Britain in 1951.[5]

The greatest strength of the Unionist party at the polls has been its ability to identify Unionism with Protestantism. Frequently this has been achieved in a genteel fashion, by calls for 'loyalist' unity and the like, with no overt appeal to sectarianism. In some constituencies, however, and especially when the party was hard pressed during the depression years, a cruder approach has been employed along the lines of the often-quoted remarks by Lord Craigavon that 'we are a Protestant parliament and a Protestant state', and by Sir Basil Brooke that 'Catholics are out to destroy Ulster with all their might and power'.[6] The problem for Unionists wishing to free their party from the sectarian style of politics has been that the replacement of the 'Protestant' appeal by any other image, such as a conservative one, would have substantially reduced their electoral support. Thus, although there has seldom been any serious objection in high Unionist circles to the appointment of a small number of individual Catholics to important public positions,[7] they have never occupied places in any degree commensurate with their numbers.[8] More important, there has never in the history of Northern Ireland been a Catholic Unionist parliamentary candidate.[9] The Orange Order has always occupied too influential a position in local Unionist politics to permit such a development. Thus, when liberal elements in the party urged the admission of Catholics in 1959, the Grand Master of the Order in Ireland denounced the proposals forcefully, and the Prime Minister of the day, Lord Brookeborough, smothered the question,

5. J. E. Sayers, 'Political parties and the social background', in T. Wilson (ed.), *Ulster Under Home Rule* (London, 1955), pp. 66–67.

6. *Parliamentary Debates, N.I.* xvi, col. 1095 (24 April 1934); M. Wallace, *Northern Ireland: Fifty Years of Self-Government* (Newton Abbot, 1971), p. 70.

7. Sir Denis Henry, the first Lord Chief Justice, was a Catholic, as was the first permanent secretary to the Ministry of Education, A. N. Bonaparte Wyse. At the local government level, where a franker sectarian spirit has often extended to those who direct affairs, discrimination in public employment has been more blatant, under Catholic-controlled councils as well as Protestant ones. See Barritt and Carter, *Northern Ireland Problem*, p. 97.

8. Barritt and Carter found that in 1959, as in 1927, 94 per cent of the senior grade posts in the Northern Ireland civil service were filled by Protestants: *Northern Ireland Problem*, p. 96. In 1969 the judiciary, from high court judges down to petty sessions' clerks, numbered 68 Protestants and 6 Catholics, while membership of nine of the most important public boards in Northern Ireland in the same year included 115 Protestants as against 16 Catholics. See Harbinson, *Ulster Unionist Party*, pp. 118–19.

9. Dr G. B. Newe, a Catholic but not an elected representative, was co-opted into the Northern Ireland cabinet for the last six months of its existence, 1971–2. Sir Denis Henry, the only Catholic Unionist MP ever, sat at Westminster from 1916 until 1921.

'which did not exist, and which probably will not arise'.[1] Under the leadership of Terence O'Neill a more liberal style of politics emerged, but the realities appear to have changed little.[2] A solitary Catholic Unionist who attempted to come forward in 1969 failed to gain the nomination in the (Nationalist-held) constituency of South Down.[3] In November 1969 after a summer of severe sectarian rioting had brought about British military intervention to maintain order in the province, Major Chichester-Clark declared that Catholics who supported the principles of Unionism had an equal right with other party members to be considered for party office.[4] But in view of the polarization of feeling which has since taken place, along with the emergence of new political groupings, the present prospects for such a development do not look very promising. No Catholic Unionists came forward in 1973 to seek election to the Assembly which replaced the disbanded Northern Ireland Parliament, or in 1975 to contest the constitutional Convention.

The party has sought to justify the adoption of what was, until recently, an intransigent attitude on the grounds that to give way on the question would be to permit the entry of more extreme Protestant groups. It is from these elements, rather than from Catholic parties (with their strictly limited number of parliamentary seats) that the Unionists have feared electoral attack. From time to time Unionists have been challenged by equally 'loyal' candidates with a radical social twist, but with the exception of the second proportional representation election of 1925 (when such candidates took four seats) and occasional forays by the Northern Ireland Labour party, they resisted these attacks with little difficulty until the changed circumstances of 1973. In 1938 a Progressive Unionist party, with an experienced ex-Unionist at the head, fought nine constituencies in Belfast, but lost heavily in all of them. Individual candidates have fared better in certain constituencies where they have been able to combine their radical views with a direct appeal to sectarianism.[5] A recent example of such a campaign was that of the Revd Ian Paisley, who combined a fundamentalist opposition to 'popery' with an emphasis on the problems of housing and unemployment, to

1. Wallace, *Northern Ireland*, pp. 72–73. It is alleged that many local Unionist associations ask only one question as a general test for membership: 'Is the individual concerned a Protestant?' (Harbinson, *Ulster Unionist Party*, p. 115).

2. For a vigorous attack on the fragility of O'Neill's liberalism see A. B. Cooke, 'O'Neill and Lord Brookeborough', *Fortnight*, 51 (November 1972). The accompanying defence of Lord Brookeborough's administration need not be regarded as an integral part of the argument. *The Autobiography of Terence O'Neill* puts the case for the defence.

3. F. W. Boal and R. H. Buchanan, 'The 1969 Northern Ireland general election', *Irish Geography*, VI. i (1969), 79.

4. Wallace, *Northern Ireland*, p. 74.

5. Notably J. W. Nixon (Ind. U.) in Woodvale, 1929–49; T. G. Henderson (Ind. U.) in Shankill, 1925–53; and N. Porter (Ind. U.) in Clifton, 1953–8. All three constituencies are predominantly working-class districts of Belfast.

undermine Terence O'Neill's liberal Unionism in 1969, and defeat O'Neill's Unionist would-be successor in the Bannside constituency in 1970.[6] Since his election Mr Paisley has created a new party by fusing his fundamentalist support in Co. Antrim with the traditional reluctance of working-class Protestants in Belfast to accept Unionist leadership. As a gesture in the direction of liberal respectability, the name of his movement was changed from 'Protestant Unionist' to 'Democratic Unionist' in 1971, but recent fluctuations in his political fortunes suggest that popular Protestant support is to be won in inverse proportion to the emphasis placed on radicalism rather than sectarianism.

Until he began to re-emphasize the 'loyalist' planks in his platform early in 1973, Mr Paisley and his Democratic Unionist party were less successful in mobilizing militant Protestant sentiment than the Vanguard movement, initially a ginger group within the Unionist party, which emerged as an independent force in time for the elections to the new Assembly. Vanguard's leader, William Craig, and some of his associates, were patently disaffected Unionist politicians with no obvious inclination to implement broad social reform.[7] Their emphasis was on the Unionist party's ineffectual handling of the security situation since 1969 and failure to resist British government intervention since 1972. But the mass of support for this movement, in Belfast at any rate, came from the paramilitary Ulster Defence Association and its industrial front, the Loyalist Association of Workers.[8] There is no doubt that one of the main political effects of the emergence of such organizations has been to broaden the social base of Protestant political representation.[9] From their earliest days they urged Mr Craig to break with the Unionist party though they were clearly anxious to take him with them in order to maintain their movement as a national one, rather than as merely the voice of working-class Protestants in Belfast. None the less, the Ulster

6. For an evaluation of Mr Paisley's position see 'The loyalist who came in from the cold', *Fortnight*, 60 (April 1973); and D. Boulton, *The UVF, 1966–73: An Anatomy of Loyalist Rebellion* (Dublin, 1973).

7. In October 1972, Mr Craig told a meeting of right-wing Conservative MPs at Westminster that he 'could mobilise 80,000 men' and was 'prepared to kill' (*Fortnight*, 49, November 1972). In 1959, when he was beginning his political career, a newspaper profile had concluded that 'the point about William Craig is that he is a moderate' (*Belfast Telegraph*, 30 October 1959).

8. Membership of the two organizations was apparently more or less identical. See the recollections of a former UDA leader in the *Sunday Times*, 28 January 1973. By 1974 the LAW had been reorganized under a new leadership as the Ulster Workers' Council.

9. The Ulster Defence Association and Vanguard almost split in July 1972 over the question of tactics to be employed in order to elicit a tougher anti-IRA line from the government. The UDA wanted (and, in Belfast, achieved) a one-day strike against all employers, and denounced Vanguard's alternative of a 'rent-and-rates strike' as 'an ill-conceived and ill-timed move which will only hurt the ordinary working-class people, who will have to pay back the money in the end'. Cited in Boulton, *The UVF, 1966–73*, p. 175.

Defence Association has maintained its paramilitary stance first and foremost, rather than risk being ensnared down what seems to be the blind alley of social questions, as the Official IRA and, for a while, the Democratic Unionists, have been. The success of the Ulster Defence Association in Protestant districts, like the success of the Provisional IRA among Catholics, seems to indicate that the militancy of the young, and radical feeling in general, can still be mobilized effectively in Ireland only be sectarian-nationalistic sentiments, and not by any direct appeal to left-wing ideology.

CATHOLIC POLITICS

Under the system of proportional representation which operated in 1921 and 1925, anti-partitionists were able to return twelve members to the Northern Ireland parliament. In 1925 they were also able to assist the return of two Labour candidates who were opposed to the border, as well as an Independent Unionist whose vigorous defence of the liquor trade meant that his election was considered a victory by one important Catholic interest group. Under the single-member system as it operated between 1929 and 1972, anti-partitionists could count on eleven seats with clear-cut Catholic majorities, while two seats in east Belfast (Dock and Pottinger) have been at one time or another truly marginal. The fluctuations in these two seats, and the bewildering variety of party labels which occur in Belfast generally, have led many observers to the erroneous view that Catholic electors did not lose by the abolition of proportional representation. In fact they made a net loss of one safe seat plus the controlling influence in another.[1]

Successful candidates for these Catholic seats have stood under three main party labels. In the twelve general elections between 1921 and 1969, 'Nationalists' won 102 electoral victories, Sinn Féiners and Republicans (all abstentionists) 12, and anti-partitionist Labour groups 19.[2] The Labour victories have all been in Belfast, all but one since 1945. All but three of the Republican victories were before 1933. Since the passage of the Representation of the People Act (NI), 1934, candidates

1. Throughout Northern Ireland's parliamentary history, Catholic voters were able to control three seats in Co. Tyrone; two each in Counties Down and Londonderry; one (later two) in west Belfast; and one each in Counties Armagh and Fermanagh. Until 1929 they also held a seat in Co. Antrim and a second seat in Co. Armagh. Following the 1929 changes in the electoral system, they were able to oust the NILP from a second 'Catholic' seat in west Belfast, though they might have been able to achieve this under the proportional representation system anyway.

2. I have included in the Republican figures a Fianna Fáil victory in South Down in 1933, although it was in fact secured *against* a Republican candidate. Not included in the Labour figure are six victories by official NILP candidates who were opposed to partition. Also excluded from these figures are three victories in Catholic seats in 1969 by independent civil rights candidates.

have been obliged to declare their intention of taking their seats if elected, while the Electoral Law Act (NI), 1962, required them to 'recognize the lawful authority of the parliament of Northern Ireland'.[3] Constitutional Nationalists, therefore, have been the leading force in Catholic politics in Northern Ireland, although there are a number of qualifications which must be made. Firstly, they have not held or contested a Stormont seat in the city of Belfast since 1946. Furthermore, their ascendancy over the abstentionist Republicans has been very much facilitated by the electoral legislation just mentioned. In elections to the Westminster parliament, where the same restrictions do not apply, Republicans have made a better showing, and it seems that from 1956 until 1970, at any rate, there was 'manifest collusion' between Nationalists and Republicans in the seats outside Belfast, to the extent that one party contested Northern Ireland elections and the other Westminster elections.[4] In contests between Nationalist and Republican candidates since 1945 each party has won two seats.

The Nationalists are usually described as the descendants of the Irish Parliamentary party of Parnell, Redmond, and Dillon, which was all but obliterated in the south of Ireland in 1918. The old parliamentarian Joseph Devlin remained leader of the Ulster Nationalists until his death in 1934, and his short-lived constituency association, the National League of the North, founded in 1928, was formally associated with the neo-Redmondite National League in the south. But these links conceal the true breadth of the Nationalist party in the north. The bitterness created by the 1922 civil war in southern Irish politics affected northern Catholics but little, partly because the battle there had been between anti-partitionists and unionists, but also because the polarization within the anti-partitionist camp continued to be between constitutional Nationalists and Sinn Féin. In effect, the pro-treaty wing of Sinn Féin in the north came over to the Nationalists in 1922. Three of the nine successful Nationalist candidates at the 1929 election had been Sinn Féiners in 1921.[5] After Fianna Fáil entered the Dáil in 1927, the northern Nationalists gradually assimilated the constitutional Republican element also, and Republicanism in the north became the preserve of the irreconcilable IRA element, just as it had done in the south. Perhaps because of their common interest in resisting IRA-Republicans, a tacit

3. Wallace, *Northern Ireland*, p. 81.
4. T. P. Coogan, *Ireland Since the Rising* (London, 1966), p. 309. The Nationalist who opposed a Republican in Co. Londonderry in 1966 was not supported by his party. In 1970, local Nationalists and Republicans agreed on compromise 'Unity' candidates in Mid-Ulster and Fermanagh and South Tyrone. Both were successful, but subsequently associated themselves with the Republican point of view. In February 1974 they were opposed for the Catholic vote by more moderate figures, and the seats were won by loyalist candidates.
5. J. H. Collins (South Down), J. Connellan (South Armagh), and C. Healy (South Fermanagh).

alliance developed over the years between the Dublin government and the Nationalists, so that by the early 1960s the latter seemed to at least one historian to be 'Fianna Fáil's faithful allies in Northern Ireland'.[6]

Until 1964, when they formally accepted the role of official opposition at Stormont,[7] or perhaps 1966 when they began to hold annual party conferences, it is misleading to talk of the Nationalists as a party at all. They were, rather, simply those MPs representing districts with Catholic majorities (excluding Belfast, since 1945), acting more or less in concert when attending Stormont, and more or less opposing IRA-Republicanism during their periods of parliamentary abstention. They had no national party headquarters, and no full-time paid organizers.[8] For much of the period they had no national constituency association. The National League of the North was forced into life to fight the 1929 election, but expired shortly afterwards. The Irish Union Association (sometimes known as the National Council for Unity) was established at a conference in Belfast in 1936, in the hope of bridging the gap between Nationalists, Republicans, and Fianna Fáil supporters, but proved even less effective.[9] In its structure, which scarcely ever existed, except on paper, it closely resembled Fianna Fáil, and it received some initial financial support from Dublin. The driving force always came from Ulster-born Fianna Fáil members like Eamon Donnelly, who was incensed at de Valera's refusal to extend his party into the north.[1] In the immediate postwar years, the Anti-Partition League emerged for a while as a more vigorous grass-roots organization, deriving some stimulus from Clann na Poblachta activity in the south (though it had no direct connection with that party), and from de Valera's 'world-wide' anti-partition campaign after his defeat at the polls in 1948. But it, too, withered away during the IRA revival of the 1950s.[2] During the 1960s emphasis shifted in Catholic political circles away from grass-roots activity in the direction of widening the policies and improving the personnel of the movement.

The widespread feeling in the early 1960s that Nationalist politicians were ineffectual 'green Tories' made it imperative to revamp the movement at the top, especially once it became reasonably clear that a

6. L. de Paor, *Divided Ulster* (London, 1970), p. 139.

7. The party relinquished this position following the Derry disturbances of October 1968.

8. R. Rose, *Governing Without Consensus* (London, 1971), p. 221.

9. McCracken, 'The political scene in Northern Ireland', in MacManus (ed.), *Years of the Great Test*, p. 153.

1. I am indebted for this information to Mr Harry O'Neill, Warrenpoint, Co. Down, whose father was a Nationalist MP from 1921 to 1938, and who was himself active in constituency politics for many years [A. C. H.].

2. A document in the possession of Mr O'Neill indicates that even active Nationalists could be unaware of the state of their movement. At a meeting of Mourne Nationalists in April 1961, the secretary was instructed to write to Belfast 'to clear the air concerning the existence of the Anti-Partition League'.

Labour government would soon take power at Westminster. Constituency organization, by comparison, was scarcely necessary, for, in the nature of politics in Northern Ireland, there were no floating voters to win over. All that was necessary in this respect was to ensure that in districts with a Catholic majority or near-majority, every eligible Catholic was registered to vote and every ineligible Protestant excluded from voting. In sectarian politics, the register is all-important. Far more than a constituency organization of the British type, a Catholic registration committee was a flexible instrument which could be put at the disposal of anti-partition candidates of any persuasion, according to circumstances.[3]

Anti-partition *arguments*, though necessary for London and the world at large, and perhaps on occasion for Dublin, were in constituency politics regarded as superfluous, as 'preaching to the converted'. For although the primary characteristic of Northern Ireland politics has been the opposition of Unionist–Protestants and Nationalist–Catholics, they have seldom ventured into one another's territory to fight elections. In only twenty-four of the forty-eight territorial seats which existed between 1929 and 1969 was there ever a contest between a Unionist and a declared anti-partitionist candidate, and only four of those seats were so contested more than four times in ten general elections. Out of 542 possible contests in territorial constituencies, including by-elections, Unionists and anti-partitionists opposed one another directly on only sixty-three occasions, seventeen of which were three- or four-cornered contests.[4] Unionists won 47 per cent of their victories without any contest, anti-partition candidates 40 per cent, and the Northern Ireland Labour party (NILP), by contrast, only 5 per cent: a figure which in fact represents only one such victory.[5]

The sectarian nature of politics in the province thus tended to cause electoral stagnation. So far as anti-partitionist politics is concerned, there was very often stagnation at the centre also. Apart from occasional flashes of excitement, usually brought about by a change of government in London or Dublin, there seemed little prospect in pursuing such aims

3. Mr James O'Reilly, for example, the last MP for Mourne constituency, entered parliament in 1958 with a declining constituency organization and a slender majority which he subsequently doubled, operating with simply a registration committee (information from Mr H. O'Neill). In Derry city during the 1920s, the Roman Catholic bishop initiated a Catholic registration committee (which survived until quite recently) because the register was going unattended while Nationalists and Sinn Féiners struggled for the leadership of the Catholic community in the city. The records of this committee have now been deposited in the Public Record Office of Northern Ireland.

4. The small number of contests between Unionists and official NILP candidates who were unequivocally opposed to partition has been omitted from this figure, as have the six contests between Unionists and People's Democracy candidates in 1969.

5. In predominantly Catholic South Armagh, 1938, when anti-partitionist parties boycotted the election.

in the northern parliament. Abstentionism was rejected as a *principle* by Nationalists after the collapse of the Boundary Commission in 1925, and gradually the other nine MPs followed Joseph Devlin's lead, entering parliament for the first time between 1925 and 1927.[6] One motive for this change of policy was certainly the knowledge that drastic boundary changes, which might have brought the new state to its knees, were no longer to be expected. Another was probably the pressure of the northern Catholic bishops, who were alarmed at the trend of the new parliament's education legislation, evolving without any formal Catholic opposition.[7] More cynical observers have suggested that Sir James Craig virtually bribed Devlin into participation in exchange for a discreet share of public patronage for the Nationalist party, but reliable evidence for (or against) such a theory is unlikely to be forthcoming. It is certainly the case that, whether or not participation was necessary for the defence of Catholic interests, it was very desirable from the point of view of Unionists who were concerned about the image of their state in London and elsewhere. As such, it was discreetly encouraged. Legislation against Republican abstentionism, such as the Representation of the People Act, 1934, was presented as a stern Unionist measure in defence of the state, but in practice it was equally helpful to non-abstentionist Nationalists.

But if abstention was no longer a principle for Nationalists after 1925, it remained in their armoury as a tactic. The entire party walked out in the spring of 1932 and remained away for eighteen months, ostensibly in protest against not being allowed to discuss certain matters which were reserved to the United Kingdom parliament. A further intention may have been to undermine as much as possible any prestige which the government might have expected to gain from the opening of the determinedly impressive parliament buildings at Stormont. Later abstention was on an individual and sporadic basis, but was more frequent among representatives from the western part of the province, where Republican-abstentionist feeling among the electorate was stronger (and where public transport links with Belfast were poor).[8] Between 1938 and 1945 only two of the eight Nationalist representatives ever attended, one of whom, the party's leader, T. J. Campbell, subsequently received a judgeship for his pains.[9] After 1945 attendance became more regular, although the refusal to participate still remained

6. *Annual Register*, 1925–7.

7. D. Kennedy, 'Catholics in Northern Ireland, 1926–35', in MacManus (ed.), *Years of the Great Test*, p. 140.

8. For an insight into the problems of attending Stormont from Co. Fermanagh, see various speeches by John McHugh in the Senate, 1940–5.

9. For a more charitable view of Campbell's motives see his autobiography, *Fifty Years of Ulster, 1890–1940* (Belfast, 1941), in which he emphasizes his role in setting an example of regular Nationalist attendance at Stormont in defence of his constituents' interests.

the ultimate weapon throughout the existence of the Northern Ireland parliament. The Nationalists had little compunction in discontinuing their short-lived role as the official opposition as a protest against the government's handling of law and order in Derry city in October 1968,[1] while the newly formed Social Democratic and Labour party withdrew from parliament in protest at the shooting by the British Army of two apparently innocent men in Derry, in July 1971, and never returned. If such withdrawals have been tactical, they have been made less with an eye on the governments in Belfast or London than with a view to forestalling criticism from their own constituents.[2]

One of the clearest characteristics of anti-partitionist politics between 1945 and 1969 was the total rift between Belfast and the rest of the province. After coming bottom of the poll in the Falls division in 1945, behind a 'Socialist Republican' and an independent Labour man who was also a Catholic anti-partitionist, the Nationalists relinquished their strongholds in the city without further struggle. When Campbell vacated Central division in 1946 to take up his judgeship, the party did not even put forward a candidate.[3] The same trend was apparent in elections for the Belfast Corporation, although there the last Nationalist hung on until 1952.[4] The abruptness of the Nationalist surrender is perhaps remarkable, but the timing of it, and the fact that it happened at all, is scarcely surprising. Relations between the city anti-partitionists and their rural associates had never been very good, except when Devlin's Ancient Order of Hibernians had been able to paper over the cracks. It was difficult during the depression years, especially for a party as lacking in dynamism as the Nationalists of that period, to find much common cause in the varied material grievances of small farmers on the one hand, concerned with derating and farm prices, and the unemployed and unskilled of the Catholic slums on the other.[5]

Perhaps more important, the Nationalist party remained conservative in outlook, despite pressure from various quarters. Anthony Mulvey, for instance, a Westminster Nationalist MP, was extremely reluctant in 1945 to support the social reform programme of the new Labour

1. De Paor, *Divided Ulster*, p. 177.
2. For the 1971 case, see the volume produced by the *Sunday Times* Insight Team, *Ulster* (London, 1972), pp. 258–9.
3. Rural Nationalists at this time found it 'hard to understand the attitude of the Belfast people to the Central election'. Malachi Conlon, Nationalist MP for South Armagh, wrote to Anthony Mulvey, Nationalist MP at Westminster for Fermanagh and Tyrone, on 7 February 1946, that 'everyone was very emphatic that it should be fought, but equally pessimistic that it would be lost' (Mulvey papers, Public Record office of Northern Ireland (PRONI), D. 1862/11).
4. Budge and O'Leary, *Belfast: Approach to Crisis*, p. 157.
5. One Protestant NILP candidate, Sam Kyle, told his Shankill constituents during the 1929 campaign that if the farmers had an unanswerable case for derating, so too did the unemployed (*Belfast Newsletter*, 20 May 1929).

government or encourage Nationalist–Labour links in Northern Ireland, and had to be urged to do so by his advisers in Dublin, who may have included de Valera himself.[6] Such resistance to social change continued to restrict the party's appeal until its virtual demise at the Stormont election of 1969. In the absence of party funds and organization, political participation becomes the preserve of those who can afford to pay their own way, and the Nationalist party therefore remained, in the words of Professor Richard Rose, 'a loose alliance of local notables'.[7] In the three general elections of the 1920s. the only ones for which detailed information is at present available, the Nationalist standard was carried, on one occasion or more, by twenty-one men, whose occupations were as follows:

TABLE 5.3

Occupations of Nationalist parliamentary candidates, 1921–9

Barristers and solicitors	6	White-collar workers	2
Hoteliers/publicans	5	Farmer	1
Newspaper owners/editors	2	Substantial businessman	1
Auctioneers	2	Journalist	1
		Full-time politician	1

Source: Extracted from J. S. Knight and N. Baxter-Moore, *Northern Ireland: The Elections of the Twenties* (London, 1972), pp. 46–56.

While the prominence of the legal profession in any modern political party is to be expected, its heavy representation here, taken along with the other groups listed in the left-hand column, suggests the predominance of the small-town middle class. There was no sign of the rejection of such leadership in rural areas until the election of 1969, but it was far less appropriate to the style of politics required by a working-class urban area, and as such was rejected far earlier.

The role of the clergy in Catholic politics, always calling for comment but always difficult to pinpoint, is probably best viewed in this context. Like the solicitor, the auctioneer, the publican, or the owner of the local newspaper, the priest in rural districts was a notable, a man with a special position from which he might influence local political opinion if

6. During 1945–6, Mulvey received frequent political advice from Gabriel Diskin, a Dublin journalist, who acted as an intermediary with de Valera—though it is not clear how much was de Valera's advice and how much Diskin's. See especially Diskin to Mulvey, nd (? August 1945): 'Regarding being doubtful of backing new social legislation, don't you see your two votes [Patrick Cunningham was a second Nationalist MP at Westminster] couldn't stop it anyway, and if you opposed such, Labour and ordinary Protestant workers would say you opposed benefits for workers'. On 6 September 1945 Diskin continued: 'Not only should there be support by you of Labour in Britain, but in the six counties also. Remember we are one-third of the voters, and one-third and one-sixth makes a half . . .' (Mulvey papers, PRONI, D. 1862/5).

7. Rose, *Governing without Consensus*, p. 221.

he so wished. We have already seen that when bitter Nationalist–Sinn Féin rivalry seemed to be weakening the position of Catholics in Derry politics in the 1920s, it was the local bishop who initiated the establishment of a Catholic registration committee. The clergy in the Newry area seem to have been instrumental in bringing about the boycotting of the 1938 election by anti-partitionists in the constituencies of South Armagh, South Down, and Mourne.[8] Although the old pre-1918 practice of priests chairing constituency nominating conventions was no longer widespread during the inter-war period, they usually continued to chair the local or branch meetings at which convention delegates were chosen.[9] On the other hand priests have almost always declined to pass judgement on a contest between two Catholic candidates.[1] Over-all, the general influence of the Catholic clergy is probably receding steadily, or at least becoming increasingly discreet, in so far as priests' signatures on a candidate's nomination papers are much less common now than they were twenty years ago. The long-established monopoly by Labour candidates of anti-partitionist representation in Belfast is indicative of the erosion of clerical leadership there. Probably, individual priests will continue to be active in politics, but their influence is now based increasingly on their personal qualities rather than on the strength of the institution which they represent.

Labour politics in Catholic Belfast since 1945 are a complicated mixture of parliamentary and city council matters, in which party labels can be more confusing than helpful. The problem is closely related, in origin, to the protracted death-throes between 1938 and 1949, of the Northern Ireland Labour party's policy of neutrality on the partition question.[2] Even though the party's crucial commitment to partition was not made until 1949, the intensity of debate during the previous decade made it plain to the average anti-partitionist in the street that whatever individual spokesman said about the border issue, the NILP was not in any active sense an anti-partitionist party. Once this was established, the NILP might still win Catholic votes against a Unionist in a predominantly Protestant constituency, but in Catholic constituencies it was finished: in the post-war period it won only the highly marginal Dock (1945) and, in special circumstances, Falls in 1969.[3]

8. Interview with Mr H. O'Neill.   9. Ibid.
  1. For example, the Bishop of Down and Connor's refusal to intervene in the Devlin–de Valera contest in Falls, 1918; and the studied neutrality of Fr Comiskey, Newry, between the Nationalist and Irish Labour candidates in South Down in 1953.
  2. The NILP is discussed below, in the section on non-sectarian politics.
  3. Paddy Devlin, who won Falls in 1969, was not a typical NILP candidate. He was a prominent opponent of partition, with a youthful association with the IRA and a more recent reputation in the civil rights movement which had eluded his much older opponent. In the 1950s he had been a member of the Irish Labour party, and he left the NILP in 1970 to join the newly formed anti-partitionist SDLP.

The confusing multiplicity of party labels in the Central, Dock, Falls, and, for a while, Pottinger constituencies between 1945 and 1969 was the result of an inability on the part of the local politicians to agree on what sort of anti-partitionist party should fill the vacuum created by the coincidental expulsion of both the Nationalists and the NILP from Belfast Catholic politics. The main difficulty was simply that there were fewer seats than there were aspirants, while—until the crisis of the late 1960s—there were no compensating pressures to encourage political unity. The various groups all had in common a radical stance on social questions and an ability to bring the socialist republican arguments of James Connolly into play when necessary, but they relied far more for support on their own efforts and individual popularity than on any formal trade union backing, while their socialism, unlike Connolly's, would scarcely have alarmed the most moderate member of the British Labour party. The new style was introduced by Harry Diamond, who won Falls as a Socialist Republican in 1945, and held it for twenty-four years. When he put up a colleague for the Central seat in 1946, however, he suffered a heavy defeat at the hands of Frank Hanna, leader of Independent Labour, by then the largest anti-partitionist group on the city council. These labels were followed in 1949 (once the split in the NILP was made permanent) by the appearance in Belfast of the southern-based Irish Labour party. Then, in the 1950s, came 'Unofficial Irish Labour', 'O'Sullivan Labour', and 'Dock Irish Labour'.

Given the partitionist stance of the NILP, it would have seemed logical for anti-partitionist socialists to unite around the Irish Labour party after 1949. Indeed, many of the prominent refugees from the NILP did so. But in terms of electoral politics, there was no room for them in Belfast (and of course practically no call from them outside the city): Diamond and Hanna, in particular, had established strong personal positions, and needed no 'new' party to assist them.[4] The party, furthermore, was Dublin-based. Indeed, its incursion into northern politics makes it unique among the southern parliamentary parties: de Valera, when in power in the late 1930s, had always refused to start Fianna Fáil in the north. Irish Labour, without the responsibilities of office for most of the period, had by comparison nothing to lose. But the experiment was not a happy one, and it must be presumed that Dublin was more forthcoming with advice and direction than it was with financial assistance. The party all but disappeared from northern politics after its resounding defeat at the hands of Independent Labour in the 1958 Belfast Corporation elections.[5]

4. In 1953 both men secured over-all majorities against Irish Labour opponents in three-cornered contests.

5. The historians of the Corporation concluded that 'the notion of a party affiliated to Dublin seemed no longer attractive'. Budge and O'Leary, *Belfast: Approach to Crisis*, p. 158.

Some semblance of unity was at last restored to anti-partitionist Labour in Belfast by Gerry Fitt, who won a city council seat in 1958 with his own ward machine, 'Dock Irish Labour'. In 1962 he came together with the old-established Socialist Republican, Harry Diamond, to form a Republican Labour party at Stormont and in the city council, where they won five seats, and soon had Independent Labour on the run. The party was little different in ideology from the Irish Labour party of ten years earlier, except that it had no formal links with Dublin.[6] By 1966, Mr Fitt had added the representation of West Belfast at Westminster to his other two public positions. With his non-sectarian rhetoric and his emphasis on social issues, very much in the style adopted by Joe Devlin in his later years, he was able to appeal effectively to the new Labour government at Westminster, and as a consequence came to surpass the Nationalist leader at Stormont, Edward McAteer, as the spokesman for Ulster Catholics. Unlike Mr McAteer and his colleagues, Mr Fitt involved himself convincingly in the aggressive, extra-parliamentary campaign for Catholic 'civil rights' in the years 1967-9. It was this reputation, combined with the authority which he gained from being an active Westminster MP, that enabled him to make the first serious effort since the inter-war period to reunite the Catholic parliamentary representatives of Belfast with those in other parts of the province.

The Nationalist party, with its roots in the rural areas and its leadership firmly in the hands of the older generation, was taken unawares by the civil rights campaign, which was transformed by the disorders of 1968-9 from a fairly typical contemporary movement of youthful protest into the main focus of Catholic political activity in the province. Like the south of Ireland in 1916-18, Catholic Ulster in 1969 had developed a new style of political aspiration for which there was as yet no formal outlet. Three of the nine Nationalist MPs were defeated in the 1969 election by independents who had been prominent in the civil rights movement. Elsewhere, the balance of parties showed little change. A hastily organized group originating in Queen's University, the People's Democracy, fought eight seats in the election. and for a while attracted considerable publicity in Ireland and Great Britain. Its ideological links were with the international 'new left', and its rhetoric was militant and anti-sectarian. It was, in effect, the left wing of the civil rights movement. It won no seats, however, and although its organizers professed satisfaction at the large number of votes they had secured in favour of non-sectarian policies in so short a time, the truth was less encouraging. Six of the party's eight contests were in Unionist strongholds, and there is no evidence that they secured there anything more

6. Budge and O'Leary, *Belfast: Approach to Crisis.* p. 158

than a rather modest turn-out of the Catholic voters.[7] Against the sitting Nationalist in remote South Fermanagh the People's Democracy candidate perhaps did well to secure even one-third of the poll, but the distribution of votes, compared with the only previous contest in 1949, provides circumstantial evidence for the view that his supporters were mainly dissident Catholics rather than Protestants.[8] Only in South Down did the People's Democracy candidate do well, securing over 48 per cent of the poll in another straight fight with a Nationalist. But the heart of the constituency was the disturbed town of Newry, and the performance can be best comprehended less as a People's Democracy achievement than as general Catholic support for a civil rights candidate. After the election, People's Democracy withered away, with the exception of Miss Bernadette Devlin, who was subsequently elected to Westminster for the predominantly Catholic seat of Mid-Ulster. Her election owed little to People's Democracy, however, for she stood now as a Catholic 'Unity candidate', put up in order to avoid splitting the Catholic vote between a Nationalist and a Republican, neither of whom would back down for the other.[9]

People's Democracy never looked like taking the lead in Ulster Catholic politics, and of course never set out to do precisely that. The Nationalist party, with its president no longer in parliament after 1969, proved unable to reassert its leadership. Thus there developed in 1969–70 a growing demand for a 'united opposition' at Stormont under the leadership of those MPs who had been active in the civil rights movement. It sought to be a genuine left-of-centre civil rights and trade union opposition, but when the NILP pulled in its horns at the end of 1969 it was left simply as a demand for unity among MPs representing Catholic seats.[1] The remaining problems were partly personal and

7. Bernadette Devlin, in South Derry, achieved the best PD performance against a Unionist. But her share of the poll, 38·7 per cent, was almost exactly the same as that gained by the previous challenger for the seat, a Nationalist who won 39·1 per cent of the poll in 1949.

8. *South Fermanagh:* 1949: Nationalist 6,680   1969: Nationalist   4,108
                                    Unionist   2,596   People's Democracy 2,100

As the total 1969 poll was lower than the 1949 Nationalist vote, it looks as though Unionists stayed at home in 1969. The constituency was declining in population, however, and losing Catholics at a faster rate than Protestants, so it is arguable that some People's Democracy support, at least, came from Protestants.

9. For an account of this episode see Miss Devlin's precocious autobiography. *The Price of my Soul* (London, 1969). Although she fought the election 'on the non-sectarian, radical socialist policies I believed in ... the difference I made to the traditional voting patterns was tiny' (p. 170). See also P. Arthur, *People's Democracy, 1968–1973* (Belfast, 1974), for a general history of the movement.

1. One of the MPs concerned was a Protestant, but since his wife and his electorate were both Catholic, his example does not represent a significant break in the sectarian pattern. Unlike the Unionists, anti-partitionist parties have never had any general objection to putting up candidates of the other presuasion. Indeed, the conversion of Protestants is the logical cornerstone of the United Ireland policy.

partly ideological. Who was to lead the new grouping, and how could the party appear sufficiently left-of-centre to satisfy working-class city Catholics, civil rights activists, and sympathetic elements in the British Labour party, without alienating the more conservative elements in Catholic political society? The tone of the new party, as it emerged in August 1970, seems to have been set by Mr Fitt.[2] It was a 'Social Democratic and Labour party' (SDLP), with an emphasis on questions of civil rights and social reform. A demand for public ownership of Irish banks, shipyards, insurance companies, and credit corporations was an attempt to deflect the jibes of the far left at the 'so-called socialism' of the less radical members of the party.[3] The goal of a united Ireland was (in the early days) placed in the background with as much discretion, and perhaps more conviction, than Joseph Devlin's National League had displayed in 1929.

Gerry Fitt's achievement was to bring together Catholic representatives from Belfast and the rest of the province under the same banner for the first time since 1945, in support of a progressive social policy which replaced 'green Tory' anti-partitionism. The price of the progressive image was the exclusion of the remaining Nationalist MPs from the new grouping, and the price of forging a new link between Belfast and other parts of the province was a sharp split with some of Mr Fitt's former Republican Labour party colleagues in Belfast.[4] But although the much-vaunted new grouping consisted ultimately of only six MPs,[5] it could count the most active and professional politicians on the Catholic side within its ranks. Despite occasional gaffes, these men were able to make the long step from Stormont constituency MP to national political stature which no one in the Nationalist party had really been able to do since the death of Joseph Devlin.

One of the main motives for forming the party had been to develop a unified Catholic opposition voice with which to address the British government. Ironically, on the introduction of mass internment of IRA suspects in August 1971, the party announced its refusal to negotiate while unconvicted men were imprisoned, so that the anticipated dialogue over Northern Ireland's future was somewhat delayed. Instead,

2. Even though he was caught on the hop by the unplanned public announcement of the party's existence. For an account of the origins of the party see *Fortnight*, 1 (August 1970). For a more sceptical account of the manoeuvring towards unity see Devlin, *Price of my Soul*, p. 193.

3. B. White, 'The SDLP', *Fortnight*, 1 (August 1970).

4. The split within Republican Labour seems to have been a personal one. If there was any ideological basis to the disagreement, it was national rather than social, for the Republican Labour MP who stood aloof from the new grouping subsequently appeared on the same platform as Provisional IRA leaders (*Fortnight*, 23 [September 1971]).

5. The three civil rights independents, one former Republican Labour man, one former NILP member, and one former Nationalist.

the SDLP's main function in its earliest years was to steer Catholic opinion as much as possible away from the IRA. Developments in the IRA, and its split into 'Official' and 'Provisional', have been described above (pp. 158–61). Suffice it to say here that the more violent Provisionals, although their appearance in the north was apparently provoked more by events south of the border than by grass-roots dissatisfaction with the Official IRA,[6] found little difficulty in surpassing their rivals once the struggle entered its full military phase. The socialist rhetoric carefully developed by the Officials since the early 1960s lost any significance it had ever possessed in actively pro-IRA districts. The Officials were able to hold off the Provisional challenge in the depressed lower Falls district of Belfast, which some observers attributed to their radical social programme. But the other main area of their residual strength was the modern Turf Lodge estate, populated mainly by people rehoused from the lower Falls.[7] It seems likely that personal links and the stature of local IRA leaders, rather than any ideological difference, have been the most decisive factors in determining local allegiance to one or the other wing of the movement. One thing, however, seems very clear at the time of writing: the IRA image as an engine for securing radical social change north and south of the border, so assiduously cultivated in the 1960s, has been very badly tarnished during the past few years.

NON-SECTARIAN POLITICS: THE NILP

Until the formation of the Alliance party in 1970, the Northern Ireland Labour party was the only political organization operating throughout the province which made any sustained effort to attract support from both sections of the community.[8] It never found this easy. Although, like any other Labour party, it has always striven to put social questions to the fore, the character of the system has required it to make constant sectarian calculations in formulating its electoral tactics. The most important characteristic of every constituency, throughout the existence of the Northern Ireland parliament, was its religious balance, and all electoral calculations had to start with this in mind. The NILP's limited degree of success has been achieved by effective manipulation of this balance, by being different things to different men, or by coming forward on a compromise platform, and not by uninhibited and uncluttered

6. *Sunday Times* Insight team, *Ulster* (London, 1972), ch. 11; J. B. Bell, *The Secret Army: A History of the IRA, 1916–1970* (London, 1970), p. 431.
7. *Sunday Times* Insight Team, *Ulster*, p. 196.
8. There is no published history of the NILP, but the subject is well covered by two important research theses: J. F. Harbinson, 'A history of the Northern Ireland Labour party, 1891–1949' (Queen's University, Belfast, MSc(Econ) thesis, 1966); and J. A. V. Graham, 'The consensus-forming strategy of the Northern Ireland Labour Party, 1949–1968' (Queen's University, Belfast, MSocSc thesis, 1972).

advocacy of social and economic reforms. It has normally advocated such views plainly enough, but the evidence suggests that its degree of success has been related less to this than to the operation of sectarian factors.

The clearest indication of this is the fact that the party has never had a 'safe seat'. At one time or another it represented eight seats, seven of which were in Belfast. But it only won two of these seats more than twice during the forty-year period 1929–69, which included ten general elections. In both the Oldpark and Pottinger divisions of Belfast it won on five occasions, while two further contests in the latter seat were won by an expelled NILP member running as an independent. Even in these two seats, however, it was vulnerable to a challenge not from critics of its policy on social and economic questions, but from Unionists who questioned its soundness on partition, and occasionally from anti-partitionist Labour candidates making the opposite allegation with a view to depriving the NILP candidate of the Catholic vote.

In such a context, the social philosophy of the NILP has scarcely been a matter of vital concern even to itself. Debate within the party has been fundamentally over electoral tactics. Ideologically, it occupies a similar position in the British Labour party, while remaining independent of it. It differs in character only in being more exclusively a trade-union-based party than its British counterpart, although of course a much smaller proportion of trade unionists vote for it than is the case in Britain. A further indication of the domination of sectarian politics is the fact that while the party is noticeably lacking in ideological tensions between socialists of different hues—members of Communist organizations, for instance, are not necessarily excluded from NILP membership —it has been riven by disputes over its attitude towards partition. Such disputes have on occasion been clothed in a socialist ideological framework, but in practice have boiled down to a reversion to sectarian politics. So, even if the party has remained non-sectarian in the sense of having Catholics and Protestants in its membership at all levels, it has by no means always been the case that its members left their views for or against partition behind them when they joined its ranks: the exigencies of electoral politics would in most cases not have permitted them to do so anyway.

From its earliest days, the political Labour movement throughout Ireland was handicapped by the need to develop an attitude to the ever-present national question. The debate centred around the Irish Trades Union Congress, founded in 1894. A Belfast Labour party was already in existence by this time, affiliated to the British Independent Labour party, and in 1897 it had some modest success in municipal politics, winning 10 per cent of the seats on the newly reformed Corporation. The first leader of political Labour in Belfast, William Walker, was a strong supporter of the British link, and led the resistance on the Irish TUC to the creation of a separate Labour party for Ireland. His school of thought went down to what was probably an inevitable defeat in 1912, however, when the annual congress voted in favour of a new national party, with a view to participating in the anticipated home rule parliament.[9] Four out of the five ILP branches in Belfast went over to the new body, including many Protestant socialists attracted by the coherence of Connolly's ideas or the vigour of Larkin's fashionable syndicalist militancy.[1] But although a small group of determined Protestant socialist republicans was thereby created, the home rule crisis of 1912–14 so polarized Belfast along traditional sectarian lines that the local Labour party, which in Walker's hands had been a unionist body, could find refuge only among the Catholic-nationalists of the Falls district. It was perhaps inevitable in Belfast that the new industrial unionism, seeking out the unskilled worker for the first time, would find itself appealing mainly to Catholics.

At the time of the first Northern Ireland parliamentary election in 1921, the Belfast Labour party was therefore an anti-partitionist body. Its three candidates all denounced the Government of Ireland Act, and apparently received financial assistance from Sinn Féin to contest the election.[2] Notwithstanding this secret arrangement, the Labour men all lost their deposits, and it seemed clear that the party would have to do some hard thinking if it was to have any future in the new system. Thus, when Ulster socialists and trade unionists regrouped as the Labour party of Northern Ireland, in 1923–4—itself an admission of the *de facto* existence of the border—they decided to adopt no firm policy towards partition.[3] Members of the party were left free to advocate what views they liked on the question. It seemed a sensible compromise, averting a division of the tiny Ulster socialist movement into two sectarian Labour parties at a time when prevailing economic conditions particularly required a strong guardian of working-class interests. In practical terms it also meant that Labour could in future select its candidates with one eye on the religious balance of the constituency concerned.

This new formation, coinciding with the rising tide of inter-war

9. Budge and O'Leary, *Belfast: Approach to Crisis*, p. 125.

1. For an account by a Belfast Presbyterian ILP member of his conversion to republican socialism see the short memoir by William McMullen, *With James Connolly in Belfast* (Dublin, 1951).

2. William McMullen, later NILP MP for West Belfast, 1925–9, remembers his nomination for East Belfast in 1921 being withdrawn because the local Sinn Féin candidate vetoed the allocation of Sinn Féin financial assistance in his case. Sinn Féin hoped, of course, that the Labour candidates would take votes from the Unionists, whereas Mr McMullen, whose trade union links were with the Catholic deep-sea dockers, was more likely to take votes from Sinn Féin. [Interview with Mr McMullen, Dublin, December 1971. A. C. H.]

3. The party's present title, the Northern Ireland Labour Party, was adopted in 1927.

unemployment and general social discontent in Belfast, brought immediate dividends. In the 1925 parliamentary election Labour's three candidates were all successful. Their backgrounds and experience are a good indication of the nature and problems of the NILP at this stage. All three were Protestants (only two of the twelve men who ever represented the party in the Northern Ireland parliament were Catholics) but their positions on the partition question were dictated less by this than by their backgrounds and electoral circumstances. Sam Kyle, in North Belfast, was a member of William Walker's branch of the ILP, which had continued its affiliation to the British rather than the Irish Labour party after 1912. He had contested the intensely Protestant Shankill division of the city in the Westminster election of 1918. His campaign, and his subsequent conduct in the Stormont House of Commons, made clear that his opposition was not to the northern parliament as such, but simply to the domination of it by the Unionist party. His links with the British Labour movement were strengthened by his marriage to Ramsay MacDonald's former private secretary, and subsequently by the absorption of the trade union of which he was an official into the British-affiliated Amalgamated Transport and General Workers' Union.

Labour's other two representatives had both lost their jobs at Harland and Wolff's shipyard, on account of their socialist activities, during the sectarian disturbances of 1914. The subsequent political development of both men was determined by their trade-union activities and their electoral circumstances. By the 1920s William McMullen had taken up James Connolly's old position of Belfast organizer of the ITGWU, a body regarded by Belfast Protestants, with some reason, as having been allied with Sinn Féin in the south during the war of independence, 1918–21. Although his background was Presbyterian, McMullen's labour connections were therefore Catholic. In 1925 he was elected to parliament for West Belfast, where most of his union membership lived, thanks largely to the surplus second preference votes of the Nationalist candidate and the transferred votes of the defeated Republican. He had been a convinced advocate of Connolly's synthesis of the national and social questions for many years, and so found little difficulty in voicing the anti-partitionist sentiments which his constituents expected of him.

The career of his colleague John Beattie was more complex. Most of Beattie's East Belfast constituents in 1925 were Protestants, like himself. But his electorate also contained a significant body of Catholics, though not large enough to invite the candidacy of an avowed nationalist. To maintain his position Beattie needed some support from both communities. His performance in the 1925–9 parliament was therefore more equivocal on the national question than that of McMullen. Meanwhile, however, his job as an official of the Blacksmiths' Society disappeared, when that body was merged with a larger union in 1925. In 1934, after several years of financial stringency, Beattie obtained a similar position with the Irish National Teachers' Organization, a Dublin-based body which, in the north of Ireland, recruited almost exclusively Catholic members. Whether the inclination to adopt a more militant anti-partitionist position came from within himself, or whether it was a response to pressure from his new employers, is not clear. Whatever the reason, Beattie underwent something of a transformation in outlook between 1929 and 1934, and for the next two decades was without rival as the leading voice of anti-partitionist socialism in Northern Ireland. He was twice expelled from the NILP, essentially for putting the interests of anti-partition before those of Labour, and although he secured the distinction—at a by-election in 1943—of becoming the only NILP candidate ever to win a Westminster seat, he had no formal connection with the party after 1944.

The fourth major figure in Ulster Labour politics between the wars, Harry Midgley, did not contest the 1925 election. His career will be discussed at this point, however, because it makes an interesting contrast to Beattie's.[4] Midgley had fought the 1921 election along with the other two Labour candidates as an anti-partitionist, and during the following decade seems to have expressed no very strong views on the subject one way or the other. He was elected to Stormont for the Dock constituency in 1933, mainly on Catholic votes, in a straight fight with a Unionist. The Union of Distributive and Allied Workers, by which he was employed as an organizer for many years, though a cross-channel union, does not appear to have exercised a decisive influence on his conduct at any stage. It seems rather that his personality and his general political interests led him into a confrontation with his Catholic constituents which turned his career in an entirely new direction. Always a man of strong and sometimes sudden enthusiasms, he became obsessed during the 1930s, as of course did many socialists everywhere, with the threat of international fascism. He spoke out strongly for the Republican side in the Spanish civil war, and in 1936 became involved in a heated and protracted quarrel with the *Irish News*, Belfast's Catholic daily paper, which portrayed Franco's rebels as the defenders of Christianity. As a consequence, a Nationalist candidate was run against him in Dock in 1938, and he was badly beaten into third place. His future potential for attracting Catholic votes seemed to be nil.

Midgley decided upon a bold course of action. During the early years of the war he cultivated his anti-fascist image, denouncing the neutral Dublin regime as a government of quislings, and attacking the

4. For a detailed discussion of Midgley's career see Harbinson, 'History of the NILP'.

Unionist government of J. M. Andrews in the north for ineffective prosecution of the war effort. The campaign paid off, and Midgley was returned triumphantly to Stormont for Willowfield, a working-class Protestant district of Belfast, at a by-election late in 1941. For a while he was once again the most prominent figure in the NILP. But he had gone far too out on a limb. Just as the party had expelled the anti-partitionist Beattie in an effort to avoid being broken on the national question so, ultimately, it turned on Midgley for antagonizing Catholic opinion in the city. He left the party at the end of 1942. Shortly afterwards, as an independent Labour member, he joined the new Unionist government of Sir Basil Brooke for the duration of the war. He contested the 1945 general election at the head of a new 'Commonwealth Labour party', which was in fact a partitionist Labour party. Although he was returned no less convincingly on this ticket against both Unionist and NILP opposition, his six running mates were all defeated. His following was now an entirely personal one. It was perhaps a surprising move, but not an entirely unpredictable one, when in 1947 Midgley joined the Unionist party, returning to the cabinet two years later. Given that he had no future in the NILP and that he had found in Willowfield a constituency which returned him triumphantly to parliament at three successive elections with a different party label each time, his action is understandable. In the situation in which he found himself after 1936, and more so after 1941, he had the choice as a politician of being broken by the operation of sectarian forces, or of attempting to manipulate them to his best advantage. To advance his own political position and that of his party at the same time had become impossible.

The careers of these men illustrate the problems and the dilemma of the NILP during the inter-war period. Only one other man represented the party in parliament during these years: Patrick Agnew, who sat for South Armagh from 1938 to 1945. He had the triple distinction of being the only Catholic NILP MP (until 1969), the only NILP candidate ever to win a seat outside Belfast, and the only one ever to win an uncontested victory. His election, however, was a fluke, coming about only because the Nationalists in south Ulster decided to abstain entirely from the 1938 election. Two of the seats which they normally held went to Unionists and the third, much to his surprise, went by default to Agnew. He was not a very prominent member of the party, made little impact in parliament, and was easily defeated by a Nationalist in 1945, despite his unequivocal opposition to partition.

During the first two decades of the Northern Ireland parliament, therefore, the NILP made no real advance. It never managed to repeat the triple success it had won in Belfast under proportional representation in the election of 1925. There is some debate as to whether its loss of two seats in 1929 was the direct outcome of the abolition of proportional

representation or whether there was simply a straight swing against it on
the part of the electors. But in the long run it is plain that the abolition
of PR harmed the party's prospects, and was intended to do so.[5] In a
large PR seat its constituency might be any body of electors which
included NILP in its preferences. Under the single-member system all
seats were 'Protestant' or 'Catholic', and the NILP had no constituencies. The best it could do was to concentrate on those few seats in
Belfast where the religious balance was close and the electors likely to
be attracted by socialist policies. As we have seen, its success was slight.

There were grounds for hope in 1945 that the post-war period would
bring better times for the party. The four old leaders had gone, the
acrimonious Anglo-Irish relations of the pre-war years appeared to have
gone, and it seemed certain that the NILP would benefit from the
massive swing to Labour which was taking place in Britain. In the
elections, which took place a few weeks before the Westminster contest,
the party made an unprecedented effort, putting forward more than
twice as many candidates as it had ever done before.[6] The result—two
victories in Belfast, making a net gain of one seat—was the best for
twenty years, but in the light of the pro-Labour swing in Britain and
the tremendous social upheaval of the war, perhaps the really remarkable
thing about the 1945 election was that so little had changed. Outside
Belfast the party failed to win even 40 per cent of the poll in any of its
seven straight fights, averaging a bare 30 per cent of votes cast. In the
city there were clear signs of a positive swing in the Oldpark division,
which was won for the first time, and one or two other seats. But in
general the figures suggest that the party did no more than achieve a
full turn out of the traditional anti-Unionist vote, which had in previous
elections been cast, if at all, for an Independent Unionist or some brand
of anti-partitionist. The challenge from Midgley's new pro-partition
Commonwealth Labour party was held off, but the credit for this
negative success is really due to the Unionists rather than the NILP.
The NILP/CLP conflicts were really fights for second place.

The NILP had scarcely more success in its relations with the British
Labour government than it had had with the Ulster electorate. It
became clear at quite an early stage that no one in the Attlee cabinet
was inclined to upset the Unionist applecart in Northern Ireland. Sir
Basil Brooke was accepted at his own estimation as a new broom who

5. See the debate on the proposed abolition of PR in parliamentary elections, 25
October 1927. *Parliamentary Debates*, NI, viii, col. 2276.
'*Lord Craigavon:* . . . what I believe we will get much better in this House under the
old-fashioned plain and simple system, are men who are for the Union on the one
hand, or who are against it and want to go into a Dublin parliament on the other
hand.'
'*Mr Beattie:* Sectarian elections.'
6. Eight in Belfast, three in Co. Antrim, and two each in Counties Armagh and
Derry: a total of fifteen.

had seen to it that the province played its part effectively in the war effort, and who was now willing and able to implement British Labour's welfare state legislation. The subsequent admission of Harry Midgley to the Unionist party lent some substance to its claim to be a more broadly based institution than the British Conservative party. The pattern was set early in 1946, when an NILP delegation travelled to London to protest against the Unionists' new Elections and Franchise Bill, which favoured business and property interests, only to be informed by the Home Secretary that the matter was entirely one for the Northern Ireland parliament.[7] It was a formula for Westminster's non-interference which was not discarded until 1969.

Only once during the Attlee years did the British Labour party intervene in the province on behalf of the NILP. Soon after Labour took office some thirty of the party's backbench MPs formed a parliamentary group, known as the 'Friends of Ireland', to work for the establishment of 'democratic Labour governments in Ireland both north and south, with a view to attaining a united Ireland by common consent at the earliest possible moment'.[8] A frankly anti-partitionist body therefore, its membership was made up largely of Labour MPs who were Catholics, or of Irish background, or who had a large Irish vote in their constituencies, along with a few members of the radical wing of the party. In May 1946, under the influence of this group, the National Executive Committee of the British Labour party agreed to co-operate with the NILP in mounting a Labour candidate to oppose the Unionist at a by-election in the Westminster constituency of Co. Down. The constituency had a substantial Protestant majority, and the Unionist ultimately carried the seat as usual. The main interest of the election lies in the fact that it remains the only occasion on which the British Labour party has participated in Northern Ireland electoral politics. But it also confirmed the 'united Ireland' strategy of those who had instigated the move, for the intention was to build a majority on a solid basis of anti-partitionist Catholic votes by detaching from the Unionists a sufficient number of Protestants voting on social issues.[9]

The Down by-election remained the high point of the Friends'

7. Harbinson, 'History of the NILP', pp. 191–2.

8. Circular headed ' "Friends of Ireland" Labour group in the British parliament', nd, enclosed with letter dated 1 May 1946 (Mulvey papers, PRONI, D. 1862/20). For the formation of the group see *The Times*, 15 November 1945.

9. See J. H. Hudson (an English Labour MP) to A. Mulvey, June 1946, shortly after the election. 'There were probably 40,000 Nationalist voters in the division, and it ought to be possible to find another 20,000 purely Labour voters. The problem for the future is how to get a good working agreement between these two so that they can go ahead on a genuinely united Irish policy' (Mulvey papers, PRONI, D. 1862/22). For a discussion of the Down by-election see Harbinson, 'History of the NILP', pp. 196–8; also the biographical entry on the Labour candidate, Desmond Donnelly, which A. B. Cooke of the Queen's University, Belfast, has prepared for his forthcoming study of parliamentary representation, 'Ulster at Westminster'.

success in involving their party in the political affairs of the province. After that the group's activities fell into two sections. On the one hand its members did effective, but politically insignificant, work in bringing cases of individual hardship under the stern residence permit arrangements to the notice of the British Home Secretary.[1] On the other a number of its members, especially Geoffrey Bing, embarked on a course of vigorous public criticism of the Northern Ireland regime and the British government's attitude towards it. At this time the internal affairs of Northern Ireland were customarily excluded from debate at Westminster under 'the convention'. But Bing and others took advantage of a minor piece of technical legislation, the Northern Ireland Bill of 1947, and the far more important Ireland Bill of 1949 (which followed the Dublin government's withdrawal from the Commonwealth), to mount a large-scale parliamentary attack on the state of affairs in Northern Ireland, emphasizing particularly the questions of gerrymandering, religious discrimination, and the Special Powers Act. These tactics were successful in drawing public attention to the problems of Northern Ireland, but far from signifying the Labour party's conversion to the anti-partition cause, they helped to bring about the reverse, by compelling Labour cabinet ministers to adopt clear-cut positions. In the 1947 debate the Home Secretary, Chuter Ede, declared that 'rightly or wrongly, this house has specifically delegated to the Northern Ireland parliament the oversight of certain matters. I have no more right to inquire into how they discharge their functions than I have to inquire into the way in which the dominions ... discharge ... self-government.'[2] By the time of the Ireland Bill of 1949, the government's attitude, as voiced by Herbert Morrison, was even more unbending. 'Quite frankly', he declared, 'this government is not going to seek and take the initiative for the purpose of losing a part of the United Kingdom ....'[3]

The British Labour party during the 1945–50 parliament was thus sharply, if not evenly, divided over Ulster. But this division was a mild one compared to the rift which developed within the NILP during the same period. Although the party had always embraced very diverse views on the national question, it had for many years been fairly successful in containing them. From the time of the Midgley row in 1942, however, and more especially after the Labour victory in Britain, the issue developed from being one which all NILP leaders, by common

1. Between 1942 and 1947, aliens, including Irish citizens from the south, needed residence permits in order to live or work in Northern Ireland. This was a United Kingdom measure, administered by the Ulster Office in London. On the abolition of residence permits the Northern Ireland parliament, for which matters relating to immigration were *ultra vires*, brought in a system of work permits, which had the same practical effect of restricting the flow of southern Irishmen across the border (*The Times*, 13 October 1947).

2. *Parliamentary Debates*, HC, 5th ser., vol. 438, cols 1446–50.

3. Ibid., vol. 464, col. 1954.

consent, regarded as tiresome and embarrassing, to one which they increasingly came to regard as of immediate and fundamental importance. From this point of view the British Labour victory, and the activities of the Friends of Ireland, helped to push the NILP towards a crisis, which could not be averted once the Dublin government's hasty and tactless declaration of a republic, in 1948, raised the climate of opinion in Ulster to a high enough temperature.

The Friends' propaganda encouraged anti-partitionist elements in the NILP to undertake talks in Dublin with the Irish Labour party, as early as the spring of 1946. But the visit of the British party's general secretary to the NILP conference later in the same year, with promises of substantial assistance at the next Westminster election, gave greater strength to partitionists in the party. As it became increasingly apparent that the British Labour leadership had no intention of reopening the border issue, it seemed to these elements in the NILP that a frank and formal acceptance of the border could end the years of wrangling, cement a firm relationship with the governing party in Britain, and increase the party's chance of future electoral success, especially in its main cockpit of Belfast. When Dublin declared a republic in the south, the pro-partitionists seized the opportunity to sweep into their camp the moderates in the party who had previously maintained that the precarious *status quo* was preferable to a virtually sectarian position. Perhaps even more important than the views of individual party members was the more practical concern of the British-based trade unions to maintain their links.[4] After unsuccessful negotiations, undertaken with a view to securing the recognition of the NILP as a regional council of the British Labour party, a special party conference of 1949 carried a resolution that 'the Northern Ireland Labour party believes that the best interests of Northern Ireland lie in maintaining the constitutional links with the United Kingdom'.[5] Thus, after twenty-five years of equivocation on the national question, the party nailed its colours to the mast.

The decision came too late to avert its total elimination from parliamentary politics at the 1949 election. Not only was its morale and its stature low after two years of internal wrangling, but external factors also operated to its acute disadvantage. The Unionists were able to extract maximum benefit from the recent declaration of a republic in the south, and succeeded in characterizing their own contest as a 'chapel gate election'. Anti-partitionist parties, they alleged, were being financed in the north by money collected at the doors of Catholic churches in the south. Just as the partitionist tide within the NILP cut it off from much of its old Catholic following, so the unfortunate coincidence of external factors made Labour issues appear irrelevant to Protestant electors. The

4. Harbinson, 'History of the NILP', p. 210.
5. Cited in Lyons, *Ireland Since the Famine*, p. 738.

party lost both its seats, and its total vote fell back almost to its 1938 level.

For nine years the party was entirely without representation at Stormont. Its re-emergence with four MPs at the 1958 election was in some ways surprising. It was in direct opposition to the trends in the Republic, where the Irish Labour party had sustained heavy losses in the 1957 Dáil election, and in Great Britain, where the British Labour party was to undergo its third successive election defeat in 1959. Further-more, the IRA's campaign along the border provided the Unionist party with an opportunity to make its traditional pan-Protestant appeal. On the other hand, the manifest failure of that campaign to upset the stability of the state, or even make much impression on Catholic public opinion, reduced its importance as an issue. The continued weakness of the British Labour party probably operated to the advantage of the NILP, rather than the reverse, in view of the widespread mistrust among Ulster Protestants of the anti-partitionist influences within it. In the main, it seems that the 1958 revival was the delayed outcome of a period of reorganization and re-thinking which followed the party's disruption in 1949.

After the split, Sam Napier was appointed as full-time secretary of the party.[6] Formal constituency organizations were developed in most Belfast seats for the first time and, most important, Napier was able to use his background as a journalist to secure vastly improved press coverage. In particular the city's only evening newspaper, the *Belfast Telegraph*, under new editorial direction, ceased to toe the official Unionist line as firmly as it had done in the past. The party was there-fore able to reap the benefits of its new policy emphasis, which had two main strands. On the one hand the new constitutional stance was stressed. An Ulster Labour group was set up to counter the anti-partitionist propaganda of the 'Friends of Ireland' group in the British Labour party. Its base was in London, but its purpose was to build the party's pro-union image in Ulster. There was no suggestion in the party's public utterances during this decade of discrimination or Protestant privilege in the province. 'I would support the constitution as firmly as any Unionist' was the pledge of one party candidate in 1953.[7] The other main strategy was to present the party as a potentially effective loyal opposition, concentrating on bread-and-butter issues like the level of unemployment in the city's main industries and Unionist attempts to raise council house rents and reduce family allowances. Stormont, in this analysis, was characterized not as repressive or sectarian, but as

6. This paragraph is derived from Graham, 'The consensus-forming strategy of the NILP', pp. 47–65.
7. David Bleakley, cited in op. cit., p. 65.

incompetent and part-time, 'the laziest parliament in the world'.[8] In the election of 1958 the party won four seats in the city, perhaps the first indication that the Tory paternalist style of the Brookeborough regime was losing its appeal to Belfast Protestants.

In the 1962 election the party more than doubled its poll, to its highest ever turnout of 76,842 votes. Much of this increase, however, is explained by the fact that it had doubled the number of candidates it put into the race. The average NILP vote per seat contested rose by less than 100, and the same four MPs were returned to Stormont, without new colleagues. The Labour revival was therefore a limited one. Subsequent events quickly showed that it was also a brittle one. By the mid 1960s the activities of the Revd Ian Paisley, which in their early stages focused on opposition to the international ecumenical movement among the Christian churches, had begun to revive the force of evangelical Protestantism in Belfast and the political militancy which tends to accompany such manifestations. This attempt to repolarize the Ulster community received a substantial boost from the excitement engendered in the Catholic camp by the fiftieth anniversary celebrations of the Easter Rising. But even before then the NILP was in difficulties. In 1963 its chairman had declared that 'the time has come when we must challenge the Catholic vested interests as well as the Protestant ones'.[9] Constituency associations were started in Catholic areas of the city, and some members of the executive began to address themselves to specifically Catholic grievances. Some sitting Labour MPs, conscious of their electors' views on these matters, were unenthusiastic about such a departure. Late in 1964 the issue came into the open, when the small parliamentary party was rocked by a row among the party's representatives on the city council over whether children's playrounds should be open on Sundays. To outsiders the episode had many of the qualities of farce. But it showed how much the party owed its limited successes of the recent past to evangelical Protestant influences rather than orthodox socialist attitudes.[1] The affair was also in part a product of the new wave of sectarian feeling which was beginning to grow in Protestant working-class districts of Belfast in opposition to the liberal attitude to community relations being struck by the new Prime Minister, Captain O'Neill. Both O'Neill's liberalism and the Paisleyite reaction against it operated to the electoral disadvantage of the NILP. At the same time, with pamphlets like 'Blueprint for Ulster', O'Neillite Unionism was stealing Labour's economic thunder. In 1965 the party

8. Bleakley, cited in Graham, 'The consensus-forming strategy of the NILP', p. 62.

9. Speech of Charles Brett to the party conference, April 1963. Cited in Graham, op. cit., p. 111.

1. For an account of the Sunday swings affair, see Budge and O'Leary, *Belfast: Approach to Crisis*, pp. 161–2.

lost two of its four seats. In 1969 it was reduced to one seat, and its vote per candidate fell to its lowest level since 1938.

Once again the fortunes of the NILP had been in direct contrast to those of the British Labour party, which returned to power in 1964 and increased its majority dramatically in 1966. Such a development was more than coincidental. Even during the period of the Attlee government, British Labour had scarcely inspired the confidence of Ulster loyalists. Mr Wilson's government, whose parliamentary following showed considerable interest in bringing about changes in Northern Ireland, was trusted far less.[2] Although the NILP was not formally associated with its British counterpart, the distinction was too subtle for the average loyalist. In the minds of many Protestants, a Labour government at Westminster meant alarms about the future of the border, which in turn produced a climate of opinion in which the NILP could not thrive. The crunch came after the fierce rioting of August 1969, when the Wilson government sent in British troops and subsequently pressured Stormont into disbanding the B Specials.[3] Mr Billy Hull, convenor of the engineering shop stewards at the Harland and Wolff shipyard and a well-known figure in the Shankill district, resigned from the NILP in protest at the British Labour government's intervention, and led a sizeable group with him into a Workers' Committee for the Defence of the Constitution, which later became the Loyalist Association of Workers and later still formed part of the Ulster Workers' Council.[4] The rhetoric of the new movement was still radical in its criticism of the traditional Unionist leadership, but it derived its main force not from this but from 'loyalist' feeling, and there can be little doubt that much of its following came from former supporters of the NILP.

The general crisis which began in 1968–9 would have accelerated the decline of the NILP anyway, but the intense hostility which Ulster Protestants then developed towards the Wilson government made the party's situation very much worse. After its disastrous showing in the local government elections of May 1973, one NILP official claimed that

2. A large proportion of the new Labour MPs elected in 1964 and 1966 were especially concerned about human rights questions, in Northern Ireland as well as further afield, according to Harold Wilson's account. Mr Wilson himself, apparently, took the initiative in suggesting the return of Sir Roger Casement's body to Dublin, after nearly fifty years, in 1965. Then in August 1966, according to his own account published five years later, Mr Wilson made it clear to Captain O'Neill at a private meeting that his government would insist on reforms in local government electoral law and in housing allocation in the province. He did nothing, however, to end the long-established Westminster debating convention of non-intervention in the domestic affairs of Northern Ireland until after the start of the troubles in 1968. H. Wilson, *The Labour Government 1964–70: A Personal Record* (London, 1971), pp. 75, 270; *The Autobiography of Terence O'Neill*, pp. 82–83.

3. Hezlet, *B Specials*, p. 223.   4. Boulton, *The UVF, 1966–73*, pp. 137–8.

'we are fighting with Harold Wilson hanging round our necks like an albatross'.[5] While it is unlikely that this was the sole cause of the NILP's near-collapse—it would of course be very comforting to place all the blame on an external factor over which the party had no control—the party certainly had cause to reflect somewhat bitterly that whenever British Labour has won power it has placed its confidence not in its socialist comrades of the NILP, but in the Unionist government—in the case of the Attlee administration—and, more recently, in the predominantly Catholic and anti-partitionist Social Democratic and Labour party.[6] Even British socialism has been unable to intervene in Northern Ireland affairs outside the sectarian framework.

POLITICS IN TRANSITION

Early in 1972 Brian Faulkner's Unionist cabinet resigned in protest at the British government's decision to take over control of security matters in the province. The Stormont parliament was suspended and direct rule imposed.[7] A senior British minister, William Whitelaw, was appointed to the new post of Secretary of State for Northern Ireland. Notwithstanding campaigns by militant Protestant groups for the total integration of Northern Ireland with Great Britain, led by Ian Paisley, and conversely for the establishment of an 'independent British Ulster', led by William Craig, it soon became apparent that the British government's intention was simply to hold the ring for a limited period while plans were evolved for a new type of provincial legislature which might encourage more fluidity in party politics than had been the case in the old parliament.[8]

The new proposals first appeared in the form of a White Paper in March 1973,[9] and were implemented by the Northern Ireland Constitution Act, which repealed most of the extant clauses of the Government of Ireland Act of 1920. The old parliament was to be replaced by a

5. *Belfast Telegraph*, 20 June 1973.
6. The Northern Ireland passages of his book *The Labour Government*, illustrate clearly Mr Wilson's tendency to regard the Catholic and socially radical positions as virtually identical in the Northern Ireland context.
7. Of the growing volume of literature dealing with the background to these events, *Ulster* (London, 1972), by the *Sunday Times* Insight team, appears to be based on extensive interviews with the politicians involved. Despite its liberal bias and inability to disclose its sources, it seems likely to be most useful to future historians. H. Kelly, *How Stormont Fell* (Dublin, 1972), by contrast, discloses few confidences, and adds little to the perceptive daily press reports of its author.
8. A paper for discussion (the 'Green Paper') issued by the Northern Ireland Office late in 1972, expressed the view that 'any shortcomings in the Northern Ireland parliamentary system hitherto may have been due to too slavish an imitation of the Westminster model in circumstances which that model was not evolved to meet'. *The Future of Northern Ireland* (London, 1972), p. 47.
9. 'Northern Ireland constitutional proposals' (Cmnd. 5259).

unicameral assembly of seventy-eight members, elected by the single transferable vote method of proportional representation, with government in the hands of a chief executive member and some executive colleagues, assisted by a number of executive committees. The powers of the Assembly were to be substantially the same as those enjoyed by the old parliament, except that police, justice, security, elections, and matters concerning the franchise would remain with Westminster, administered by the Secretary of State. The office of Governor would be abolished. Further constitutional details, including the relationship between the executive and its committees, as well as the implementation of the provision that 'executive powers will not be concentrated in representatives from one community only [ie Protestant or Catholic]',[1] were to be negotiated between the Secretary of State and the party leaders, following the election of the Assembly. The provision of the 1949 Ireland Act that Northern Ireland would not be taken out of the United Kingdom without the consent of its local parliament was replaced by an assurance that such a development would require the consent of the majority of the electorate as expressed in a referendum.[2]

One of the intentions behind these changes was to disperse the monolithic power which the Unionist party had exercised in the old parliament, on the assumption that if political competition could be seen to hold out some hope of success to non-Unionists, then the disaffected spirit which had provided the background to political violence and abstention for so long would be removed. In fact the very appearance of the new proposals broke up the Unionist monolith, but not quite in the way that had been anticipated. Whereas Mr Whitelaw's original hope was perhaps that the system would produce in the Assembly a sizeable group of moderate members to hold the balance between the sectarian parties, the outcome was rather different. In the elections of June 1973 the NILP managed to return only one member, and the new Alliance party eight.[3] The great majority of first preference votes went to clearly identifiable 'Protestant' or 'Catholic' candidates. For this reason the results were characterized by the press as a setback for the British government's policy.

But the election destroyed the traditional two-party system none the less. In effect there were two separate elections taking place at the same time. The contest for representation of the Catholic community was fought between the SDLP on the one hand and an assortment of groups

1. Cmnd. 5259, p. 14. The 'executive committees' came to nothing and executive members were later permitted to style themselves ministers.
2. Northern Ireland Constitution Act, 1973, clause 1. Such a referendum cannot be held more frequently than once every ten years. At the first poll, in March 1973, there was an overwhelming majority for remaining in the United Kingdom, swollen because anti-partitionist parties advised their supporters to abstain.
3. See below, pp. 217–18.

more or less sympathetic towards the IRA on the other,[4] mainly over the question of whether or not the community's representatives should participate in the new system at all while political prisoners were interned without trial. In this contest the SDLP was more successful than had been anticipated, winning nineteen seats and eliminating all other anti-partition parties. It was a vote of confidence in the leaders who had emerged in 1968–9, and a rejection of IRA policy.

In the Protestant community an entirely separate, but even more bitter contest was being fought, ostensibly over whether or not the broad outlines of the constitutional proposals should be accepted as a workable basis for the new Assembly. Brian Faulkner's Unionists, pledged to make the Assembly work, were returned as the largest single party, with twenty-two seats plus one independent supporter. Mr Faulkner, for long Ulster's most deft politician, had surprised some of his critics by asserting his leadership so strongly on an unpopular issue. His Assembly following was smaller than he must have hoped for, but —ironically, in view of his right-wing reputation—the possibility remained that he would succeed in persuading a sizeable section of the party to implement the reformed system, and perhaps even shake off the influence of the Orange Order in the process, where his predecessor and rival, Terence O'Neill, had so patently failed.

The battle was by no means won, however, for twenty-seven Protestant candidates were returned on a platform of unequivocal opposition to the Assembly and a return of the old parliament. They included ten dissident members of the Unionist party, as well as Mr Paisley's Democratic Unionists and Mr Craig's new Vanguard Unionist Progressive party, who made up a 'Loyalist Coalition', and two other Loyalists. The constitutional proposals were certainly at the centre of this debate, but the situation is too complex to be analysed simply in terms of Unionist moderates versus Loyalist right-wingers. In part at least, the contest between Unionists and Loyalists was a more explicit form of the old struggle of lower-middle and working class elements to break the predominantly upper class grip on Protestant representation.[5]

The immediate outcome of the Assembly election was thus a state of unprecedented political flux. There seemed to be reasonable grounds for believing that, while the Ulster electorate still preferred to vote

4. Republican Clubs candidates advocated thorough-going socialist policies. Despite their non-sectarian handling of the issues, they were generally regarded as the political wing of the Official IRA. The Provisional IRA ran no candidates, but advised its supporters to abstain from voting or to spoil their ballot papers. The old Nationalist party, while closer in political outlook to the SDLP which was supplanting it, made tentative gestures towards an abstentionist viewpoint in a vain effort to regain its position. The vestigial Republican Labour party adopted a similar position, with equal lack of success.

5. For a thoroughgoing exposition of this view, see Boulton, *The UVF, 1966–73*, especially pp. 184–8.

under its direction. The UWC called for an indefinite general stoppage to coincide with the ratification of the Sunningdale agreement by the Assembly. At first its impact seemed limited, but as the days passed the strikers developed a network of paralysing roadblocks, while roaming 'pickets' were able to close down shops and other services altogether, except in large Catholic districts. There was clear evidence of both widespread support and widespread intimidation.

Power to respond lay not with the executive but with the Labour government at Westminster. Leaders of the three executive parties flew to London, and returned with the impression that the Prime Minister had agreed to implement a series of measures which would maintain essential services and generally resist the stoppage.[8] Possibly because of army advice on the security position, possibly because of doubts as to whether army personnel could operate the power stations, Mr Wilson appeared to change his mind overnight, and instead made a television broadcast which was in effect limited to abuse of the strikers, and which can have served only to strengthen their resolve.[9] The government would not crush the strike, but neither would it negotiate with the strikers, who were not elected representatives. In the circumstances the stoppage became increasingly solid and the situation more critical. It was resolved only by the resignation of the Unionist ministers, which brought an end to both the stoppage and the executive. The Assembly was prorogued, direct rule restored, and a few weeks later a new white paper announced plans for the election of a 78-seat Convention to draft another new constitution for Northern Ireland. This time the decision was to lie with a representative body of Ulstermen, with the proviso only that there be a broad measure of acceptance from both communities. Meanwhile Provisional IRA violence and the sectarian assassination campaign continued at a high level.

After two years the Whitelaw policy was in ruins. It had always been something of a gamble, but for some considerable time it seemed that it might work. Its collapse was in some part due to bad luck. Had it not been for the unexpected February election, the UWC and their associates might have had less confidence and the government considerably more in dealing with them. Had the executive been able to develop a programme of wide-ranging social reform in the interests of both communities, then unionist electors might have been able to see some advantage in a new broom. As it was, all they saw were frequent television appearances by SDLP ministers, who were by and large

8. For an account of these events by an SDLP member of the executive, see P. Devlin, *The Fall of the Northern Ireland Executive* (Belfast, 1975), pp. 22–24. For a general study of the crisis see R. Fisk, *The Point of No Return* (London, 1975).

9. Fisk, p. 198, makes the additional point that by this stage the Prime Minister was reluctant to commit himself to the maintenance of the executive, believing that it would soon disintegrate as a result of Unionist defections.

more prominent in the executive than their Unionist colleagues, and so gave the impression that power-sharing meant 'Catholic government'.

But the SDLP had also contributed to its own downfall by being too successful in the Sunningdale negotiations. Reluctant to enter government at all while internment without trial continued, it insisted on making the Council of Ireland link appear as significant as possible. Yet the Dublin government, on the other hand, was unable to balance this by taking any clear steps towards ending the use of the Republic as a haven by IRA offenders from the north. Had the SDLP felt able to enter a power-sharing executive simply for its own sake, taking a risk with its electorate over the Irish dimension as well as internment, then the basis for Loyalist opposition would have been narrower. As it was the SDLP stood firm at Sunningdale (though it began to show more flexibility later, when it was too late), leaving the power-sharing Unionists to take what was, in retrospect, a far greater gamble. If the cause of this lapse of judgement was anything other than mortal politicians operating in unfamiliar waters, it lies at least to some extent in the segregated character of the political system. The SDLP, like the parties on the other side of the divide, was a political force which operated seriously only in its own, ie Catholic, constituencies. Its function was to undercut popular support for republican extremism, and indeed its long honeymoon with the Heath government was based largely on its effectiveness in achieving this. Its politicians had reached this position by looking to their own constituency and leaving the Protestants to theirs. Once it became a party of government, it was in the SDLP interest to include the difficulties of the moderate Unionists in its tactical considerations, but it did not do so until it was too late.

During the twelve months that followed the fall of the executive, the pace of political change reflected the bankruptcy of constitutional ideas on all sides. The Westminster election of October 1974 and the Convention election the following May, with over-all UUUC votes of 58 and 54 per cent respectively, confirmed the opposition of most Protestants to power-sharing with the SDLP at ministerial level, but did not indicate any clear alternative way of advance. A number of discussion papers were put out by the British government, designed to show that Ulster was dependent on the British purse, and also to draw attention to experiments in inter-communal government in other parts of the world. It seemed clear that the major British parties had set their minds against total integration of the province into the United Kingdom, implying as it did both an increase in the number of Ulster MPs at Westminster and (given the administrative complications involved) an end to flexibility on the Ulster question in general. The UUUC, with 46 out of 78 Convention seats after May 1975, had declared its unequivocal opposition to power-sharing in government, except in the form of back-bench committees along Congressional lines, which the SDLP seemed unprepared to accept. The only bright spot was the shaky continuation of a Provisional IRA ceasefire, begun at the end of 1974. Uneasiness about the security situation scarcely abated however, partly because of the steady continuation of sectarian murders in Belfast and elsewhere, partly because of a widespread feeling that the ceasefire was no more than a tactical one on the part of the Provisionals, likely to end with the anticipated breakdown of the Convention.

Discussion among political observers in mid 1975 centred around the merits or otherwise of schemes for institutionalized power-sharing, such as that laid down by the Whitelaw plan. It was argued in some quarters that the precedents for these arrangements were not encouraging.[1] While this view was doubtless partly an attempt to put a brave face on the fact that the UUUC seemed likely to veto such a scheme anyway, there was some evidence from Belgium and Cyprus that such institutional provisions tended to harden community divisions, and from Holland that communities divided on religious rather than linguistic lines can evolve effective coalitions without institutional prompting. There has thus been a certain amount of speculation on the nature of the party political system that is evolving in the light of proportional representation and the changed circumstances since 1972. While the UUUC has indicated its potential as a Protestant monolith in three successive elections, it is a three-party coalition which has not yet attained even the minimum level of domination which the Unionist party was able to maintain in the old Stormont parliament.[2] A 1 per cent swing in the eight most marginal returns at the Convention election would have reduced the number of UUUC seats to thirty-nine, exactly half the total.[3] It is thus not yet established that an unrestricted assembly under PR would produce one-party government *ad infinitum*.

In these circumstances, the condition of the other parties becomes crucial. The SDLP managed to survive the humiliating collapse of Sunningdale and the executive, and the continuation of internment, with the loss of no more than two seats from its 1973 total, and has the advantage of an inner core of experienced and full-time politicians, which would have been the envy of some Unionist cabinet-makers, and which no Catholic party has enjoyed since the formation of the state. The standard of moderate Unionism, meanwhile, seems to have come to rest very firmly in the hands of Brian Faulkner, until 1972 a most

1. See, for example, *Fortnight*, 99 (21 February 1975). For a wider study see A. E. Alcock, *Protection of Minorities* (N.I. Constitutional Convention paper, 1975). I am grateful to Dr Alcock for a copy of this paper, which was commissioned by the Office of the Chairman for circulation to Convention members [A.C.H.].

2. At the PR general election of 1925 the Unionists won 32 seats out of 52 (62 per cent). The 1975 UUUC total was 46 out of 78 (59 per cent). The average Unionist total, 1921–69, was 70 per cent of the seats.

3. *Fortnight*, 104 (9 May 1975).

improbable-looking champion. His party, formed during the summer of 1974 as the Unionist Party of Northern Ireland (UPNI), lost control of almost all the branches of the old Unionist party, and was in reality no more than the rump of the pro-Sunningdale Assembly Unionists. It was cut down to five seats at the Convention election, and seemed to be competing for a slender middle ground to which the Alliance party had already staked a more convincing claim. The party trimmed its financial sails very sharply after the election, and it may be that it has no further role. On the other hand it remains the only power-sharing *Protestant* party within the terms of the 1972 green paper. At the least its continued existence maintains a mild degree of uncertainty for the UUUC. If the UPNI has lost its voters it has retained more than its share of experienced Unionist leadership.[4] The official Unionists in particular are thin on leaders, and unless and until the UUUC becomes a single party there remains a slim possibility that the demagogic approach of Mr Paisley or the social-cum-sectarian militancy of the trade union and paramilitary wing of Vanguard may stimulate a re-alignment of the Unionist parties in distinction from the Loyalists.

Perhaps the most remarkable outcome of the Assembly election was the almost complete collapse of the NILP. The standard press view is that it lost the slender corpus of moderate opinion which exists in Northern Ireland to the new Alliance party. The pattern of transferred votes in the 1973 election lends some support to such an interpretation: when NILP candidates were eliminated, as most of them were at an early stage, three times as many of their votes went to Alliance candidates as to any other party (see Table 5.4); the NILP, which obtained

TABLE 5.4

Distribution of NILP transfers to other parties,
1973 and 1975 elections (percentage)

1973 (16,020 transfers)		1975 (4,709 transfers)	
Alliance	41	Alliance	38
SDLP	13	SDLP	5
Unionists	13	UPNI	18
Loyalists	9	UUUC	18
Other NILP, and non-transferable votes	24		21
Total of first preferences	18,675		9,102

Note: In each election two cases are excluded, where technicalities of the counting procedure make it impossible to identify NILP transfers separately.

Source: Extracted from the detailed counts listed in the *Belfast Telegraph*, 30 June 1973 and 3 May 1975.

4. All its five Convention members have been both Assemblymen and Stormont MPs, as compared to 6 out of 19 official Unionists, 1 out of 14 Vanguard members, and 2 out of 12 DUP.

45,113 votes in 1969, before the formation of Alliance, slumped to 18,675 first preferences in 1973.

It should not be forgotten, however, that the NILP was already in difficulties in the years before 1970, when the Alliance party was founded, its vote having fallen from a peak of 76,542 in 1962. The party's rate of decline was faster after 1969, but it lost a larger number of supporters between 1962 and 1969. The losses it then made were not to a rival moderate party, but to politicians operating, sometimes very blatantly, within the sectarian framework. On the Protestant side seats were lost to old-style Unionists, or to men like John McQuade, the militant loyalist docker who, as a Unionist, took the Woodvale seat from Labour in 1965 and, on the Catholic side, to Paddy Devlin, who transferred from NILP to SDLP in 1970, taking his supporters with him.

Since 1973 the party's downward trend has continued. Following the shift of moderate support to Alliance has come the loss of left-of-centre Catholic opinion to the SDLP. The party has thus been obliged to fall back on what would normally be considered a Labour Party's natural power base: the unionized working class of the city. But this meant in effect the very elements most aggressively opposed to power-sharing and the Irish dimension. It should not have been all that surprising therefore, when the NILP Assembly member abstained from voting on the ratification of the Sunningdale agreement in May 1974, and when a number of prominent NILP members involved themselves in the UWC stoppage.[5] The appearance of its Convention election manifesto in March 1975 confirmed that the NILP was no longer a party which advocated institutionalized power-sharing in government. The pattern of NILP transfers to other parties at the Convention election indicates clearly that the electorate was sensitive to these changes (see Table 5.4). But the continued decline in the total number of first preference votes suggests that the change of policy, in the short-run at least, has further undermined the party's credibility. The changing distribution of transfers between the SDLP and the Loyalists/UUUC is the outcome simply of a far greater absolute decline on the Catholic side. There is, at this stage, no indication that the party has yet managed to do any more than slow down the movement against it in working-class Protestant areas.

The Alliance party, formed in 1970 by a group of previously non-political figures in Belfast, was considerably more effective in its first two general elections than the NILP ever was in fifty years at attracting votes on a non-sectarian basis. Alliance may well prove in the long run to be no more than a sparkling flash in the pan, as Clann na Poblachta was in the south. It is essentially a one-issue party, a reaction of moderate opinion against the bitter partisanship and violence of recent years.

5. Devlin, *Fall of the N.I. Executive*, p. 61.

Despite rumours of an impending radical take-off in social policy,[6] it retains a middle-class suburban image and power base. This, however, need not necessarily be a barrier to some further progress. Its relative success certainly lends support to the internal critics of the orthodox NILP analysis. Labour's appeal against sectarianism to the working class (which, after all, includes the most overtly sectarian elements) on a platform of common social and economic grievances has, in existing circumstances, been unrealistic. Alliance's greater success suggests that the first generation of converts to non-sectarian politics will be found, if at all, among the middle classes. If this be conceded, then Labour's social policies act not as an alternative to sectarian rhetoric at the hustings but as an additional hurdle. For not only does the party ask people to vote in the same camp as their traditional opponents, but it calls on them to embrace radical social views as well. To state the argument in terms of nationalism and socialism, it seems likely that if non-sectarian politics is introduced successfully into Northern Ireland, it will not be by stressing socialist ideals in the hope of mitigating sectarian feeling, but by confronting the issue directly and presenting a non-sectarian vote as a patriotic vote, a vote in Ulster's 'national' interest. On the other hand, the immediate way of advance for radical social politics seems to lie, if anywhere, within a segregated framework.

Postscript. Alongside bombings and murders, the stalemate over power-sharing continued throughout the winter of 1975–6. In September 1975 William Craig called for a three-year all-party coalition of reconstruction, on a voluntary (ie non-institutionalized) basis, to be followed by a return to orthodox party government. He was vigorously opposed by the other UUUC leaders however (although he alleged that they too had been privately favourable to the scheme), and led a much-reduced Vanguard party out of the UUUC. The Convention failed to present an agreed report to Westminster, and was dissolved in March 1976. The government announced an indefinite continuation of direct rule, phased out internment, and ended special category status (in effect, prisoner-of-war conditions) for future 'political' prisoners. Its policy, perhaps perforce, had become a complete reversal of the Whitelaw approach. The search for a political solution was to be set aside as peripheral, rather than central, to the security problem, which in turn would no longer be treated as acute and requiring extraordinary measures, but as chronic and ongoing, best handled by treating political terrorism as ordinary crime.

6. See *Fortnight*, 64 (June 1973).

CHAPTER SIX

Some Conclusions

Nationalism in Ireland, as elsewhere, has been more directly concerned with securing the power of the nation to direct its own destiny than with achieving prosperity or social progress as such. In a number of countries, this instinct for national self-assertion has developed into expansive nationalism, manifesting itself as an urge for power over others. The tension between working-class and middle-class political aspirations in modern states in the late nineteenth and early twentieth centuries frequently channelled itself into a struggle between socialism on the one hand and expansive nationalism or imperialism on the other.

In most of Ireland, where the struggle was for the mere establishment of the national state, sustained conflict between national aspirations and the striving of the lower classes for an increased political voice did not arise, prior to independence. The two aims appeared to coincide: the class enemy was the national enemy; the repressive economic masters were the foreign political masters. The fight by workers and small farmers for improved living conditions and a larger share of political power was regarded by them as part of the national fight, within which it became subsumed.

Since the post-treaty split of 1922, this unity in the south of Ireland has disintegrated. But the result has not been the emergence of a frankly class-based politics. The modest performance of the Irish Labour party, the oldest-established party in the state, is evidence of that. Since independence, as before, radical social aims have been voiced with any vigour only as a function of disaffected nationalism: in the land war of the 1880s, in Sinn Féin between 1916 and 1921 and republican Sinn Féin, 1923–6, in the early Fianna Fáil and in Clann na Poblachta. Left-wing forces have had little or no success when they have tried to take the lead in the national movement or work independently of it, as they did in the 1913 Dublin strike, the sporadic agrarian disturbances of 1918–23, Saor Eire and the Republican Congress in the 1930s, the various phases of the Communist movement in Ireland, or the social radicals who have been active in the IRA since 1962.

Just as the left has, in effect, been captured by radical republicanism, so the mainstream of Irish national politics has moved steadily to the right over the same period, incidentally heading off any development of a conservative party, such as the first Farmers' party, outside the national framework. In the case of the majority, pro-treaty wing of Sinn Féin, this development took place between the 1916 rising and the last years of the Cumann na nGaedheal administration. On the anti-treaty side the same trend is apparent, from the radical republicanism of the civil war period and the economic war, to the conservative period which began with the signing of the Anglo-Irish agreement of 1938. Once the treaty had been effectively dismantled, as it was by this agreement, the *raison d'être* for the 1922 split in the ranks of Sinn Féin was removed. It became increasingly difficult to distinguish between the policies of the two major parties, and the sociological differences between them have blurred accordingly. On the crucial issue of neutrality during the Second World War they acted with almost perfect consensus. The Republic was finally instituted not by Fianna Fáil but by a taoiseach from the old pro-treaty side. Revival of the national language and reunification of the country remain formal goals of both parties, but it seems reasonably clear that the bulk of opinion on each side regards both as unrealistic in the present circumstances. While it may be argued that Fine Gael stands slightly to the right of Fianna Fáil in that it represents a narrower spectrum of class and opinion, in seeking power it has consistently shown itself willing and able to ally with politicians who are both more strongly republican than Fianna Fáil and more radical on social questions. If Fianna Fáil is a coalition of interests, the Fine Gael-led alternative governments have differed only in being coalitions with the bones showing.

What, then, of nationalism and socialism in recent years? Firstly, it must be noted that the concept of the 'east–west gradient', used in Chapter Two of this book to analyse Irish society and politics in the revolutionary period, which particularly attracted the interest of scholars in the German edition,[1] cannot be applied effectively to the contemporary situation. Recent work by economists makes clear that 'the traditional dividing line [between east and west] more or less down the Shannon had been outmoded by 1966'.[2] It is no longer possible to speak of the western counties, as a group, as being poorer or more

1. For example, Basil Chubb, *Government and Politics of Ireland*, p. 51.
2. T. J. Baker and M. Ross, 'The changing regional pattern of Ireland', *Economic and Social Review*, i (1970), 164.

economically backward than those to the east: the increased prosperity of dairy farming in Munster, the impact of the Shannon industrial zone on Clare and Limerick, and the general effect of tourism and the increase in motor-cars, has effectively blurred what was once a clear-cut distinction. This socio-economic change seems to be reflected politically by the declining influence of militant republicanism in these areas. Whereas Sinn Féin won four Dáil seats in 1957 in the north-west border areas and in Kerry, and did well elsewhere in the west, in 1973 it won no seats and fared badly everywhere. The social basis for militant republicanism in western districts has been cut away, and surviving republican spirit there is to a great extent vestigial. In the last few years, militant and socially radical nationalism has been strongest in urban areas, especially in Dublin and Belfast. In its style of operation—direct action—and the issues on which it has concentrated—housing and employment—it has borne a close resemblance to contemporary extra-parliamentary reform movements in many western countries. In Ireland this movement has looked for its momentum to militant nationalism.

Since the German edition of this book appeared in 1959, the nationalist style of politics has been increasingly set aside by the politicians of the major southern parties (apart from a brief bout of excitement when Armageddon was scented in the north in 1969), just as their predecessors set aside social radicalism. This is partly explained by the eventual retirement of the veterans of the revolutionary generation. Their successors have, probably inevitably, grown up in a less strident national atmosphere. Recent members of the Dáil are considerably less likely to have had a Gaelic League background, for instance, than the leaders of the revolutionary generation.[3] In the trade union movement a deep split along national lines, which seemed insoluble in 1945, was healed without difficulty in 1959. If party politics in the south are still formally based on the old national lines, there is now little pretence that such lines retain any real significance. The two major parties continue to exist because they already exist and are well established. They are both, and have been for some years, 'catch-all' parties—though with differing degrees of success—rather than nationalist parties.[4] Since the late 1940s, the articulation of militant national sentiments has not been a major vote-catcher and, perhaps for this reason, has been left increasingly to the radical fringes of politics.

The politics of Northern Ireland differ from those of the south in that national issues retain a real and central, not merely a formal, significance. The character of Irish nationalism in the north has inevitably been affected by various developments in the south since 1921. But unlike that

3. A. Cohan, *The Irish Political Elite* (Dublin, 1972), p. 60.
4. Chubb, *Government and Politics of Ireland*, pp. 75–76.

of the south it is still an unfulfilled nationalism, and retains some characteristics of pre-independence nationalism. Apart from the division between Belfast and the rest of the province between 1945 and 1970—which is similar to that between Larkinite Dublin and the rest of the south earlier in the century—Irish nationalists in Ulster have been little aware of any conflict of interest between nationalism and social reform. One party has always been able to dominate Catholic political representation, and the recent wholesale shift of support from the Nationalist party to the Social Democratic and Labour party reflects less a move by Ulster Catholics to the left than a desire for Catholic political unity, combined with an awareness of the advantages of presenting an appropriately progressive image to the British Labour party.

But Irish nationalism is not the only nationalism in the north. What, for the sake of clarity, we may term Orange nationalism is equally nationalist in temper. Though it may be pro-British, it is not simply British nationalism or patriotism, but a force with a unique character of its own.[5] It has some of the characteristics of an expansionist or imperialist nationalism, for—although it does not seek to claim new territory—one of its driving forces has always been an aggressive belief in the superiority of its own way of life to that of its southern neighbour. Like Irish and other nationalisms, however, it has preached a community of class interests within the national group: landowner, industrialist, and worker, each with their role to play, in harmony with one another. The nature of the Ulster Unionist Labour Association is an indication of the status of social questions in this system, and the history of that association is the best evidence in the Ulster context for the argument that nationalism is a middle-class ideology.

None the less, there are clear indications in recent Ulster history that even if nationalism is in some senses a middle-class ideology, the most outspoken nationalism is socially radical and aims itself specifically at the rural and urban working class. Independent Unionists, almost always of a militantly 'Protestant' hue, have been more successful in working-class districts of Belfast than anywhere else in Ulster. Wherever they have stood they have backed up their main arguments—that the Unionist party has not been sufficiently 'loyal'—with an emphasis on social issues. The Paisley–O'Neill contest in the Bannside constituency in 1969 is one recent example of this. Indeed it may be argued, and it may be the secret of the recent success of the loyalist coalition in Ulster politics, that an orthodox left-of-centre party such as the NILP could not hope to succeed in Northern Ireland politics because it could

5. This of course is not an argument for an independent Ulster state, any more than observations about Slovak national characteristics would make a case for an independent Slovakia. For some acute strictures on nationalism and politics in continental Europe see E. Kedourie, *Nationalism* (London, 1960), pp. 92–140.

never appeal effectively outside Belfast. Militant loyalism is, in such a situation, apparently the only effective way of getting Protestant workers in the city and small farmers in the country to join forces behind a radical candidate.

Just as anti-treaty republicanism proved more attractive than the Irish Labour party to the poorest classes in the south in the 1920s, so in the north today the NILP is no match for the Protestant militancy of the DUP and Vanguard. Middle-class nationalism in power has been most effectively challenged, or at least embarrassed, by a cruder and more extreme nationalist appeal, on both sides of the border. Whether such appeals have been characterized by their opponents as 'communist' or as 'fascist', they have in practice had a great deal in common. They are both appeals against the prevailing national orthodoxy to the men of little or no property, and as such have been more effective than any appeal which traditional Labour parties have made.

Whether radicalism in these cases is merely a stalking-horse for nationalism (Irish or Orange), or vice versa, is hard to say. Electors take from party manifestos what appeals to them most, while politicians in office often find themselves in different circumstances or under other pressures than those which applied when they formulated their beliefs or drew up their party programmes. Fianna Fáil, the most successful nationalist *and* radical party in Ireland since 1921, changed its character almost entirely between the early 1930s and the 1960s. Nationalist–radical parties in general possess considerably more political flexibility in areas of the world which have nationality problems than do Labour parties, which tend to appear by contrast as very colourless when confronted with the state's most burning issues. On the other hand their very flexibility, while making them more likely to win power, suggests that in the long run, like Fianna Fáil, they will not be very reliable vehicles for the passage of wide-ranging social reform.

APPENDIX 1

Land reform since 1870 and its effect on the social structure of Ireland

In preparing this book, it was necessary to pay considerable attention to the fundamental social changes which have taken place in Ireland since 1870 as a result of agrarian reform. A number of ideas which suggested themselves during the course of the study advanced the central theme only indirectly, so that in order to avoid deviation a number of interesting developments had to be omitted from the main analysis. It seems worth while to include some of this material in an appendix, so as to make clear the changes in social structure which underlay political events.[1]

In 1870 the twenty million acres of Irish land were in the hands of a few thousand proprietors who received rent from half a million tenants, to the extent of about £12–15 million pa, some £10–12 million of which was collected in the area of the present Irish Republic. Today, farmers in the Republic who have not yet become the freehold owners of their property have to bear only about 20 per cent of this charge, in

1. There are a number of useful studies of the Irish land question. The most readily available source material is in the *British Parliamentary Papers*, which contain detailed annual reports and statistics on the Irish land question down to 1921. From 1922 the annual *Reports of the Irish Land Commission* (Dublin, Stationery Office), as well as the *Statistical Abstracts of the Irish Free State*, provide similar information. In addition, *Thom's Directory* contains useful summaries of the main statistics. Elizabeth Hooker's *Re-adjustments of Agricultural Tenure in Ireland* is a thorough yet concise survey, well supported with statistical material and diagrams, which steers judiciously clear of any partisan attitude towards either the Irish–English conflict or the conflict between Free Staters and Republicans. J. E. Pomfret's *The Struggle for Land in Ireland* is also useful, but does not deal with developments after 1923. The work of Mortiz Bonn, a German economic historian, covers the pre-independence period, as far as the beginnings of the new legislation. A useful survey of the work of the Congested Districts Board was written by its first secretary, W. L. Micks. Perhaps most useful of all for social and economic data in a broad geographical setting is T. W. Freeman's major textbook, *Ireland*. See the bibliography for details of all these books.

the form of land annuity payments for the purchase of the land.[2] In 1870, the demand of most tenants was simply for the 'three Fs': *fixity of tenure*, with protection against arbitrary eviction; *fair rent*, to be appropriate to the agricultural value of the land, as assessed by an impartial body; and *free sale* by a departing tenant of his interest in the holding, so that compensation would be payable for any increase in the value of the holding brought about by the tenant's improvements. The last of these was a right which had been long established by custom in Ulster.[3] As a result of Land Acts passed by Gladstone's governments in 1870 and 1881, the 'three Fs' were secured, and the principle of 'dual ownership' thereby established. The act of 1881 also brought into existence the Irish Land Commission, a government agency created to administer the new agrarian legislation. Reform, however, always lagged behind the increasing demands of the tenants. As farm prices went on declining and agrarian discontent continued in the 1880s, exclusive ownership of the land by the tenants became the popular demand. The Ashbourne Land Purchase Acts of 1885, 1888, and 1889 accepted the principle, and a government loan of £5 million was advanced to provide money for tenant purchase. With such legislation Conservative governments, though almost totally unsympathetic towards Irish nationalism, made practical contributions to reform which were no less valuable than the measures introduced by the Liberals.[4] The decisive step, however, was the Land Act brought in by the Conservative, George Wyndham, in 1903, by which future sales were to proceed by whole estates rather than individual holdings. New loans were raised which, it was hoped, would finally settle the problem within a reasonable time. In 1909 some coercive power was given to the Land Commission for the first time by the Liberal, Augustine Birrell. His Act, as well as revising the finances of the purchase scheme, provided for compulsory purchase orders against reluctant landlords in the congested western districts.

One aspect of the agrarian problem was concerned with the relationship between landlord and tenant. A further difficulty was the hopeless congestion and excessive number of uneconomic smallholdings which made certain districts in the west perpetual centres of destitution and disorder. To ease this congestion, and establish economic farming units, the Congested Districts Board (CDB) was set up in 1891. Initially one-sixth and, after 1909, one-third of the land of Ireland came under the authority of this body. Its main responsibilities were the enlargement

2. Much of what follows is based on K. R. O'Shiel, 'The work of the Land Commission', a paper read at the Civics Institute of Ireland, in December 1944 (duplicated copy in the possession of Mr O'Shiel).

3. But see B. L. Solow, *The Land Question and the Irish Economy, 1871–1903* (Cambridge, Mass., 1971) for some important new insights.

4. For a discussion of Conservative policy see L. P. Curtis Jr, *Coercion and Conciliation in Ireland, 1880–92* (Princeton, 1963).

and consolidation of holdings, improvement of farming methods, afforestation, and the development of fisheries, industries, and trade. It became one of the most successful agencies created by the British government in Ireland. It purchased the equivalent of five-eighths of the land of the original CDB area for redistribution to small farmers,[5] so that the number of uneconomic holdings, below 10 acres, was reduced from 43,730 in 1881 to 36,110 in 1911, while the number of holdings between 10 and 100 acres rose from 67,351 to 75,138. The number of holdings over 100 acres was also reduced, from 44 per cent down to 25 per cent of the total CDB area.[6] One sign of the improved condition of the seven counties in which the CDB operated was the sevenfold increase of private deposits in savings banks between 1881 and 1911.[7] The activities of the board also included the building of new farmhouses, with the result that one-roomed huts almost completely disappeared. Whereas £565,014 was spent on emergency relief operations in the years 1879–91, only £100,000 was needed between 1891 and 1908, when the payments were terminated.[8] Thus the need to interfere fundamentally with the rights of property in order to improve conditions was recognized long before the creation of the Irish Free State. Besides small farmers whose uneconomic holdings required additional land before they could become viable farms, there were tenants who had been evicted during the land war of the 1880s. Many of them emigrated, and little was done for those who remained behind until the Evicted Tenants Act of 1907. Seven years later the claims of 3,587 applicants had been met, and by 1923 only 191 valid cases remained to be dealt with.[9]

Soon after the establishment of the Free State, agrarian legislation entered a new phase. In August 1923 the Hogan Act removed the remnants of dual ownership by making the Land Commission owner of all leasehold land. The Commission paid off the remaining landlords, sold their land to the tenants, and took over the duties of the CDB, which was disbanded. The price for expropriated land was no longer to be assessed freely, but reckoned according to the level of rent in 1911. The subletting of land transferred in this way was prohibited, in order to prevent the task of the Commission becoming like that of Sisyphus.[1] In response to the campaign against annuities, the Fianna Fáil government halved the annuity payments in 1933, and all arrears older than ten years were annulled.

The authority of the Commission was again extended and, in accordance with de Valera's party programme, emphasis changed to the provision of land for the landless. For the first time the Commission was authorized to expropriate land for this purpose, and distribute it to

5. E. R. Hooker, *Re-adjustments of Agricultural Tenure in Ireland* (Chapel Hill, North Carolina, 1938), p. 137.   6. Ibid., p. 141.   7. Ibid., p. 143.
8. Ibid., p. 146.   9. Ibid., p. 155.   1. Ibid., pp. 84 and 104.

people previously ineligible. This caused some concern, and it was feared that the attempt to cater for landless men might create a new wave of uneconomic holdings.[2] Another apparent danger was that by an Act of 1936 the process of legal expropriation became very much easier. This threatened a farmer's security of tenure, which was one of the original aims of agrarian reform.[3] In the event, however, these fears have proved groundless, and the reforms of the 1930s did little to alter the general direction of land reform. Increased prosperity has been the farmer's best guarantee of security, while Fianna Fáil's gesture towards the landless man soon proved to be no more than a gesture.

TABLE A.1

Changes in owner-occupied land,
1870–1929 (percentage)

	Owners	Tenants
1870	3·0	97·0
1906	29·2	70·8
1916	63·9	36·1
1929	97·4	2·6

Source: Hooker, *Agricultural Tenure*, p. 120. The 1929 figures are based on land area, others on the number of landholders.

Although size of holdings is not, by itself, an ideal guide to the prosperity of a farming community, it is the only general guide available in the absence of realistic Poor Law Valuation ratings for the entire period. Because land rates differ greatly from area to area—in Connaught, for example, they are generally far lower than in Munster and Leinster—a comparison according to area and value has been drawn up, and this is set out in Fig. A.1.

Ignoring the smallest groups of holdings, of less than one acre or £4 pa, this shows that in Leinster the correlation between acreage and value is quite close, whereas in Munster many of the holdings are quite poor. In Connaught it is clear that the land is generally poorer than in the other two provinces, since the curve in the value column is sharply to the left of that in the acreage column. This must be borne in mind as a corrective factor when we look at the figures over a wider period (see Fig. A.2). From 1861 to 1888 there was a sharp decline in the number of the smallest farms, those of less than 5 acres, mainly as a consequence of eviction and emigration in the decades after the famine and during the land war.[4] Particularly in Connaught, where this class

2. Ibid., pp. 112 ff and 165 ff.   3. Ibid., pp. 114, 167.
4. Only the three southern provinces are included in this analysis. Of the remaining three counties in the Republic, Donegal's pattern follows that of Connaught, while Cavan and Monaghan follow Leinster.

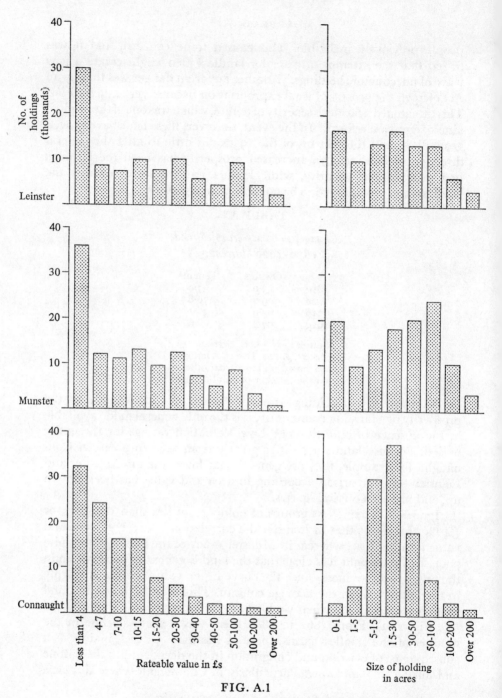

FIG. A.1

Distribution of agricultural holdings in
Leinster, Munster, and Connaught, 1932

Source: *Statistical Abstracts*, 1932, p. 39.

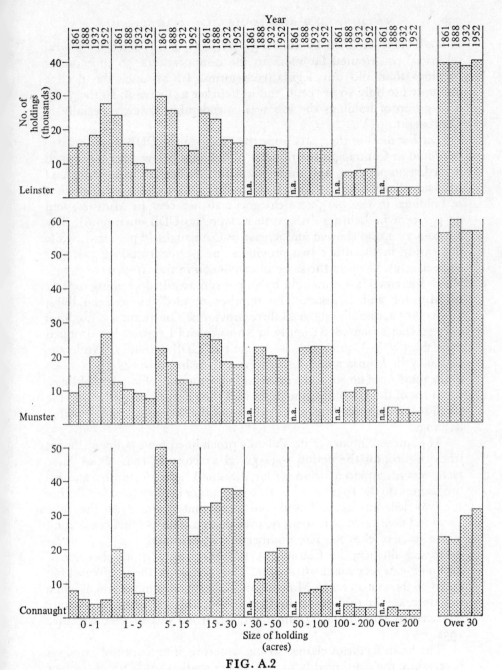

FIG. A.2

Distribution of agricultural holdings in
Leinster, Munster, and Connaught in selected years

Sources: *Thom's Almanac and Directory, 1866,* p. 833; *Parliamentary Papers,* 1889
[c. 5785], lxxxiii. 215; *Statistical Abstracts,* 1932, 1952.

of landholder declined by almost 34 per cent, this process of 'natural selection' contributed far more to the disappearance of uneconomic holdings than did any legislative reforms. In Munster the decline amounted to only 19 per cent, and in Leinster 24 per cent. In the 5–15-acre group of holdings the loss was considerably lower, especially in Connaught.

During most of the years from 1888 to 1932 the CDB was in operation, and in Connaught the number of holdings below 5 acres dropped a further 30 per cent, and there was a further decline in Leinster and Munster. Particularly striking is the more rapid decline in the number of holdings in the 5–15-acre category: 26 per cent in Munster, and 33 per cent in Leinster (where there were no CDB operations). The 15–30-acre group showed an increase in Connaught (7 per cent), while decreasing in the other two provinces (21 per cent and 22 per cent respectively). We find the same phenomenon in the 30–50-acre group, which increased in Connaught by 30 per cent, while decreasing slightly in Munster and Leinster. The number of medium-sized holdings, 50–100 acres, rose slightly in all three provinces. The number of holdings over 100 acres increased slightly in Munster and Leinster, but dropped very sharply in Connaught, as a result of CDB activities. While the tendency in Munster and Leinster was therefore towards an increase in the number of larger and a decrease in the number of smaller holdings, the work of the CDB in Connaught had the effect of strengthening the small-to-medium holding at the expense of the very small and the large holdings.

The limited impact of de Valera's proclaimed land policy is shown in the figures for the period 1932–52. His victory in 1932, as we have seen, was an apparent triumph for the small farm electorate, and his programme in the 1930s was hostile to the larger landowners. But during the two decades that followed, the trend that started with the 1870 Land Act continued only steadily, with no sign of any rapid acceleration of the pace of change. The number of 1–5-acre and 1–15-acre farms decreased further; in Connaught the 15–30-acre group became a declining category for the first time. The increase in the number of big farms of 100–200 acres in Munster and Leinster was maintained, while the decrease in this group in Connaught, as well as of farms over 200 acres in Munster and Connaught, was in no way accelerated after 1932.

The main factor of change in the structure of agricultural holdings is certainly the continued high level of emigration. Although it cannot be taken as a rule that only the poorest classes of a population emigrated, it was nevertheless the class of small farmers in Ireland which decreased most sharply during the decades of high emigration, thereby helping to enlarge the holdings of those who stayed behind. Over the years, emigration probably played a larger role in changing the structure of landholding than did any legislative measures.

The Land Commission regards its work as still uncompleted, in spite of the drastic and revolutionary changes which have taken place in the last eighty years. 130,000 tenant farms are not yet the absolute property of their tenants, and 28,000 of these must still be merged in order to form economic units. There are still many thousands of land-hungry or landless country people, in a land prolific in children, who still hope to satisfy their desire for land one day. Yet there are limits to the number of people which even the best-farmed land can support, and in the opinion of some experts those limits have been almost reached already.[5]

5. This paragraph has been left exactly as Dr Rumpf wrote it in the late 1950s. That the observations no longer apply to the circumstances of today is an indication of how much rural Ireland has changed since the original edition of this book appeared [A. C. H.].

APPENDIX 2

Irish political groupings in the twentieth century

ALLIANCE PARTY. A non-sectarian party formed in 1970 in response to the disturbances in Northern Ireland. It has had some success in attracting support from both Protestants and Catholics, especially in middle-class areas of Belfast, and won a number of Assembly, Convention, and local council seats. But there is little indication at present that it has made much inroad into the traditional blocs of support for Protestant and Catholic candidates.

ANCIENT ORDER OF HIBERNIANS. A Catholic benevolent society, founded by Irish emigrants in America in the mid nineteenth century, and subsequently imported into the home country. In America it had no more precise political commitment than a general sympathy with Irish national aspirations. In Ireland, however, between 1900 and 1918, it became an important constituency organization for the Irish Parliamentary party, especially in Ulster, where it came to be regarded as the Catholic equivalent of the Orange Order. Since independence it has not been influential in southern politics. In the north its sympathies are still with constitutional nationalism, but it no longer occupies a position in Catholic politics in any way equivalent to that held by the Orange Order on the Protestant side.

ANTI-TREATY PARTY. *See* Sinn Féin, third phase.

AONATACHT EIREANN (*Irish Unity*). A republican splinter-group which broke away from Fianna Fáil in 1971 in protest against the leadership's conciliatory attitude to the Northern Ireland disturbances. It differs from Sinn Féin in its readiness to participate in constitutional politics in the Republic. It has not made an appearance in Northern Ireland politics, nor did it win any seats in the Dáil election of 1973.

BLUESHIRTS (*Army Comrades Association*). Ireland's nearest approach to a fascist movement in the 1930s. During the summer of 1932 a benevolent association for veterans of the Free State Army, the Army Comrades Association began to accept membership applications from the general public. In the election campaigns of 1932 and 1933 the Association played an increasingly prominent part in defending the right of Cumann na nGaedheal speakers to free speech, and perhaps also in denying such rights to Fianna Fáil speakers. It became essentially a street-fighting force, in opposition to the 'communist' IRA. In April 1933 it obtained a new leader and martyr, General Eoin O'Duffy, who had been dismissed by Fianna Fáil from his post as Commissioner of Police. Under his leadership the movement adopted the uniform of a blue shirt, and was renamed the National Guard. Faced with the rising tide of street violence and what were, in retrospect, slightly hysterical allegations that O'Duffy was a would-be Mussolini, ready to snatch control of the state, the government suppressed the National Guard. At this stage the opposition politicians of Cumann na Gaedheal and the National Centre party entered into an alliance with O'Duffy and his Blueshirts, the outcome of which was the new Fine Gael party, with O'Duffy as leader. The Blueshirts continued to exist as the League of Youth. O'Duffy proved an inept politician, however, and resigned his leadership of Fine Gael in 1934. The Blueshirts faded away gradually, and O'Duffy's last political gesture was to lead a small force to Spain to fight for Franco in 1936.

CLANN NA POBLACHTA (*Family of the Republic*). A political party formed in Dublin in 1946 on a platform of swift action to end partition, establish an Irish republic, and implement radical social reform. Although many of its leading figures had at least some old links with the IRA, it differed from other IRA splinter-groups in its readiness to participate fully in constitutional politics, and in its relative degree of success. It won ten seats in the Dáil in 1948, and participated in the inter-party government of 1948–51. Its influence soon helped to bring about the declaration of the republic, but some of its members were at the centre of the controversy over the mother-and-child welfare scheme in 1951, and it never recovered its momentum. It gave only outside support to the second inter-party government, and although it retained one member in the Dáil until 1965, it had virtually ceased to exist as a party several years earlier.

CLANN NA TALMHAN (*Family of the Land*). Founded at Galway, in 1938, to represent the interests of the smaller, especially western, farmers in the Dáil. It won ten seats in 1943, and took part in both inter-party governments, 1948–51 and 1954–7. By 1961 its party organization had withered away, and its last TD retired from politics in 1965.

COMMONWEALTH LABOUR PARTY. Founded by Harry Midgley following his departure from the NILP. Very much a vehicle for its leader, it contested the 1945 Stormont election on a partitionist, pro-British platform, but brought Midgley no new parliamentary colleagues. When he joined the Unionist party in 1947, it quickly faded away.

CONGRESS OF IRISH UNIONS. See Irish Trades Union Congress.

CUMANN NA NGAEDHEAL (*Community of Irishmen*). The governing party in the Irish Free State, 1922–32. Founded by the pro-treaty members of the Dáil after the split in Sinn Féin, it formally adopted its new name and organization in April 1923. During a decade of power, its cautious attitude towards social and economic reform, its thorough-going commitment to the British Commonwealth, and its stern suppression of the IRA, won it the support of many former Unionists and a generally conservative reputation in the country at large. It fell from power in 1932 and, after a second general election defeat in the following year, merged with some smaller groups to form a new party, Fine Gael.

DEMOCRATIC UNIONIST PARTY (*DUP*). Formerly the Protestant Unionist party, a group of radical right-wing militants who appeared in Belfast city politics in the late 1950s. The Revd Ian Paisley, Moderator of the Free Presbyterian Church, became the dominant figure in the movement after 1964, winning its first parliamentary seats—at both Stormont and Westminster—in 1970. The new name was adopted in 1971, partly as a means of effecting a merger with some dissident Unionist politicians, partly in order to give the party a more respectable image in British government circles. For a while the leadership revealed an unexpected flexibility in its political outlook, but the effect on its popular following was clearly a negative one. Before the 1973 Assembly elections the DUP moved to re-establish its natural power-base, forming a Loyalist Coalition with the VUPP. In 1974 they were joined by the official Unionist party in a more formalized United Ulster Unionist Council (UUUC).

FARMERS' PARTY. A minor party in the Free State Dáil from 1922 to 1932, at one time holding 15 seats. Its organization was based on the Irish Farmers' Union, and it represented particularly the interests of the larger farmers. In 1932 it merged into the National Centre party.

FENIANS. See Irish Republican Brotherhood.

FIANNA FAIL (*Soldiers of Destiny*). Convinced of the sterility of Sinn Féin's policy of abstention on principle from the Free State Dáil, de Valera attempted in 1926 to lead that party in a new direction. Having failed to carry a majority of the activists with him, he and his followers left to found Fianna Fáil. The new party quickly showed at the polls that it commanded the lion's share of anti-treaty opinion, and in 1927 it entered the Dáil. It won power in 1932 and has since been the dominant party in the state, holding office for thirty-four of the following forty-one years. In the early days its image was one of small-farmer radicalism and sympathy with the aspirations, if not the methods, of the IRA. The long years of power made their mark, however, and more recently it has come to be regarded as the party of the new national establishment.

FINE GAEL (*United Ireland party*). The second-ranking party in the Irish state since its foundation in 1933 from a merger of Cumann na nGaedheal, the National Centre party, and the Blueshirt movement. Its flirtation with the fascist-style politics of the Blueshirts was a passing phase in its development, a panic response to the electoral triumphs of Fianna Fáil and the apparent re-emergence of the IRA. Much of the corporative/vocational theory that was bandied about derived more from the Vatican than from the rhetoric of the continental dictators. Fine Gael has remained an essentially conservative and middle-class party. It perhaps comes slightly closer to being 'the Catholic party' than any of its rivals, but it also probably commands the support of the majority of Protestants in the state. In recent years its leadership has come to include an element which places more emphasis on progressive social reform. Although never holding power independently, it has been the main component of three coalition governments, 1948–51, 1954–7, and 1973– .

GAELIC ATHLETIC ASSOCIATION (*GAA*). Founded in 1884 to promote traditional Irish sports, especially hurling and Gaelic football. Its early leaders included a strong Fenian element, and the movement rapidly developed an aggressively republican spirit at grass-roots level. Athletes who participated in 'English' sports were excluded, as were members of the Royal Irish Constabulary. The GAA is thought to have furnished the hard core of the rank-and-file of the Irish Volunteers. In more recent years it has been concerned solely with the administration of sports, although even today many Irish politicians owe their local popularity to a GAA background.

GAELIC LEAGUE. Founded in 1893 by a non-political Protestant, Douglas Hyde, and other Gaelic scholars, in order to revive the Irish language and urge the cultural necessity of 'de-anglicizing' Ireland. It remained formally non-political until 1915, when militant nationalists gained control, arguing that cultural de-anglicization was impossible without political independence. In recent years the League has become a relatively staid Irish language pressure group. Despite the fairly short period of its formal political commitment, it played a significant part in building the 'Irish-Ireland' climate of opinion which ensured widespread public support for the struggle of 1916–21.

IRISH CITIZEN ARMY. Recruited by James Connolly and James Larkin in 1913 from members of the ITGWU, in order to prevent disruption at their political meetings. Its membership never rose much above three hundred. A small contingent led by Connolly took part in the 1916 rising alongside the Irish Volunteers.

IRISH CONGRESS OF TRADES UNIONS. *See* Irish Trades Union Congress.

IRISH LABOUR PARTY. Founded in 1912 by resolution of the ITUC, of which it was a constituent part until 1930. Its early radicalism was replaced after 1916 by tactical and ideological caution. The party did not contest the 1918 election, in order to avoid being split over the national issue. It re-entered politics in the 'treaty' election of 1922, but has never been able to achieve more than third-party status in southern politics. It was second partner in the coalition governments of 1948–51, 1954–7, and 1973– . It has been the only major southern-based party to operate in Northern Ireland. During the 1950s it was an influential force in Belfast Catholic politics, but its activities in the north now seem to have virtually ceased, although it still maintains a branch in the border town of Newry.

IRISH NATION LEAGUE. A short-lived political movement in 1916–17. It sought to provide a militant alternative to the Irish Parliamentary party without the abstentionism of Sinn Féin or the militarism of the Irish Volunteers. Late in 1917 it became a constituent part of the new Sinn Féin, and so embraced both these things. Its leaders were mainly Catholic lawyers in the north of Ireland, and its opponents christened it 'The league of the seven attorneys'.

IRISH PARLIAMENTARY PARTY (*Irish Nationalist party*). The voice of constitutional nationalism at Westminster before independence. It was the dominant force in Irish politics from its formation by Isaac Butt in the 1870s, through the decade of Parnell's leadership and the long vigil of Redmond and Dillon, until its annihilation at the polls by Sinn Féin in 1918.

IRISH REPUBLICAN ARMY (*IRA*). A name first adopted by the Irish Volunteers during the Anglo-Irish war, 1919–21. The movement has maintained a continuous existence down to the present day, although it has undergone more splits and changes of direction than even Sinn Féin, in recent years its political counterpart. The first split was the departure of the pro-treaty element in 1922 to become the basis of the Free State army, while the remainder—probably the majority— soldiered on in the established guerrilla style against the new Dublin regime as against the old. Since 1923 there has been no formal military campaign against the Dublin government, but its authority has never been recognized, and there have been sporadic incidents in the south throughout the state's existence. During the early 1930s, especially, the IRA was much in evidence as a street-fighting force, in opposition to the right-wing Blueshirts. In 1939 it mounted a destructive, but politically ineffective, bombing campaign in English cities; during the Second World War it failed in both its objectives, winning active support from Nazi Germany, and bringing about an uprising in Northern Ireland; and from 1956 to 1962 it mounted a drawn-out, but again politically ineffective, campaign against the Northern Ireland security forces along the border.

From time to time, radical or revolutionary socialist elements within the movement, despairing at the sterility of the 'military' policy, have sought to lead it along new paths. In the early 1930s the dissenters tried to form new parties, notably Saor Eire and the Republican Congress. More recently, in 1962, the IRA itself began to drift away from its military emphasis in favour of involvement in non-violent direct action in support of assorted socialist and radical issues in Dublin and elsewhere. This approach, and the move to end parliamentary abstentionism, did not find favour with many veterans of the 1956 campaign. When the upheaval in Belfast came in 1969, catching the IRA unprepared for military action, these elements took their chance. They failed to carry a majority on the Army Council in Dublin, but subsequently appealed on a platform of military preparedness to the grass-roots of the movement, with great success. They formed a 'Provisional' Army Council, and in effect created a second IRA, which has dominated the headlines since 1971. The 'Official IRA' continues to exist but has come increasingly to resemble the left-wing splinter-groups of the 1930s.

IRISH REPUBLICAN BROTHERHOOD (*IRB*). A secret society formed in Ireland and in the United States in 1858, for the purpose of planning and directing the overthrow of British rule in Ireland by force of arms. It had two main periods of activity. A rising in Ireland was planned for 1865, with the intention of utilizing the military skills of Irishmen returning from service in the American civil war. The scheme fizzled out, however, in a series of bomb attacks and other isolated incidents in England, and a half-hearted 'invasion' of Canada from the United States, in 1867. The IRB during this period of its activity is usually referred to by historians by its alternative name, the Fenian movement, in order to distinguish it from the second phase of activity. There was some nominal continuity, on both sides of the Atlantic, over the next forty years, but most of the leaders of the reformed IRB after 1907 were young men, taking only inspiration from the ideals and methods of the

Fenians. To all intents and purposes, they revived an entirely moribund movement. The IRB planned and led the 1916 Dublin rising, operating clandestinely within the command structure of the Irish Volunteers. Many of its leaders were afterwards executed. The movement continued to exist, at least until 1922, although its activities after 1916 remain shrouded in secrecy. During this period of more open conflict with Britain, when Michael Collins was its most prominent member, its continued existence was a source of considerable bitterness and suspicion within the republican movement at large. Whether at the same time its operations substantially furthered the cause of Irish independence is, in the absence of evidence, hard to say.

IRISH SOCIALIST REPUBLICAN PARTY. A small group of thorough-going socialists organized by James Connolly in Dublin between 1896 and his departure for America in 1903. A useful focus for socialist ideas, it made no impact on practical politics.

IRISH TRADES UNION CONGRESS. Founded 1894, as an association of craft unions, about half of which, the 'amalgamateds', had headquarters across the water in Britain. Following the adhesion of the ITGWU after 1909, the Congress became more broadly based within the working class, although a large proportion of its membership has remained in amalgamated unions. In 1912 the Congress agreed to establish an Irish Labour party, and the two bodies remained fused together until 1930. From its earliest times, the movement had contained a large proportion of Protestant members in the industrial north, and so was highly anxious, especially in the 1912–21 period, to avoid formal commitment on 'national' questions. The advent of partition did not affect the structure of the movement, but in 1945 it was badly split by the withdrawal of the ITGWU and some smaller unions to set up a new body, the Congress of Irish Unions, which would only accept affiliation from unions with headquarters in Ireland. Although the manoeuvre may be judged a failure, in that it took only a third of trade union membership with it, and so failed to break the ITUC, the split continued for fifteen years. Reunion was finally achieved in 1959, when the two bodies merged to form the Irish Congress of Trades Unions, open to unions based outside Ireland provided arrangements were made to safeguard the autonomy of Irish members. Trade unionists in Northern Ireland continued their affiliation to the ITUC after partition. The majority of members there were in amalgamated unions, and in 1945 the ITUC authorized them to set up a separate Northern Ireland Committee to look after local affairs. This arrangement was continued after 1959 by the reunited ICTU which, in 1964, amended its constitution in such a way as to give the Northern Ireland Committee real autonomy. The latter then received formal recognition from the Northern government for the first time.

IRISH TRANSPORT AND GENERAL WORKERS UNION (*ITGWU*). Founded by James Larkin in 1909. Under his leadership it was a small, militant force, the focus of syndicalism in Dublin. After 1916 his more cautious successors developed it into the country's biggest and most powerful union. Its tone remained intensely national, and in Northern Ireland its membership has been almost entirely Catholic. In 1944–5 its 'national' standpoint brought about major splits in both the Irish Labour party and the Irish Trades Union Congress. It is still Ireland's largest union.

IRISH UNIONIST ALLIANCE. Formed originally as the Irish Loyal and Patriotic Union, in Dublin in 1885, it adopted the shorter title in 1891. Its purpose was to produce propaganda against home rule, and organize support for Unionist parliamentary candidates. Unionists in Ulster increasingly went their own way, however, and in 1905 formed their own Ulster Unionist Council. The IUA therefore became more and more a southern Unionist movement, and as such its social base was far too narrow for it to be able to move effectively from the field of propaganda into electoral politics. Its membership in 1913 was a mere 683. It split in 1917–18 over whether to accept the inevitable and work for a compromise home rule settlement, or fight on to the end. In 1922 it converted itself from a political movement into a relief organization.

IRISH VOLUNTEERS. Founded in November 1913 in Dublin by a group of nationalists of various shades of opinion, in response to the formation of the UVF in the north. It was regarded as an embarrassment by the Irish parliamentary party, but many party supporters joined the ranks, and in the spring of 1914 John Redmond made a successful take-over bid for the leadership of the movement, which at that stage numbered close on 200,000 men (although it did not compare with the UVF in its standard of training and equipment). When, at the outbreak of the war, he began to urge volunteers to enlist in the British army, the movement split. The great majority of the rank-and-file became the Redmondite National Volunteers, with no very obvious purpose, while the majority of the activists continued as the Irish Volunteers, some 10,000 strong. From the beginning the IRB was a discreet, but dominant, force in the leadership of the latter. The Dublin contingents of the Irish Volunteers carried out the 1916 Rising, and the Volunteer structure remained the basis for subsequent guerrilla operations from 1918 onwards. Gradually the Volunteers came to be known as the IRA, although the Irish name, *Oglaigh na hEireann*, continued unchanged. The National Volunteers, a force unwanted by its leaders, ceased to exist during 1917.

LAND LEAGUE. Founded in 1879, amidst acute agricultural depression, to lead Irish tenant farmers in a fight for rent reductions and improved conditions. For two years it occupied the centre of the stage during the series of disturbances known as the land war, but it was suppressed by the government late in 1881. It was replaced for a while by the Ladies' Land League, but after 1882 the leaders of the Irish national movement preferred to rely for grass-roots organization on more manageable constituency associations.

LEAGUE OF YOUTH. *See* Blueshirts.

LOYALIST ASSOCIATION OF WORKERS (*LAW*). A reaction against the conciliatory approach of the official trade union movement in Northern Ireland to the Northern Ireland disturbances. Formed early in 1972 to organize industrial action in defence of what it considered to be Protestant interests, it demonstrated its ability to call short general strikes at will. Centred on the Harland and Wolff shipyard, it appeared to be influential in most of the larger industrial concerns in the Belfast area. It was closely associated with the UDA and the VUPP. By 1974 it had merged into a somewhat more broadly based Ulster Workers' Council.

NATIONAL CENTRE PARTY. An attempt to re-establish the Farmers' party in Free State politics, on a broader political platform. Founded in 1932, it won eleven Dáil seats in the election of the following year. In the Dáil it sought to establish a middle ground between the two major parties, but rapidly found itself forced by its opposition to the main policies of Fianna Fáil into alliance with Cumann na nGaedheal. The two parties, along with the leaders of the Blueshirt movement, formed themselves into a new party, Fine Gael, within less than a year of the Centre party's foundation.

NATIONAL GUARD. *See* Blueshirts.

NATIONAL LABOUR. A small group of Labour party TDs who broke away from the Irish Labour party in 1944, alleging that it was Communist dominated. In fact the split was closely linked to the dispute within the trade union movement. All the dissidents were TDs sponsored by the ITGWU. The party was reunited in 1950.

NATIONAL LEAGUE. A moderate constitutional party, founded in 1926 to compete in southern politics. Led by William Redmond, son of the old Irish Parliamentary party leader, its backing came from supporters of the old party, from men who had served in the British forces during the First World War, and from the licensed trade. It won eight Dáil seats in 1927, but shortly afterwards attempted unsuccessfully to form a blatantly opportunist coalition with Labour and Fianna Fail and lost much of its credibility. It was dissolved in 1931, when Redmond and many of its followers joined Cumann na nGaedheal. Its links with the old Parliamentary party enabled it to form a more convincing alliance with the constitutional nationalists in the north, led by Redmond's former colleague Joseph Devlin. The National League of the North was founded, accordingly, in 1928. But in circumstances where Nationalists could win all the Catholic seats in the north without a constituency organization it proved superfluous, and quickly faded from the scene.

NATIONAL LEAGUE OF THE NORTH. *See* National League.

NATIONAL VOLUNTEERS. *See* Irish Volunteers.

NATIONALIST PARTY. The main voice of Catholics in Northern Ireland politics from 1921 until its demise at the general election of 1969. It was a political party only in the very limited sense that a group of MPs at Stormont recognized one of their number as leader. There was little party discipline, and on vital matters such as parliamentary attendance or abstention, decisions were taken not at the top but at constituency level. There was no regular party organization in the constituencies, decisions being taken by a group of notables or a 'representative' convention nominated by various bodies. Detailed electoral work, if done at all, was carried out by registration committees. The party was beginning to reorganize itself during the 1960s when it was overtaken by the pace of events in which it had played little part.

NORTHERN IRELAND CIVIL RIGHTS ASSOCIATION (*NICRA*). Formed in Belfast early in 1967. Its object was to agitate for the improvement of the position of Catholics in Northern Ireland, especially in respect of housing and employment, using techniques of non-violent protest along the lines exploited successfully by Martin Luther King in America. Between 1967 and 1969 the small IRA element within the movement was present to monitor its activities rather than to direct them. Since 1970, however, the leadership of the movement appears to have fallen increasingly under IRA influence.

NORTHERN IRELAND LABOUR PARTY (*NILP*). Formed in Belfast, in 1923, from the loose association of branches which had originally been established under the aegis of the old British Independent Labour party. Until the emergence of the SDLP, whose socialist credentials it has called into question, the NILP was unquestionably the leading labour party in the province, despite having never won more than four parliamentary seats. It took a neutral, some would say evasive, line on partition until 1949, when it carried a resolution in favour of maintenance of the union with Britain. Since then it has inevitably been challenged by anti-partitionist labour elements, notably the Irish Labour party during the 1950s, but it maintained its non-sectarian position, and did not enter into any visible decline until the reappearance of serious inter-communal tension in the 1960s.

ORANGE ORDER. A fraternal association, founded in the north of Ireland in 1795. Its purpose was to maintain the position of Protestants in Ulster society. In style and organization it closely resembled the Masonic lodges. For half a century after the formal dissolution of the Grand Lodge in 1836, it was widely regarded as disorderly and plebeian. After 1886, however, when the threat of home rule appeared, the gentry and business and professional classes in the province came to appreciate its usefulness as a political force: it was vigorously in favour of the union with Britain and it cut across class barriers. The links between the Order and the Unionist party, forged at that time, have never been broken. The Order nominates about one-eighth of the delegates to the Ulster Unionist Council. This is not the full measure of its influence, however, for almost all Unionist MPs since 1921 (and earlier) have been members. The apparently serious split in Protestant politics between Unionists and Loyalists in 1973 posed a new problem for the Order, in that its leaders supported Unionist politicians, but inclined more to Loyalist policies. The formation of the United Ulster Unionist Council in 1974 thus eased the Order's position. The Order has some strength outside Ulster, most notably in Glasgow, Liverpool, and Toronto.

PEOPLE'S DEMOCRACY. A radical socialist group, founded by students at Queen's University, Belfast, late in 1968, in the hope of giving a socialist slant to the civil rights campaign in Northern Ireland. Though not a political party, it contested the Stormont election of 1969, but without success. In the polarization of the two communities which followed, it was dismissed by most Protestants as a Catholic organization. It disappeared from the headlines as quickly as it had captured them, and after 1970 had little more than a nominal existence.

PRO-TREATY PARTY. *See* Cumann na nGaedheal.

PROVISIONAL IRA. *See* Irish Republican Army.

REPUBLICAN CLUBS. Formed in a number of towns in Northern Ireland during the late 1960s, the Clubs sympathized with the views, and to an extent duplicated the membership, of Sinn Féin and the IRA north of the border. The movement took the 'Official' side in the IRA split, and subsequently became the equivalent of Official Sinn Féin on the northern side of the border. In the elections it opposed the SDLP in a number of predominantly Catholic areas on a 'non-sectarian' platform of socialist republicanism, but without success.

REPUBLICAN CONGRESS. One of a series of attempts during the 1930s by a group of left-wingers in the IRA to establish a revolutionary political front which might bring about a radical restructuring of society in the south as well as the north of Ireland. Founded in 1934, it petered out within a year or so. (*See also* Saor Eire.)

REPUBLICAN LABOUR PARTY. Formed by Gerry Fitt, following his election to Stormont in 1962. It brought together some independent Catholic Labour politicians in Belfast with former members of the Dublin-based Irish Labour party who were anxious to have a locally controlled movement. It held seats at Stormont and on the city council for a number of years, but was reduced to a rump in 1970 when Mr Fitt and others joined in the formation of the more broadly based SDLP. It ran some candidates in the Belfast district and Assembly elections in 1973, but none were successful.

REPUBLICANS. *See* Sinn Féin and IRA.

SAOR EIRE (*Free Ireland*). A left-wing splinter group of the IRA, formed in 1931 in order to concentrate on political rather than military action. It was suppressed by the government within a few months, though many of the same leaders reappeared in the Republican Congress movement a few years later. At the end of the 1960s the name was revived by a small, anonymous revolutionary group based in Dublin, which claimed responsibility for a series of bank robberies in the republic.

SINN FEIN (*Ourselves Alone*). A party label so closely linked with the struggle for independence that the proprietorship of it has been, on occasion, much sought after. Historians now distinguish four main phases of its existence: (i) 1905–17. A party founded by Arthur Griffith to achieve full *de facto* independence for Ireland, not necessarily a republic, by means of passive resistence and general abstention and withdrawal from British institutions, including parliament. It contested one by-election, without success, and was not formally involved in the 1916 rising. The press and the police none the less seized on the party's exotic name to describe militant nationalists and rebels in general, and so its future was assured. (ii) 1917–22. A fusion of all the militant groups which emerged in the aftermath of the rising, the original Sinn Féiners being an influential, but far from dominant, element. It won almost all the seats in southern Ireland in the 1918 general election, and its elected representatives made up Dáil Eireann, 1919–22. (iii) 1923–6. After the treaty split, the anti-treaty republicans regrouped under the old label which, surprisingly, had not been taken up by their Free State opponents. This third phase came to an end in 1926 when de Valera narrowly failed to persuade the party to abandon the principle of abstentionism, and left with his supporters to form Fianna Fáil. (iv) After 1927 the party's existence was almost nominal for many years. Since the 1950s it has co-operated closely with the IRA, becoming in effect the political front of the latter organization, with much duplication of membership. When the IRA split at the end of 1969, Sinn Féin followed suit, and now has two wings, both with headquarters in Dublin: 'Official Sinn Féin' (Gardiner Place), and 'Provisional Sinn Féin' (Kevin Street). Amidst this confusion runs one thread of consistency: no Sinn Féin candidate has ever sought election to Westminster, Stormont, or the Dáil on any platform other than that of abstentionism.

SOCIAL DEMOCRATIC AND LABOUR PARTY (*SDLP*). Founded in Belfast in 1970, on a non-sectarian, left-of-centre platform, it rapidly became the leading voice of Ulster Catholics, in Stormont and elsewhere. Its main components were a number of active civil rights campaigners who had been returned to Stormont as Independents, and the bulk of the small Republican Labour party, supplemented by breakaway elements from the Nationalists and the NILP and some smaller groups without political representation. The violent developments of 1971–2 caused the party to adopt a more nationalistic tone. Perhaps partly for this reason, it was able to trounce its rivals for the Catholic vote in the 1973 and 1975 elections, though at the same time it seems to have retained the discreet backing of the British Labour party.

SOCIALIST REPUBLICANS. A small group of slightly left-of-centre Catholic politicians, active in Northern parliamentary and Belfast city politics in the late 1940s and 1950s. Some members later joined the Republican Labour party.

SOUTHERN UNIONISTS. Those supporters of the union with Britain who lived outside the six north-eastern counties. Formerly a part of the Irish Unionist party, they emerged as a distinct group, opposed to partition, during the Irish Convention of 1917–18. Since 1921 they have ceased to exist as a political body in the south, although the 'Protestant vote' has remained an important consideration in some constituencies along the border.

ULSTER DEFENCE ASSOCIATION (*UDA*). A street army which appeared in very large numbers in the Protestant working-class districts of Belfast and other Ulster towns following the suspension of Stormont in 1972. Its membership was said to duplicate very closely that of the LAW, while politically it is associated with Vanguard. It should not be confused with the Ulster Defence Regiment, a part-time force within the British Army, although there have been allegations of widespread double-membership.

ULSTER UNIONIST LABOUR ASSOCIATION. Founded in 1917–18, on the suggestion of the Unionist party leader, Sir Edward Carson, in order to retain the votes of Protestant workers in the north of Ireland in face of the vigorous challenge from socialism and republicanism which was expected at the end of the First World War. A small number of trade unionists were returned to Westminster as Unionists in 1918, and to the Northern Ireland parliament in 1921, but they were no more than a token. The association continues to exist, but has never played an important role in Unionist politics.

ULSTER UNIONIST PARTY. Stimulated by the activities of the Irish Unionist Alliance, Irish Conservative MPs, and those Liberals who opposed home rule came together at Westminster in a common Unionist front within the Conservative party in the years after 1886. The elected representatives were in practice almost all from Ulster constituencies, where there existed a far broader base of public support than was available in the south. In 1905 this distinction was formally recognized by the establishment in the north of a central organization of grass-roots bodies, the Ulster Unionist Council—which in effect functioned like the annual conference of a British party. After 1921 the Ulster Unionist MPs at Westminster have continued as a group within the Conservative party, while the party at home, known simply as the Unionist party, has been the dominant force in Stormont politics. Apart from a general readiness to accept progressive social legislation financed by United Kingdom taxation, the party's complexion, excepting a few individual figures, has been somewhat right-wing Conservative. None the less it was not effectively challenged for the support of the Protestant community until the emergence of the DUP/VUPP Loyalist Coalition in the elections of 1973. Early in 1974 the party threw off the new 'power sharing' politics of its leadership, and entered into an electoral coalition with the DUP and VUPP, known as the United Ulster Unionist Council. The representatives of this group at Westminster have not taken the Conservative whip.

ULSTER VOLUNTEER FORCE (*UVF*). A very large private army, founded in 1912 on full military lines, officered by the social élite of the province, to resist the imposition of home rule. Highly disciplined throughout its existence, it was responsive to the dictates of the Unionist leadership both in the crisis of 1912–14 and later, when it was converted *en masse* into a division of the British Army. The force was virtually destroyed at the battle of the Somme in 1916. The name was revived in 1966 by a small group of Protestant extremists in Belfast. For some time its name appeared only spasmodically, in connection with individual acts of violence, but during 1973–4 it began to seek political limelight and a volunteer political party was formed, though with no initial success. In some respects, a left-wing rival to the UDA.

ULSTER WORKERS COUNCIL (*UWC*). A body of loyalist trade unionists, based particularly on the shipyards and power stations, but with apparently widespread influence throughout the working-class Protestant districts of Belfast and elsewhere. It first appeared in May 1974, when it directed the general strike which brought down the power-sharing executive.

UNIONIST PARTY OF NORTHERN IRELAND (*UPNI*). A new party formed by Brian Faulkner and his associates in 1974 after they lost control of the Ulster Unionist party. Its policies appear to differ little from those of the Alliance party.

UNIONIST PARTY. *See* Ulster Unionist Party.

UNITED IRISH LEAGUE. An agrarian organization, formed in 1898 to better the conditions of tenant farmers, and especially to press for compulsory redistribution of the western grasslands to small tenant-purchasers. As the edge was gradually taken off agrarian discontent after the 1903 Land Act, the UIL became simply a constituency association for the Irish Parliamentary party in most districts. It withered away following the collapse of that party at the polls in 1918.

UNITED ULSTER UNIONIST COUNCIL (*UUUC*). An electoral agreement which served to prevent competition between members of the DUP, VUPP, and the Unionist party in the Westminster elections of 1974, and the 1975 Convention election. Subsequently the umbrella for a regular coalition between these parties.

VANGUARD UNIONIST PROGRESSIVE PARTY (*VUPP*). The Vanguard movement was formed in Northern Ireland in 1972 by a group of right-wingers and out-of-office dissidents to act as a ginger-group within the Unionist party. The force of the movement, however, came from those working-class and small-farm Protestant districts which were at the same time spawning the UDA and LAW. These elements had turned away from the manoeuvrings of the DUP following the internment crisis of autumn 1971, and now put increasing pressure on the Vanguard leadership to form a new party. This was done, apparently not without some reluctance, in time for the 1973 Assembly election. Ironically, the election was ultimately fought on a Loyalist Coalition platform alongside a DUP which had meanwhile returned to the fold. In the autumn of 1975, the movement split over the issue of admitting the SDLP into an emergency coalition to restore devolved government to Ulster. Vanguard, though not the majority of its Convention members, withdrew from the UUUC to work for its new policy.

WORKERS' UNION OF IRELAND. When James Larkin returned to Ireland in 1923 after eight years in America, he attempted to regain control of his creation, the ITGWU. His successors had no time for what they regarded as his destructive flamboyance, and he was effectively excluded. The following year, along with his brother Peter, he formed the WUI as a breakaway union of general workers. It won over a fair proportion of former ITGWU members in Larkin's old citadel of Dublin, and although it had little impact elsewhere, it became one of the country's larger unions. It was refused affiliation by the ITUC, until the withdrawal of its old rival from that body in 1945.

Election results since 1921

DAIL EIREANN GENERAL ELECTIONS 1922–73

Election	Anti-treaty	Pro-treaty	Labour	Farmers	Independents	Others	Number of seats
1922	35	58 Cumann na nGaedheal	17	7	11	—	128
1923	44 Fianna Fáil	63	14	15	17	—	153
1927 (June)	44	47	22	11	14	15[1]	153
1927 (Sept.)	57	62	13	6	12	3[2]	153
1932	72	57	7	4	11	2[3]	153
1933	77	48 Fine Gael	8	—	8	12[4]	153
1937	69	48	13	—	8	—	138
1938	77	45	9	— Clann na Talmhan	7	—	138
1943	67	32	17	14	8	—	138
1944	76	30	8	11	9	4[5]	138
1948	68	31	19	7	12	10[6]	147
1951	69	40	16	6	14	2[7]	147
1954	65	50	19	5	5	3[8]	147
1957	78	40	13	3	8	5[9]	147
1961	70	47	16	2	6	3[10]	144
1965	72	47	22	—	2	1[11]	144
1969	75	50	18	—	1	—	144
1973	69	54	19	—	2	—	144

Source: Meenan, *Irish Economy since 1922*, p. 407, updated.

1. 8 National League, 5 Sinn Fein, 2 Independent Republicans.
2. 2 National League, 1 Independent Labour.   3. 2 Independent Labour.
4. 11 National Centre Party, 1 Independent Labour.   5. 4 National Labour.
6. 10 Clann na Poblachta.   7. 2 Clann na Poblachta.
8. 3 Clann na Poblachta.   9. 4 Sinn Féin, 1 Clann na Poblachta.
10. 2 National Progressive Democrats, 1 Clann na Poblachta.
11. 1 Clann na Poblachta.

NORTHERN IRELAND GENERAL ELECTIONS:
HOUSE OF COMMONS, 1921–69
ASSEMBLY, 1973, CONVENTION, 1975

Election	Unionist	Unof U[1]	NILP	Ind. Lab.[2]	Nat.	Rep.[3]	Lib.	Others	Number of seats
1921	40	0	0	0	6	6	0	0	52
1925	32	4	3	0	10	2	0	1	52
1929	37	3	1	0	11		0	0	52
1933	36	3	2	0	9	2	0	0	52
1938	39	3	1	1	8	0	0	0	52
1945	33	2	2	3	10	0	0	2	52
1949	37	2	0	2	9	0	0	2	52
1953	38	1	0	3	7	2	0	1	52
1958	37	0	4	2	8	0	0	1	52
1962	34	0	4	3	9	0	1	1	52
1965	36	0	2	2	9	0	1	3	52
1969	36[4]	3	2	2	6	0	0	3	52
		Loyalists		SDLP			Alliance		
1973	33[5]	17[6]	1	19	0	0	8	0	78
	UUUC	UPNI							
1975	46[7]	5	1	17	0	0	8	1[8]	78

Source: Elliott, *Northern Ireland Parliamentary Election Results, 1921–72*, p. 96, updated.

1. Including Independent Unionists, Progressive Unionists, Protestant Unionists and Independent O'Neill Unionists.

2. Including Independent Labour, Commonwealth Labour, Federation of Labour, Irish Labour, Republican Labour and Socialist Republican.

3. Including Republicans, Sinn Féin, Fianna Fál, Anti-Partitionists, and Republican Clubs.

4. 24 pro-O'Neill and 12 anti-O'Neill.

5. 22 pro-White Paper, 10 anti-White Paper, and one independent pro-White Paper.

6. 8 DUP, 7 VUPP, and 2 independent loyalists.

7. 19 Unionists, 14 VUPP, 12 DUP, one independent.

8. Independent loyalist.

Bibliography

GENERAL WORKS

BELL, J. B. *The Secret Army: A History of the IRA, 1916–70* (London, 1970).

CHUBB, F. B. *The Government and Politics of Ireland* (Stanford and London, 1970).

COOGAN, T. P. *Ireland since the Rising* (London, 1966).

—— *The IRA* (London, 1970).

FARRELL, B. *Chairman or Chief? The Role of the Taoiseach in Irish Government* (Dublin, 1971).

FREEMAN, T. W. *Ireland: A General and Regional Geography* (London, 1950, 4th edn, 1969).

HOGAN, J. *Election and Representation* (Cork, 1945).

LONGFORD, EARL OF, and O'NEILL, T. P. *Eamon de Valera* (London, 1970).

LYONS, F. S. L. *Ireland since the Famine* (London, 1971, 2nd edn, 1973).

LYSAGHT, D. R. O'C. *The Republic of Ireland* (Cork, 1970).

McCRACKEN, J. L. *Representative Government in Ireland: a Study of Dáil Eireann, 1919–48* (London, 1958).

MACDONAGH, O. *Ireland* (Englewood Cliffs, New Jersey, 1968).

MANNING, M. *Irish Political Parties* (Dublin, 1972).

MEENAN, J. *The Irish Economy since 1922* (Liverpool, 1970).

MITCHELL, A. *Labour and Politics in Ireland, 1890–1930* (Shannon, 1973).

O'LEARY, C. *The Irish Republic and its Experiment with Proportional Representation* (Notre Dame, Indiana, 1961).

ROSS, J. F. S. *The Irish Electoral System* (London, 1959).

WHYTE, J. H. *Church and State in Modern Ireland, 1923–70* (Dublin, 1971).

OFFICIAL PUBLICATIONS
United Kingdom

Agrarian Outrages, Ireland, 1919–21. [Cmd. 709, 859, 1025, 1165] (London, 1919–21).

Agricultural Statistics of Ireland, 1889–90. HC (1890), lxxix. 371.

Articles of Agreement for a Treaty between Great Britain and Ireland, 1921 [Cmd. 1560] (London, 1921) ('The Treaty').

Board of Trade. Statistical Abstracts for the Commonwealth, lxxi, 1947–50 (London, 1951).

Census of Population (Ireland), 1911 [Cd. 5691, 6 049–52].

Congested Districts Board for Ireland. Annual Reports, 1893–1923.

Future of Northern Ireland, The: A Paper for Discussion (London, 1972) ('The Green Paper').

Government of Ireland Act, 1920 [10 & 11 Geo. 5. Ch. 67].

Irish Land Commission. Annual Reports, 1882–1922.

Northern Ireland Constitution Act, 1973 (1973 c. 36).

Northern Ireland Constitutional Proposals, 1973 [Cmnd. 5259] (London 1973) ('The White Paper').

Royal Commission on the Rebellion in Ireland, 1916. Report and Minutes of Evidence [Cd. 8279, 8311] (London, 1916) ('The Hardinge Commission').

Irish Free State and Republic

Bureau of Military History, 'Chronology, 1913–21' (Dublin, 1947–51, unpublished).

Census of Population, 1926, 1936, 1946, 1951, 1956, 1961, 1966.

Dáil Eireann. Minutes of Proceedings of the First Parliament of the Republic of Ireland, 1919–21: Official Record (Dublin, 1921).

Dáil Eireann. Official Report: Debate on the Treaty between Great Britain and Ireland, Signed in London on 6 December 1921 (Dublin, 1922).

Dáil Eireann. Official Report for the Periods 16–26 August 1921 and 28 February to 8 June 1922 (Dublin, 1922).

Dáil Eireann. Parliamentary Debates: Official Reports (Dublin, 1922).

Dáil Eireann. The Constructive Work of Dáil Eireann: The National Police and Courts of Justice (Dublin, 1921).

Dáil Eireann: General Election Results with Detailed Accounts of the Transfer of Votes (Dublin, 1944, 1948, 1951, 1954, 1957, 1961, 1965, 1969, 1973).

Department of Industry and Commerce. Statistical Abstracts, 1931–   .

Department of Social Welfare. Reports, 1947–   .

Irish Land Commission. Annual Reports, 1923–   .

Report of the Commission of Inquiry into Banking Currency and Credit [P. No. 2628] (Dublin, 1938).

Reports of the Commission on Emigration and other Population Problems 1948–54, [Pr. 2541] (Dublin, 1956).

Reports of the Tariff Commission, 1926–39 (Dublin, Stationery Office).

Report of the Commission on Vocational Organisation (Dublin, 1926).

Saorstat Eireann: Official Handbook (Dublin, 1932).

Second Programme for Economic Expansion [Pr. 7239, 7670, 8244, 8703, 9949] (Dublin, 1964–7).

Northern Ireland

Census of Population, 1926, 1937, 1951, 1961, 1966.

House of Commons Debates, 1921–72.

ALCOCK, A. E. *N.I. Constitutional Convention,* Protection of Minorities (1975).

OTHER REPORTS AND INQUIRIES

Congress of Irish Unions. Annual Reports, 1946–59.

Fianna Fáil, 1926–51: The Story of Twenty-five Years of National Endeavour and Historic Achievement (Dublin, 1951).

Fine Gael, *Fine Gael and Labour: A Plan to Benefit all Sections of the Community* (Dublin, 1934).

Governmental Policy and Constitution of Oglaigh na hEireann (IRA) Adopted by the General Army Convention, 1933.

IBEC Technical Services Corporation, *The Industrial Potentials of Ireland: An Appraisal* (Report written by Stacy May) New York, 1952.

Industries of Ireland, The, Thirty Years of Progress (Dublin, 1957).

IRISH CONGRESS OF TRADE UNIONS. *Annual Reports,* 1960– .

IRISH LABOUR PARTY. *Annual Reports,* 1931– .

—— *Report of a Special Congress,* 1930.

IRISH LABOUR PARTY AND TUC. *Annual Reports,* 1914–30.

IRISH TRADES UNION CONGRESS. *Annual Reports,* 1896–1913, 1931–59.

—— *Official Statement Relating to the Disaffiliation of the ITGWU, 1944.*

NATIONAL COUNCIL FOR CIVIL LIBERTIES. *Report on the Operation of the Northern Ireland Special Powers Act* (London, 1936).

WORKS OF REFERENCE

Dod's Parliamentary Companion (London, 1832–   ).

ELLIOTT, S. *Northern Ireland Parliamentary Election Results, 1921–72* (Chichester, 1973).

FLYNN, W. J. (ed.). *The Irish Parliamentary Handbook* (Dublin, 1932–   ).

The Irish Who's Who (Dublin, 1923).

McCABE, A. (ed.). *The Irish Year Book* (Dublin, 1921).

STAMP, L. DUDLEY. *An Agricultural Atlas of Ireland* (London, 1931).

THOM's *Irish Almanac and Official Directory* (Dublin, 1844–   .)

NEWSPAPERS AND PERIODICALS

Unless otherwise stated the place of publication in each instance is Dublin.

For a more detailed list of republican journals see J. B. Bell, *The Secret Army* (London, 1970), pp. 454–7.

Belfast Telegraph.

Cork Examiner.

Fortnight (Belfast), 1970– .

Hibernia, 1882– .

Irish Bulletin, 1919–21.

Irish Communist, 1934– .

Irish Freedom, 1910–14.

Irish Independent.

Irish News (Belfast).

Irish Press, 1931– .

Irish Times.
Manchester Guardian, Commercial supplement, 15 March, 10 May 1923
  (Manchester).
The Newsletter (Belfast).
Northern Whig (Belfast), (to 1963).
An t'Oglach, 1918–22.
An Phoblacht, 1925–36.
The Republican Congress, 1934–6.
The Republic of Ireland, 1922.
The Round Table (Ottawa), 1911– .
Sinn Féin, 1905–14, 1923–5.
United Irishman, 1948– .
Voice of Labour, 1921–7.
The Workers' Republic, 1915–16.

THE HISTORICAL BACKGROUND

ARENSBERG, C. M. *The Irish Countryman* (London, 1937).
—— AND KIMBALL, S. T. *Family and Community in Ireland* (Cambridge, Mass.,
  1940, 1968).
BAUMGARTEN, P. M. 'Die politischen und nationalen Ziele Irlands', *Irische
  Blätter,* vols 1–2 (1917–18).
BECKETT, J. C. *The Making of Modern Ireland, 1603–1923* (London, 1966).
BLACK, R. D. C. *Economic Thought and the Irish Question, 1817–70* (Cambridge,
  1960).
BLUNT, W. S. *The Land War in Ireland* (London, 1912).
BONN, M. J. *Modern Ireland and her Agricultural Problems* (Dublin, 1906).
—— *Irland und die irische Frage* (Munich and Leipzig, 1918).
BOYCE, D. G. *Englishmen and Irish Troubles: British Public Opinion and the
  Making of Irish Policy, 1918–22* (London, 1972).
BOYLE, J. W. (ed.). *Leaders and Workers* (Cork, 1966).
BRINGMANN, R. *Geschichte Irlands: Schicksalsweg eines Volkes* (Bonn, 1953).
BROWN, T. N. *Irish-American Nationalism, 1870–90* (New York, 1966).
BURKE, J. F. *Outlines of the Industrial History of Ireland* (Dublin, 1940).
BUCKLAND, P. J. *The Anglo-Irish and the New Ireland 1885–1922* (Dublin, 1972).
—— *Irish Unionism, 1885–1923: A Documentary History* (Belfast, 1973).
CARTY, J. (ed.). *Ireland: A Documentary Record, from the Great Famine to the
  Treaty, 1851–1921* (Dublin, 1951).
CHART, D. A. *An Economic History of Ireland* (Dublin, 1924).
CLARKSON, J. D. *Labour and Nationalism in Ireland* (New York, 1925).
CONNELL, K. H. *Irish Peasant Society* (Oxford, 1968).
CONNOLLY, J. *Labour in Irish History* (Dublin, 1910).
—— *A Socialist at War, 1914–16* (London, 1941).
—— *Labour and Easter Week,* ed. D. Ryan (Dublin, 1950).
—— *Socialism and Nationalism,* ed. D. Ryan (Dublin, 1948).
CONNOLLY, M. 'James Connolly, socialist and patriot', *Studies,* xli (1952),
  293–308.

CULLEN, L. M. *An Economic History of Ireland since 1660* (London, 1972).
—— *Six Generations: Life and Work in Ireland from 1790* (Cork, 1970).
—— (ed.) *The Formation of the Irish Economy* (Cork, 1969).
CURTIS, E. *A History of Ireland* (London, 1936).
—— AND McDOWELL, R. B. (eds). *Irish Historical Documents, 1172–1922* (London, 1943).
CURTIS, L. P. *Coercion and Conciliation in Ireland, 1880–92: A Study in Conservative Unionism* (Princeton, 1963).
—— *Anglo-Saxons and Celts: A Study of Anti-Irish Prejudice in Victorian England* (Bridgeport, Conn., 1968).
DAVITT, M. *The Fall of Feudalism in Ireland* (London, 1904).
EDWARDS, R. DUDLEY, and WILLIAMS, T. D. (eds). *The Great Famine* (Dublin, 1956).
ENGELS, F. *The Condition of the Working Class in England in 1844* (London, 1892).
FARRELL, B. *The Founding of Dáil Eireann: Parliament and Nation-Building* (Dublin, 1971).
—— 'Labour and the Irish political party system: a suggested approach to analysis', *Economic and Social Review*, i (1970), 477–502.
FIGGIS, D. *Recollections of the Irish War* (London, 1927).
FOX, R. M. *James Connolly: The Forerunner* (Tralee, 1946).
—— *Green Banners: The Story of the Irish Struggle* (London, 1938).
—— *The History of the Irish Citizen Army* (Dublin, 1942).
FROMME, F. *Irlands Kampf um die Freiheit: Darstellung und Beispiel einer völkischen Bewegung bis in die neueste Zeit* (Berlin, 1933).
GOOD, J. W. *Irish Unionism* (Dublin, 1930).
GREAVES, C. D. *The Life and Times of James Connolly* (London, 1916).
GREEN, E. R. R. *The Lagan Valley, 1800–50* (London, 1949).
GRIFFITH, A. *The Resurrection of Hungary: A Parallel for Ireland* (Dublin, 1904).
GWYNN, D. R. *The Life of John Redmond* (London, 1932).
—— *The History of Partition, 1912–25* (Dublin, 1950).
GWYNN, S. L. *The History of Ireland* (London, 1924).
HAMMOND, J. L. *Gladstone and the Irish Nation* (London, 1938, 1964).
HENRY, R. M. *The Evolution of Sinn Féin* (Dublin, 1920).
HEPBURN, A. C. 'The Ancient Order of Hibernians in Irish Politics, 1905–14', *Cithara*, x (1971), 5–18.
HETZEL, F. 'Die irischen Agrarfragen' (Heidelberg University doctoral dissertation, 1929).
HOCTOR, D. *The Department's Story: A History of the Department of Agriculture* (Dublin, 1971).
HOGAN, D. *Four Glorious Years* (Dublin, 1953).
HOLT, E. *Protest in Arms: The Irish Troubles, 1916–23* (London, 1960).
HOOKER, E. R. *Readjustments of Agricultural Tenure in Ireland* (Chapel Hill, North Carolina, 1938).
JASPERT, W. *Irland* (Berlin, 1938).
JONES, T. *Whitehall Diary, Vol. III: Ireland, 1918–25*, ed. K. Middlemas (London, 1971).
JOYCE, P. W. *A Social History of Ancient Ireland* (London, 1903).

Kee, R. *The Green Flag: A History of Irish Nationalism* (London, 1972).

Kelly, R. J. 'The agricultural labourers of Ireland', *New Ireland Review*, xx (1905), 297–305.

Larkin, E. *James Larkin: Irish Labour Leader, 1876–1947* (London, 1965).

—— 'The Roman Catholic hierarchy and the fall of Parnell', *Victorian Studies*, iv (1961), 315–36.

—— 'Mounting the counter-attack: the Roman Catholic hierarchy and the destruction of Parnellism', *Review of Politics*, xxv (1963), 157–82.

—— 'Socialism and Catholicism in Ireland', *Church History*, xxxiii (1964), 462–83.

Lecky, W. E. H. *A History of Ireland in the Eighteenth Century* (London, 1902).

Lenin, N. 'The Easter 1916 Rising in Ireland', *Labour Monthly* (April 1929).

Locker-Lampson, G. *A Consideration of the State of Ireland in the Nineteenth Century* (London, 1907).

Longford, Earl of (Frank Pakenham). *Peace by Ordeal* (London, 1935, 2nd edn, 1972).

Lyons, F. S. L. *The Irish Parliamentary Party, 1890–1910* (London, 1951).

—— *The Fall of Parnell* (London, 1960).

—— *John Dillon: a Biography* (London, 1968).

Macardle, D. *The Irish Republic* (Dublin, 1937).

MacBride, M. G. *A Servant of the Queen: Reminiscences* (London, 1938).

McCaffrey, L. J. *The Irish Question, 1801–1922* (Lexington, Kentucky, 1968).

MacDonagh, M. *The Home Rule Movement* (Dublin, 1920).

McDowell, R. B. *The Irish Convention, 1917–18* (London, 1970).

Mac Giolla Choille, B. (ed.). *Intelligence Notes, 1913–16* (Dublin, 1966).

Mansergh, P. N. S. *The Irish Question, 1840–1921* (London, 1940, 1965).

Martin, F. X. (ed.). *The Irish Volunteers, 1913–15* (Dublin, 1963).

—— (ed.) *Leaders and Men of the 1916 Rising* (London, 1967).

—— and Byrne, F. J. (eds). *The Scholar Revolutionary: Eoin MacNeill, 1867–1945, and the Making of the New Ireland* (Dublin, 1973).

Micks, W. L. *The History of the Congested Districts Board* (Dublin, 1925).

Miller, D. W. *Church, State, and Nation in Ireland, 1898–1921* (Dublin, 1973).

Moody, T. W. (ed.). *The Fenian Movement* (Cork, 1968).

—— and Beckett, J. C. (eds). *Ulster since 1800: A Political and Economic Survey* (London, 1955).

—— —— (eds). *Ulster since 1800: A Social Survey* (London, 1957).

Morris, W. O'C. *Ireland, 1798–1898* (London, 1898).

Müller-Ross, F. 'Die irische Grenzfrage, Ulster, Irland und Grossbritannien' (Berlin University doctoral dissertation, 1930).

—— *Irland: Die andere Insel* (Leipzig, 1939).

Norman, E. R. *The Catholic Church and Ireland in the Age of Rebellion, 1859–73* (London, 1965).

Nowlan, K. B. (ed). *The Making of 1916: Studies in the History of the Rising* (Dublin, 1969).

O'Brien, C. C. *Parnell and his Party* (Oxford, 1957).

—— (ed.). *The Shaping of Modern Ireland, 1891–1916* (London, 1960).

O'Brien, G. *The Economic History of Ireland from the Union to the Famine* (London, 1921).

O'Brien, W. *Forth the Banners Go: Reminiscences*, ed. E. MacLysaght (Dublin, 1969).

—— and Ryan, D. (eds). *Devoy's Postbag, 1871–1928* (Dublin, 1948, 1952).

OBroin, L. *Dublin Castle and the 1916 Rising* (Dublin, 1966).

O'Connor, Sir J. *A History of Ireland, 1798–1924* (London, 1925).

O Cuiv, B. *Irish Dialects and Irish-speaking Districts* (Dublin, 1951).

O Faolain, S. *Constance Markievicz, or the Average Revolutionary* (London, 1934).

—— *The Irish* (London, 1947).

O'Hegarty, P. S. *A History of Ireland under the Union* (London, 1952).

Paul-Dubois, L. *Contemporary Ireland* (Dublin, 1908).

Phillips, W. A. *The Revolution in Ireland, 1906–23* (London, 1923).

Pomfret, J. E. *The Struggle for Land in Ireland, 1800–1923* (Princeton, 1930).

Prokorny, J. *Irland* (Perthes *Kleine Völker-und Länderkunde*) (Gotha, 1916).

Regan, J. X. *What Made Ireland Sinn Féin* (Boston, 1921).

Reidy, J. 'The IRB', in Joy, M. (ed.), *The Irish Rebellion of 1916* (New York, 1916).

Ryan, D. *James Connolly* (Dublin, 1924).

Ryan, W. P. *The Labour Revolt and Larkinism* (London, 1913).

—— *The Pope's Green Island* (London, 1912).

—— *The Irish Labour Movement* (Dublin, 1920).

Shaw, F. J. 'The canon of modern Irish history—a challenge', *Studies*, lxi (1972), 115–53.

Smith-Gordon, L., and Staples, L. C. *Rural Reconstruction in Ireland: A Record of Co-operative Organisation* (London, 1917).

Strauss, E. *Irish Nationalism and British Democracy* (London, 1951).

Usher, A. *The Face and Mind of Ireland* (Dublin, 1949).

Ward, A. J. *Ireland and Anglo-American Relations, 1899–1921* (London, 1969).

Wells, W. B. *Irish Indiscretions* (Dublin, 1916).

Williams, T. D. (ed.). *The Irish Struggle, 1916–29* (London, 1966).

—— (ed.). *Secret Societies in Ireland* (Dublin, 1973).

THE SOCIAL STRUCTURE OF NATIONALISM AND REPUBLICANISM

Barry, T. *Guerilla Days in Ireland* (Dublin, 1949).

Beaslai, P. *Michael Collins and the Making of a New Ireland* (Dublin, 1926).

—— *Michael Collins, Soldier and Statesman* (Dublin, 1937).

Bennett, R. *The Black and Tans* (London, 1959).

Breen, D. *My Fight for Irish Freedom* (Dublin, 1924).

Butler, E. *Barry's Flying Column: The IRA's Cork No. 3 Brigade, 1919–21* (London, 1971).

Forester, M. *Michael Collins: The Lost Leader* (London, 1971).

Freeman. T. W. A series of articles on 'The changing distribution of population in counties Donegal, Kerry, West Cork, Mayo and Sligo', *Journal of the Statistical and Social Inquiry Society of Ireland, 1940–44*.

—— 'The congested districts of western Ireland', *Geographical Journal*, xxxiii (1939).

—— 'Farming in Irish life', ibid. cx (1947), 38–59.

GREAVES, C. D. *Liam Mellows and the Irish Revolution* (London, 1971).

HOOKER, E. R. *Re-adjustments of Agricultural Tenure in Ireland* (Chapel Hill, North Carolina, 1938).

JOHNSTON, J. 'The devolution of Donegal', *Manchester Guardian* supplement, 15 March 1923.

KERRYMAN LTD. *With the IRA in the Fight for Freedom, 1919 to the Truce: The Red Path of Glory* (Tralee, 1952).

MACARDLE, D. *The Irish Republic* (Dublin, 1937).

MACCARTHY, J. M. *Limerick's Fighting Story, 1916–21* (Tralee, 1948).

NEESON, E. *The Civil War in Ireland, 1922–3* (Cork, 1966).

O'CONNOR, B. *With Michael Collins in the Fight for Irish Freedom* (London, 1929).

O'DONOGHUE, F. *No Other Law: The Story of Liam Lynch and the Irish Republican Army, 1916–23* (Dublin, 1954).

O'HEGARTY, P. S. *The Victory of Sinn Féin* (Dublin, 1924).

O'HIGGINS, B. *Sinn Féin and Freedom* (Dublin, 1933).

O'MALLEY, E. *On Another Man's Wound* (Dublin, 1936). Reissued as *Army without Banners* (London, 1967).

O'NEILL, B. *The War for the Land in Ireland* (London, 1933).

O'SHIEL, K. R. 'The work of the Land Commission', in King, F. C. (ed.), *Public Administration in Ireland*, vol. ii (Dublin, 1944).

PYNE, P. 'The third Sinn Féin Party, 1923–6', *Economic and Social Review*, i (1970), 29–50 and 229–58.

TAYLOR, R. *Michael Collins* (London, 1958).

VALERA, E. DE *The Alternative to the Treaty: Document No. Two* (Dublin, 1923).

YOUNGER, C. *Ireland's Civil War* (London, 1968).

THE CONSERVATIVE PERIOD

BITTSCHEID, W. 'Irlands Aufstieg zum Dominion' (Cologne University doctoral dissertation, 1929).

COSGRAVE, W. 'Irlands künftige Politik', *Zeitschrift für Geopolitik* (1929).

—— 'Die wirtschaftliche Entwicklung Irlands', *Das Neue Europa* (Zurich, 1930).

GILMORE, G. *The Republican Congress, 1934* (Dublin, 1934, 2nd edn, 1966).

GWYNN, D. R. *The Irish Free State, 1922–7* (London, 1928).

—— *Eamon de Valera* (London, 1933).

GWYNN, S. L. 'Ireland since the Treaty', *Foreign Affairs* (January 1934).

HANCOCK, W. K. *Survey of British Commonwealth Affairs: Problems of Nationality, 1918–36* (London, 1937)

HAND, G. J. (ed.). *Report of the Irish Boundary Commission, 1925* (Dublin, 1969).

HARKNESS, D. W. *The Restless Dominion: The Irish Free State and the British Commonwealth of Nations, 1921–32* (London, 1969).

HOGAN, J. *Could Ireland Become Communist?* (Dublin, 1935).

JOHNSON, D. S. 'The economic history of Ireland between the wars', *Irish Economic and Social History*, i (1974), 49–61.

KOHN, L. *The Constitution of the Irish Free State* (London, 1932).

LENNHOFF, E. *De Valera* (Lübeck, 1933).

MACMANUS, F. (ed.). *The Years of the Great Test, 1926–39* (Cork, 1967).

MALONE, A. E. 'Party government in the Irish Free State', *Political Science Quarterly*, xliv (1929).

MANSERGH, P. N. S. *The Irish Free State: Its Government and Politics* (London, 1934).

—— *Britain and Ireland* (London, 1942).

MOSS, W. W. *Political Parties in the Irish Free State* (New York, 1933).

MURPHY, J. A. 'The new IRA, 1925–62', in Williams, T. D. (ed.), *Secret Societies in Ireland* (Dublin, 1973).

NEVIN, D. 'Radical movements in the twenties and thirties', ibid.

O'DONNELL, P. *The Gates Flew Open* (London, 1932).

—— *There Will Be Another Day* (Dublin, 1963).

O FAOLAIN, S. *The Life Story of Eamon de Valera* (Dublin, 1933).

O'SULLIVAN, D. *The Irish Free State and its Senate* (London, 1940).

PAUL-DUBOIS, L. *The Irish Struggle and its Results* (London, 1934).

RYAN, D. *Unique Dictator: A Study of Eamon de Valera* (London, 1936).

VALERA, E. DE. *A National Policy Outlined* (Dublin, 1926).

—— *Fianna Fáil and its Economic Policy* (Dublin, 1928).

WHITE, T. DE VERE. *Kevin O'Higgins* (London, 1948).

THE REPUBLICAN EPOCH

BAKER, T. J., and ROSS, M. 'The changing regional pattern in Ireland', *Economic and Social Review*, i (1970), 155–67.

BAUER, R. *Irland, die Insel der Heiligen und Rebellen* (Leipzig, 1938).

—— *Irland im Schatten Englands* (Berlin, 1940).

—— 'Hauptprobleme der irischen Volkstumspolitik', *Volk und Reich, Politische Monatshefte*, x (November, 1934), 827.

CHUBB, F. B. 'Vocational representation and the Irish Senate', *Political Studies*, ii (1954), 97–111.

—— 'Ireland 1957', in Butler, D. E. (ed.), *Elections Abroad* (London, 1959).

COHAN, A. *The Irish Political Elite* (Dublin, 1972).

GARVIN, T. 'Continuity and change in Irish electoral politics', *Economic and Social Review*, iii (1972).

HARKORT, P. G. 'Der Irisch-Englische Handelskrieg' (Kiel University doctoral dissertation, 1938).

HARRISON, H. *Ireland and the British Empire* (London, 1937).

IRELAND, D. *Eamon de Valera Doesn't See It Through* (Cork, 1941).

JOHNSTON, J. *Irish Agriculture in Transition* (Dublin, 1951).

KAIM-CAUDLE, P. R. *Social Policy in the Irish Republic* (London, 1967).

KELLY, R. S. *Ireland's Bloodless Revolution, 1932–6* (Chicago, 1936)

KING, F. C. (ed.). *Public Administration in Ireland*, 3 vols (Dublin, 1944–54).

McBRIDE, S. *Our People—Our Money* (Dublin, 1943).

McMANUS, M. J. *Eamon de Valera: A Biography* (Dublin, 1947).

MacManus, F. (ed.). *The Years of the Great Test, 1926–39* (Cork, 1967).

Manning, M. *The Blueshirts* (Dublin, 1971).

Murphy, J. A. 'The new IRA, 1925–62', in Williams, T. D. (ed.), *Secret Societies in Ireland* (Dublin, 1973).

O'Brien, C. C. *States of Ireland* (London, 1972).

—— 'Ireland in international affairs', in Edwards, O. D. (ed.), *Conor Cruise O'Brien introduces Ireland* (London, 1969).

O'Duffy, E. *The Labour Policy of Fine Gael* (Dublin, 1934).

O Faolain, S. *De Valera* (London, 1939).

Sheehy, M. *Divided We Stand* (London, 1955).

—— *Is Ireland Dying? Culture and the Church in Modern Ireland* (London, 1968).

Stoye, J. *Irland frei von England! Was will de Valera?* (Leipzig, 1938).

Tierney, M. 'Modern Ireland: two interpretations', *Studies*, xli (1952), 257.

Valera, E. de. *Ireland's Stand: A Selection of Speeches during the War, 1939–45* (Dublin, 1946).

Westropp-Bennett, T. W. *Pro Domo Sua: Speech in Defence of the Senate* (Dublin, 1934).

Whyte, J. H. 'Ireland', in Rose, R. (ed.), *Electoral Behaviour: A Comparative Handbook* (New York, 1974).

Williams, T. D. (ed.). *Ireland in the War Years and After, 1939–51* (Dublin, 1969).

NORTHERN IRELAND

Akenson, D. H. *Education and Enmity: The Control of Schooling in Northern Ireland, 1920–50* (Newton Abbot, 1973).

Arthur, P. *The People's Democracy, 1968–73* (Belfast, 1974).

Baker, S. E. 'Orange and Green', in Dyos, H. J., and Wolff, M. (eds), *The Victorian City: Images and Realities*, vol. 2 (London, 1973).

Barritt, D. P., and Carter, C. F. *The Northern Ireland Problem: A Study in Group Relations* (London, 1962, 1972).

Beckett, J. C., and Glasscock, R. E. (eds). *Belfast: The Origin and Growth of an Industrial City* (London, 1967).

Blake, J. W. *Northern Ireland in the Second World War* (Belfast, 1956).

Boal, F. W., and Buchanan, R. H. 'The 1969 Northern Ireland General Election', *Irish Geography*, vi (1969), 78–84.

Boulton, D. *The UVF, 1966–73: An Anatomy of Loyalist Rebellion* (Dublin, 1973).

Boyd, A. *Holy War in Belfast* (Tralee, 1969).

Boyle, J. W. 'The Belfast Protestant Association and the Independent Orange Order, 1901–10', *Irish Historical Studies*, xiii (1962), 117–52.

Buckland, P. J. *Ulster Unionism and the Origins of Northern Ireland, 1886–1922* (Dublin, 1973).

Budge, I., and O'Leary, C. *Belfast: Approach to Crisis* (London, 1973).

Callaghan, J. *A House Divided* (London, 1973).

Campbell, T. J. *Fifty Years of Ulster, 1890–1940* (Belfast, 1941).

Devlin, B. *The Price of my Soul* (London, 1969).

Devlin, P. *The Fall of the Northern Ireland Executive* (Belfast, 1975).

EDWARDS, O. DUDLEY. *The Sins of our Fathers: The Roots of Conflict in Northern Ireland* (Dublin, 1970).

ERVINE, ST. J. *Craigavon: Ulsterman* (London, 1949).

FISK, R. *The Point of No Return: The Strike which broke the British in Ulster* (London, 1975).

GRAHAM, J. A. V. 'The consensus-forming strategy of the Northern Ireland Labour Party, 1949–68' (Queen's University of Belfast, MSocSc thesis, 1972).

GRAY, T. *The Orange Order* (London, 1972).

HARBINSON, J. F. *The Ulster Unionist Party, 1882–1970: Its Development and Organisation* (Belfast, 1973).

—— 'A history of the Northern Ireland Labour Party, 1891–1949' (Queen's University of Belfast, MSc (Econ) thesis, 1966).

HARRIS, R. *Prejudice and Tolerance in Ulster: A Study of Neighbours and 'Strangers' in a Border Community* (Manchester, 1972).

HESLINGA, M. W. *The Irish Border as a Cultural Divide* (Assen, Netherlands, 1962, 2nd edn, 1971).

HEZLET, SIR A. *The B Specials* (London, 1972).

ISLES, K. S., and CUTHBERT, N. *An Economic Survey of Northern Ireland* (Belfast, 1957).

JOHNSON, D. S, 'The economic history of Ireland between the wars', *Irish Economic and Social History*, i (1974), 49–61.

JONES, E. *A Social Geography of Belfast* (London, 1960).

KELLY, H. *How Stormont Fell* (Dublin, 1972).

KENNEDY, D. 'Catholics in Northern Ireland', in MacManus, F. (ed.), *The Years of the Great Test, 1926–39* (Cork, 1967).

KNIGHT, J. S., and BAXTER-MOORE, N. *Northern Ireland: The Elections of the Twenties* (London, 1972).

LAWRENCE, R. J. *The Government of Northern Ireland: Public Finance and the Public Services, 1921–64* (Oxford, 1965).

McCLELLAND, A. 'The later Orange Order', in Williams, T. D. (ed.), *Secret Societies in Ireland* (Dublin, 1973).

McCRACKEN, J. L. 'The political scene in Northern Ireland, 1926–37', in MacManus, F. (ed.), *The Years of the Great Test, 1926–39* (Cork, 1967).

—— 'Northern Ireland, 1921–66', in Moody, T. W., and Martin, F. X. (eds), *The Course of Irish History* (Cork, 1967).

McMULLEN, W. *With James Connolly in Belfast* (Dublin, 1951).

MANSERGH, P. N. S. *The Government of Northern Ireland: A Study in Devolution* (London, 1936).

MOGEY, J. M. *Rural Life in Northern Ireland* (Belfast, 1947).

The Autobiography of Terence O'Neill (London, 1972).

PAOR, L. DE. *Divided Ulster* (London, 1970).

ROSE, R. *Governing without Consensus* (London, 1971).

STEWART, A. T. Q. *The Ulster Crisis, 1911–14* (London, 1967).

SUNDAY TIMES INSIGHT TEAM. *Ulster* (London, 1972).

WALLACE, M. *Northern Ireland: Fifty Years of Self-Government* (Newton Abbot, 1971).

WILSON, T. (ed.) *Ulster under Home Rule* (London, 1955).

Index